Praise for DIG THIS GIG

Could there possibly be a more timely book? The job market has never seemed so forbidding. But through beautifully rendered vignettes, Laura Dodd introduces us to an array of gutsy and determined young people diving into interesting and sometimes novel careers. We meet genetic counselors, adventure guides, and food bloggers. We get a first-hand view of whole new fields that are starting to take off because of technological, demographic, and cultural shifts. We hear poignant war stories from renowned leaders. This book is full of smart, practical career advice, much of it earned through hard experience, and all of it deeply relevant for any young person attempting to gain a toe hold in a daunting job market.

—**David Barstow,** Pulitzer Prize–winning investigative reporter for *The New York Times*

Not everyone can have Jeffrey Sachs as a personal career mentor. But they can have him and other successful people in *Dig This Gig*, which is an honest and thorough look at what work truly means. As Laura Dodd interviews everyone from a genetic counselor to a TV reporter to a policy analyst, she gets to the root of how people find their calling as opposed to how they find their jobs. *Dig This Gig* is not going to give you the secrets to becoming rich, famous, and powerful. But it will tell you how to find or create a job that makes your life meaningful, and that's even better.

—**Lilit Marcus,** author of *Save the Assistants*

A great job isn't the one that looks good on a resumé. It's the one that fires you up, engages your soul, and makes you feel alive. *Dig This Gig* is better than going on twenty informational interviews. Maybe you have years to waste, trying out this job and that for a few months each. If not, read *Dig This Gig* and figure it out before you get started.

—**John Bowe,** author of *Gig: Americans Talk About Their Jobs*

dig this gig

Find Your Dream Job— Or Invent It

Laura Dodd

CITADEL PRESS
Kensington Publishing Corp.
www.kensingtonbooks.com

CITADEL PRESS BOOKS are published by

Kensington Publishing Corp.
119 West 40th Street
New York, NY 10018

All Kensington titles, imprints, and distributed lines are available at special quantity discounts for bulk purchases for sales promotions, premiums, fund-raising, educational, or institutional use. Special book excerpts or customized printings can also be created to fit specific needs. For details, write or phone the office of the Kensington special sales manager: Kensington Publishing Corp., 119 West 40th Street, New York, NY 10018, attn: Special Sales Department; phone 1-800-221-2647.

CITADEL PRESS and the Citadel logo are Reg. U.S. Pat. & TM Off.

First printing: April 2011

10 9 8 7 6 5 4 3 2 1

Printed in the United States of America

Library of Congress Control Number: 2010931896

ISBN-13: 978-0-8065-3245-5
ISBN-10: 0-8065-3245-9

To my mom,
who always encouraged me to explore,
but never let me feel lost.

Contents

Prologue

Some people accused us of running away, and in truth, they were partially right. But looking back, we were running to find something. It just happened to take traveling halfway around the world to realize that.

The three of us, best friends from high school, had up and left good jobs and comfortable lives in the United States for an adventure. A year had passed since college graduation, and already we felt job burnout creeping in. Before it was too late we needed to live, we impatiently explained to our incredulous parents. Really live.

And now we were "really living" in a ten-by-ten shoebox of a room in a beach shack near Sydney, Australia. In one corner, Nina and Callie shared a mattress on the floor. I slept an arm's reach away. Having commandeered an extra twin box spring to stack in the corner, I managed to squeeze six more inches of distance between my face and the dingy, dank carpet. Our roommates across the hall were a revolving cast of Brazilian surfer guys with spotty English skills and barely-there board shorts.

For work, we found minimum-wage under-the-table jobs. I was a waitress at a "gourmet" pizza restaurant, Nina scooped ice cream near the main promenade, and Callie served espresso and lattes to tourists. Among the three of us, we were able to smuggle home enough left-overs to clear a few days of free meals—breakfast, lunch, and dessert.

The work was admittedly a brain-break compared with our jobs back home. Stateside we had dutifully stepped on the age-old career treadmill that society proselytized: graduate from college, start entry-level jobs, put in four decades, and retire.

We were right on schedule. A year out of school our professional titles were nod-worthy: production assistant on a hit television show in Los Angeles (me), publicity assistant at a major publishing house in New York City (Nina), and veterinarian technician at an exotic animal clinic in New Orleans (Callie).

Now, Down Under, when we crossed paths in our cubbyhole from various work shifts, we traded notes. The work gripes were a little less sophisticated (shrieking kids and lousy tips versus shrieking actors and lousy clients), but the angst-ridden career questions persisted all the same: "What would it be like to be a . . . ?" or "How do you even get into *that* job?"

The underlying current of these group sessions—during happy hours, on the ferry, running errands—was a deeper conversation about work and how one decides which career, or career*s*, to pursue. After all, a lot of the indecision paralyzing my peers, I thought, was rooted in not knowing what people actually do all day at their jobs. There was an insatiable curiosity to understand not only the gritty details of life at the office, but also the more nuanced aspects of career journeys—the how and why people choose to do what they do.

Some people might have thought we were lazy or whiny, or both. Work is work. Yes, but we had an urge to be part of something bigger. To do work that mattered. Really mattered.

And it wasn't just the three of us ex-pats who grappled with the "What should I do with my life?" conundrum. I'd refill a water glass for a table full of travelers who looked about my age and eavesdrop

work debates, or be in line at the Internet café and overhear back-
packers sharing career dilemmas.

At times our old jobs, the ones we had abandoned, sounded pretty
good. For Callie especially. She spoke endlessly about the animals at
the clinic, and her duties of feeding and x-raying the monkeys and
snakes and ferrets that cycled through. She wanted to apply to vet
school, and working as a technician provided experience that might
impress the graduate admissions office.

Nina had majored in communications in college, and though she
wasn't crazy about the publishing world, she had speed-dial access to
public relations veterans. Now she settled for less-prestigious recognition. When she bragged to her boyfriend, temporarily left behind in
the States, that she had received "employee of the month" at the ice
cream shop, the accolade felt silly.

And me? I had done the waiting-tables thing before, so there were
definitely the "What was I thinking?" moments. How foolish had I
been to purposely stall what was a promising start in the production
world?

For direction, I looked to the "professionals." Surely they would
have the answers to the simple questions reverberating among my
twentysomething generation: What are jobs really like on a day-to-day
basis? How do people break into off-the-radar fields? Is what you do
who you are?

I came up short. The college career counselors were focused on
shuttling students off campus and into any workplace. Work was
work, remember? Career websites displayed drop-down search menus
that led to scrolls of listings of nebulous job titles. The well-meaning
armchair consultants and book authors critiqued the trends and gen-
erational comparisons. Major media outlets chimed in, too, to try
to distill what made this generation tick and what was up with its
wanderlust habits.

It seemed everyone was talking about the twentysomethings, not to them. Where were our unvarnished voices, speaking about jobs from the trenches? Not summed up in a quote or two, but in honest, specific, here's-what-it's-really-like conversations.

So, I started asking my peers about how they made a living and how they felt about it. No pressure. No agenda. Merely candid chats about work. The visceral reactions ran the gamut—pride, embarrassment, hope, anxiety.

A few casual talks became a few dozen, and soon the discussion mushroomed into hundreds of interviews. Once the concept evolved into a formal book project, I emailed everyone I knew to help recruit twentysomethings interested in talking about their gigs. I described the concept—a career book for our peers, by our peers—and asked them to press "forward" to their friends with a request for their friends to do the same.

They did. Before long, I had a virtual, viral network of twentysomethings working a variety of jobs all over the country. The idea resonated so strongly with people that they were contacting ex-boyfriends and ex-girlfriends or hometown family friends they hadn't spoken to in years to contribute their experiences. In the meantime, I clipped news articles with quotes from college grads who I thought sounded interesting and cold-contacted them asking to hear more about their stories.

With more than enough war tales to work with, it was time to organize the voices into chapters. I chose eight fields—some because they were growing industries, others because folks were putting a new twist on an old one.

The result of these over-a-beer-style talks is what you now hold in your hands: a book profiling thirty-two young adults in the workforce—working ordinary and extraordinary gigs—and telling with candor what it means to do what they do. Some I know personally; others I met for the first time during this project. All of them demystify their titles and the glib "HR" descriptions to uncover behind-the-scenes details so that the rest of us—and some of them, too—can make informed decisions in the future. The young adults who appear in these pages reviewed their profiles and were invited to make factual notes, an effort to both ensure accuracy and inspire additional thoughts on aspects of their work they might not have shared initially.

To add gravitas to the stories of the twentysomethings' job adventures and misadventures, I also invited industry leaders to share theirs. Mentors are a kind of old-fashioned notion but crucial to charting career courses. They can serve as sounding boards, confidants, and references. The mentors in this book have decades on us in age, with the job titles and career wisdom to prove it.

The format for the mentor's insights is a bit different from the written profiles of your peers. The mentors' reflections are told entirely in first person—as if they were speaking directly to you, one-on-one. Each chapter wraps with an excerpt from our interview that has been transcribed and edited by topic and space. They draw from their early days and share mistakes and turning points that stand out to them with the clarity of 20-20 hindsight. Now, within these pages, you have eight mentors representing a cross section of corporate and nonprofit organizations, as well as government agencies and academic institutions. Not a bad start.

A common thread links all these stories: *It is hard*. It is hard to pursue a dream. It is hard to take a risk. It is hard to sustain your momentum and your belief in your goals in order to see them through.

Just as quickly, however, another common thread emerges: *It is all worth it*. The sweat, the tears, the false starts. But don't take my word for it. Read these stories from your peers and the insights from your mentors, and go out and blaze your own path.

And remember, people who perceive you to be running away don't understand that someone else is seeing you arrive.

dig this gig

1

Healthcare Gigs

Beyond the MD Option

INTRODUCTION

Virgil, the classical Roman poet, summed it up succinctly: "The greatest wealth is health."

Our generation "gets it." Health consciousness is nonnegotiable. If you don't have your health, you don't stand much chance of working, much less pursuing a career you love.

But it's not just about fitness—healthcare is a hotbed of job growth, ironically, thanks in large part to our parents. The industry will generate 3.2 million new wage and salary jobs between 2008 and 2018, more than any other industry, mostly in response to the accelerated growth in the aging population, according to the U.S. Bureau of Labor Statistics.

Many of those jobs will be related to caretaking for the elderly—the number of home health aides is estimated to increase by 50 percent and physical therapist assistants by 33 percent, suggests BLS. Familiar titles such as registered nurses, dental hygienists, and medical assistants are expected to flourish in coming years, too. The surge is across the board: ten of the twenty fastest-growing jobs are healthcare related, according to BLS.

With the movement to prioritize health comes new jobs that are gaining traction, like naturopathic medicine and genetic counseling. Profiled here are four gigs plucked from the plethora of options out there—two with a new twist on traditional jobs and two that explore less traveled (for now) routes.

Chrissie Norton is a nurse for dual-disorder patients in Durham, North Carolina. Her patients suffer from mental illness and substance abuse, and they are often the population most people would prefer to ignore—which is exactly what drew Chrissie to the position. "I wanted to talk with people," she says simply, a modus operandi that some feel contradicts conventional medicine's acute focus on "fixing" the illness, not so much the person.

The job is not without its challenges. "How can I help someone be 'healthy' if they are using drugs every day or if they are living in a different place every time I see them?" she continuously asks herself, having dealt with multiple patients who drift from place to place. Part of the answer, perhaps, is to just keep showing up.

You can't cover healthcare without addressing the business side. Someone, somewhere, whether in a private company or a government-sponsored program, is watching the bottom line. And at the core of the healthcare-as-a-business conundrum is the insurance industry, often painted as coldhearted arbiters intent on making a profit at the expense of the patient.

Brent Smith works as an insurance salesman in New York City. His sales pitch is part of a new school of thought that employers and employees are beginning to warm to—a hybrid model of personal responsibility and employer participation.

Take smoking and obesity, for instance. Studies suggest a healthy employee is a more productive employee. Companies are listening and getting inventive with ways to motivate workers into taking better care of themselves. Employers are offering incentives to their workers to quit smoking and lose weight—anything from cash to gift certificates to reducing an employee's premium, or contributing to a health savings account (Brent will explain a little more about this trend).

The concept is not based on charity—smokers cost an additional $1,850 a year to insure, and obese workers cost private employers $45 billion a year in medical costs and lost productivity, according to the National Business Group on Health.

Speaking of new-age careers in healthcare, here's one that has roots dating back thousands of years: naturopathic medicine. "It's a traditional form of family medicine that emphasizes the prevention of disease and the use of natural, non-toxic therapies," says Dr. Nick Bitz, a twentysomething naturopathic doctor based in Vail, Colorado. In his practice, Nick advocates the use of herbal medicine, nutrition and nutritional supplements, detoxification and hydrotherapy, among other methods, to bring about "optimal health and well-being."

Judging from medical school enrollment numbers, the field is growing in popularity. In 2000, 1,908 NDs graduated from U.S.-accredited naturopathic medical schools. Five years later, the figure jumped to 3,265 graduates. Almost a decade later, there are no signs of interest plateauing.

A healthcare profession with much less of a historic foundation, but with all the guns pointed at the value of preventative care, is genetic counseling. Generally defined, genetic counselors help patients through the before, during, and after process of getting a genetic test to forecast health issues. Chrissy Seelaus, a counselor specializing in cancer testing, will elaborate.

The field is exploding. Less than a decade ago, the number of genetic tests available to consumers was in the hundreds; today, more than a thousand tests are available to patients, according to the National Society of Genetic Counselors. And to help walk patients through this unchartered territory are genetic counselors specializing in a range of up-and-coming areas, including prenatal, pediatrics, neurology, and cardiology.

Sidney Wolfe, MD, founder and director of Public Citizen's Health

Research Group, a consumer nonprofit advocacy group, and this chapter's mentor, aims to treat healthcare from a large-scale perspective and address systemic problems. "My view is that by improving the public health on a large-multiplying basis, I can have more impact than I would practicing medicine," he says.

On the job he is a tireless, relentless patient advocate. Outside the office, however, he may be slightly less vehement, but no less passionate about whatever he takes on—even for fun. You can't reach him by cell phone (because he doesn't have one), and he tunes out of email when not at work. But give him a hiking trail to trek or put him in front of a grand piano, and he is content.

CHRISSIE NORTON
Nurse for Dual Disorder Patients
Durham, North Carolina
Age: 27

It's the middle of the workweek in Durham, North Carolina, and Chrissie Norton is preparing to attend a funeral. She hasn't been to one since her mother passed away eight years ago, and she's nervous it'll stir up emotions she has struggled to manage.

Technically, Chrissie really shouldn't be going to this memorial service. The deceased woman was her patient. Healthcare industry standards generally frown upon "getting attached," and warn attending could be crossing a boundary.

But what they'd been through in the past year, as nurse and patient, defied boundaries. There's no denying they were an odd team. Sheila,* the patient, was a bipolar, alcoholic, heroin-addicted mother of two young children, whom she abandoned years ago. Chrissie, the

*The patient's name has been changed.

caregiver, was a free-spirited nursing student, who grew up going to cotillions and was the daughter of adoring, affluent parents.

When they first met, Sheila had recently moved from a tent in the woods into city-subsidized housing. Acclimating to each other was difficult. "She was a very tough patient—bad attitude, stubborn, resisted most treatment," says Chrissie, recalling the time Sheila refused to allow her bed to be moved against the wall to prevent her from injuring herself by falling out in a drunken stupor, as she did frequently.

Breakthroughs were few and far between—the day Sheila agreed to have bed guardrails installed counted as a small victory. Getting her to the dentist to address her rotting teeth was another.

But Sheila was in the depths of her addiction, a place where no one could reach her. Efforts and pleas to stop fell on deaf ears. At fifty years old, she died from multiple organ failure, years of alcohol and drug abuse finally taking their toll.

Chrissie is a nurse for chronic substance abusers and the severely mentally ill. Think incorrigible alcoholics, homeless drifters, and repeat domestic abuse offenders. Think the headaches on society for whom people have a hard time rousing empathy. Think Sheila.

"I know they can be considered a drain on society. I see that when I step away. But they're people and they deserve respect and care," Chrissie says.

Empathy. It's one of Chrissie's great gifts, and occasionally, her Achilles' heel. At twenty and a junior in college, she had her own bout with demons. Mourning her mom's death from cancer brought her to her knees, and she sank into a deep depression. The once gregarious soccer player skipped classes to sit in her room in her pajamas, shades drawn, and drink. Daytime soaps played on repeat, fast-food trash piled up in the corner. Friends were dismissed when they staged an intervention. Chrissie sank deeper.

A year passed like this and slowly Chrissie clawed her way out, aided by a grief-counseling group she started on campus. It was only by talking to people who had experienced a crushing loss, as she had, that made the difference. "We all spoke the same language," she says. "I learned that I wasn't alone, that I wasn't crazy, and that things would not stay like this forever." Only those who have been through it understand: one never completely heals; one merely learns to cope.

Connecting with people is Chrissie's forte, but making a living out of it didn't occur to her. After graduation, she moved to Asheville, North Carolina, and tried the corporate thing, working as a receptionist at a swank hotel. "We had to wear an ascot and follow a stupid script: 'I'd be *delighted* to upgrade you.' 'I'd be *delighted* to show you to your room.'"

I'd be *delighted* to get the hell out of here, she thought to herself. But where to? She counseled herself, "Well, I like biology and science comes pretty easy to me and I like helping people." How about nursing?

After some thought, she packed up her stuff, drove four hours east, and unpacked in Chapel Hill, North Carolina, where she was accepted to graduate school, and could begin her nursing career chapter. One semester into a two-year program and she wanted to kick herself. The assignment on the first day of clinic: give a 350-pound, schizophrenic male a suppository.

"I started dry-heaving." *This* is what nurses do? She panicked. The mental disorder she could handle; the gory side she could not. Two more years? "I didn't even know if at the end of all this I wanted to be a nurse."

To make matters worse, everyone else seemed, well, *delighted* to be there. Chipper nursing students lined up for the day's demonstrations: inserting a catheter, changing a wound dressing, taking blood pressure. "I was not your typical nursing student. I was the student who wanted to talk to the person in the hall in restraints for throwing her feces across the room and smearing it into her wounds. The patient who everyone walked by, without a second thought."

Patients like Sheila.

As a last-ditch effort before quitting outright, Chrissie met with a mentorlike professor who explained that there was another side of nursing. "I didn't have to go and be miserable in a hospital," she recalls of the "phew" moment. Nurses, she learned, could do community mental health by incorporating their training in a social work–type position—a combination of counseling and medicine, like checking blood pressure, giving injections, assessing mental status, and providing motivational support.

Her first nursing job was in community mental health on a team that worked with patients suffering from dual disorders. Now her shift begins at an office building where there's no trace of a catheter or colonoscopy bag. Motivational posters tacked to the wall and images of famous people who have battled mental illness—Beethoven, Abe Lincoln, Charles Dickens—serve as "you're not alone" reminders. Chrissie, who earns $22 an hour, and her team—a group of thirteen mental health care providers specializing in psychiatric support and substance abuse counseling—meet each morning at 8:00 a.m. to discuss crisis calls received the night before and update other pending cases.

Afternoons are spent in the field, sometimes literally. Chrissie helped one of her patients move his tent from one part of the woods to another because the area had flooded. "Eighty percent of our work is done in the community. You learn a lot from going into someone's space," she says, whether it is an apartment, a street corner, or a jail cell. "This can be pretty stressful depending on the circumstances. A lot of our clients live in unsafe neighborhoods. Others live among the elements—heat, rain, snow, insects—which can make providing services difficult and somewhat uncomfortable."

There's something to be said about showing up. In person. On the patient's terms. When treating a patient in an office building or a hospital, "it's easy to get upset if he's not taking his medications or has started using drugs again. But when you go to them and see their day-to-day environment, you realize he's living with twelve people in a boarding house and his brother steals his medicine."

The circumstances don't excuse the behavior, but they can help explain it. The more Chrissie knows about the patient, disorders and otherwise, the better nurse she can be. "I cannot have expectations for them. It's their recovery, not mine." When a patient has a setback, the starting point is reset. "We'll pick up where you are right now," she tells patients, because today's progress means nothing tomorrow. "With these patients, so much changes every day. A patient you see today may be stable, but tomorrow he is in the hospital."

Few people can keep up the intensity for long. It's an emotionally draining job, and turnover is high. Even Chrissie may not be immune to the long-term strain. "I don't want to do this forever. It burns you out. There are no immediate rewards from your work."

The rewards may not be immediate, but they are every bit as gratifying. "I've had the opportunity to work with survivors," she says proudly. "My clients are some of the strongest people in the world. They have endured hardship, trauma, prejudice, and pain and keep struggling despite adversity. I have more respect for these individuals than words can express. They are my teachers."

Postscript from Chrissie . . .

If I had to do it all over again, I would . . . Go to school for social work. Think more about "careers" in college. Traveled when I had the chance.

If I knew then what I know now, I would . . . Have graduated high school, traveled for a year, gone to college with a career in mind.

Three characteristics or personality traits you need to do this job:

1. Patience
2. Sense of humor

3. Belief that all people should be treated with respect. Belief that all people deserve genuine and authentic care no matter what their current, past, or present issues or behaviors may be.

Don't even try this if . . . You need instant gratification or need to see immediate results of your work. You don't believe in harm reduction, but instead demand abstinence. You think substance use is a character flaw or that mental health problems aren't as real as physical health problems.

Brent Smith
Health Insurance Salesman
Brooklyn, New York
Age: 25

Rush hour in mid-town Manhattan is not a pleasant scene; in the subway, it's downright grimy. Commuters are cranky, tired, and ready to get home. Nevertheless it's the unsavory setting where Brent Smith chose to stage his heart-healthy intervention, and a metaphorical "ground zero" to begin building his career in healthcare.

"I'll give you one dollar—no strings attached—to take the stairs," he shouts to weary commuters pouring off the subway and mechanically exiting via escalators. "Free money!"

For effect, he waves a bulging wad of dollar bills to entice them to take the aerobic route. The bribe is partially successful: a few takers trickle out of the escalator queue, snatch the bill, and begin the climb.

This is just one quirky scene from an amateur thirty-minute movie called *SickCare* that Brent produced about people and the unhealthy state of healthcare. The-stairs-versus-escalator vignette is purposely lighthearted, but Brent's underlying message is deadly serious: people should take responsibility and ownership for their health. "Eighty percent of medical costs in the United States today are from preventable illnesses," he says, and he should know: he spends his days poring over the dollars as a salesman for one of the largest U.S. health insurance companies.

Brent is an advocate for a new way of doing business in healthcare insurance. The current system is broken, he argues, and in order to fix it, both the business model and Americans' attitudes need an extreme makeover.

His philosophy is this: "Bad behavior is contagious. If most of your friends are overweight, there's a good chance you are, too. The good news is that healthy habits, such as weight loss and smoking cessation, have also been proven to be contagious. We have to stop the ball rolling any farther before we start pushing it the other way. The goal right now should not be for people to lose weight, but to just stop gaining it."

Restless to get out from behind the desk where he makes hundreds of sales calls and onto the street, Brent shot *SickCare* as a "man-on-the-street" documentary—part tongue-in-cheek, part disturbing peephole. In one on-camera exchange, he challenges a mother and son about their health priorities. Turns out, Mom will spend $25 on an oil change for her car several times a year but won't see her primary care physician for an annual checkup for the same price.

The experiment also underscored a few things he already knew: people love to hate health insurance companies. "A lot of people think that we are the devil," he says. "We're an easy target, but I never take it personally." For years, the industry has been accused, sometimes fairly, of profiting off the sick. Few people understand how insurance companies work behind closed doors. The middlemen, the piles of paperwork, and the lack of transparency contribute to a frustrated public opinion.

Brent, admittedly one of those middlemen, concedes the process can be confusing, but he insists the tarnished reputation doesn't apply to him. "I don't consider myself a slick sales guy," he says. "I've never sold—and don't want to sell—anything to someone who doesn't need or want it."

A health insurance salesman's main responsibility is to attract new business for the company. Insiders call it "hunting," and Brent, a 6-foot 2-inch alpha male who was president of his college fraternity, is a natural fit. "It takes time, relentless attitude, ego, and the ability to be told 'No' a thousand times and still be hungry knowing that a 'Yes' (or a 'Kill') is right around the corner," he says. "I'm hunting every day."

Brent covers midsize companies with 250 to 5,000 employees. Take, for instance, a high-end women's shoe store. Figuring out how to insure the employees can be complicated—it involves layers of middlemen sifting through background information (i.e., medical claims filed the previous year, locations of the doctors they visited, analysis of claims over $25,000) to assess the insurance company's risk and rates. Simply put: high risk begets high premium; low risk begets low premium.

Once the risk and subsequent rates are sorted out, Brent moves in to sell the shoe store's executive on why his customized insurance plan is best suited for her employees. As a carrot to employers angling for reduced premiums, Brent may include a smoke cessation program with incentives for employees to quit smoking. "A healthy employee is a more productive employee," he reminds them.

And this, the Sales Pitch, is the bullpen where Brent thrives.

The opportunity to close a deal with profit-oriented executives triggers his self-confidence, in part, because he's been preparing since he was a kid. At ten years old, he started a paper route, rising every morning at 6:00 a.m. to deliver to a dozen houses in the neighborhood. When he realized his customers wanted specialized delivery service—the paper tucked inside the screen door, thrown on the lawn, or tossed at the foot of the driveway—Brent adjusted his routine. Within a few weeks he doubled the number of household subscribers.

At twelve, he added fresh-baked bread and homemade pies to the operation. Family helped (Mom lent her bread maker; Grandma donated her famous crust recipe) and the preteen spent many evenings baking. The fifth grader watched his profit margin climb 200 percent, earning him a respectable $40 per week.

By sixteen, Brent was working at his father's business, power washing, staining, and sealing decks averaging $2,000 per project. He added professional accessories to his sales come-on: a clipboard, company shirt with logo, customized carbon copy bid sheets, and a photo album with other projects' before and after snapshots. A 1986 rusty Ford Ranger pickup truck that he had bartered for a power washing job and $100 cash became his "company" ride.

In college, his entrepreneurial spirit meshed with a growing interest in healthcare—his own. After putting on forty pounds within two years, he took a critical view of his diet and workout regime, prescribing his own extreme makeover. He traded late-night chicken wings for strict servings of protein, carbs, and fruit. "The goal was to never feel hungry and never feel full." By graduation, he had dropped to his precollege weight.

At a job fair on campus, an insurance company recruiter noticed Brent's upbeat nature, a key component to be successful in sales. They chatted and before long, Brent was taking the online math and social preference test required to apply. Questions like "Would you rather hang out at a party or rebuild an engine in a garage by yourself?" weeded out the introspective candidates. Of the thirty applicants who took the test, less than half were invited to interview. Brent was one of them, and he cruised through.

A sixteen-week paid training session in Hartford, Connecticut, followed. On the agenda were a range of sessions from learning the history of healthcare in America (a bit of trivia: company-sponsored employee benefits started in World War II when companies were in such need of workers they actually had to compete for them), to dinner etiquette (mind your manners: the head of the table is not the power position. It's actually the person in the middle who has the broadest view of everyone at the dinner or meeting).

But the most essential take-away for the new hires was the importance of relationship building, a talent that came easy to Brent. Win-
ing and dining clients and gifting New York Yankees tickets, all on the
company's dime, were prime opportunities to schmooze. "We talk
about personal stuff, family stuff," he says of his ways to engage clients.
"Sales is about trust. No matter how good my product is, nobody will
want to buy from me if they don't trust me."

In the best-case scenario, the trust translates to clients—and sales.
The more business he brings in for the company, the more money he
earns. "My job is risky. If I don't hustle and market myself correctly,
I'm doing a lot of work and only making the base salary of fifty-five
thousand dollars. When the year resets, I'm a bum as far as my company is concerned."

It took him four years to hit his stride, but when he did, it was a
bonanza. After racking up nine sales, including a casino, a real estate
company, and a health center, for a compensation paycheck of over
$150K, he was in line for a status-enhancing spot among the top
25 percent of sales colleagues.

But it wasn't always a six-figure income, free lunches, and sporting events. "My first three years I didn't make a single sale." And
the burden of finding new clients depends on his initiative. "As a sales
rep, you write your own ticket. No one checks to see if I'm at my
desk."

That self-propelling focus shows no signs of tapering. Selling insurance for a large company is a primer for his main goal: opening
his own business, possibly one with a holistic approach to employees'
health. His business model would cherry-pick elements he's learned
on the job, plus a few out-of-the-box ideas he's mulling. It may involve a hybrid system: the employer pays 100 percent of preventative care (like annual checkups), and contributes to a health savings
account—both measures designed to empower the employee to take
responsibility for his healthcare.

"I'm the first to admit I have so much to learn, but here is what I've figured out so far: bad behaviors lead to risks, risks lead to disease, and disease leads to high cost," he says, leveling the issue to its most basic chain of events. Understand and address the behavior, Brent reasons, and the rest may become more manageable. Good health is a bottom line that makes sense. And cents.

Postscript from Brent . . .

If I had to do it all over again, I would . . . Not have false started.

If I knew then what I know now, I would . . . Have relaxed. It's never as important in hindsight.

Three characteristics or personality traits you need to do this job:

1. Competitiveness/ego
2. Empathy
3. Time management

Don't even try this if . . . You aren't highly self-motivated.

NICHOLAS BITZ
Naturopathic Doctor
Vail, Colorado
Age: 29

When was the last time your doctor asked you what you ate for breakfast? Or consulted with you for an hour and a half? Or instead of prescribing drugs from the corner pharmacy, he sent you to the local farmer's market?

This is everyday protocol in Dr. Nick Bitz's office. He is a naturopathic doctor working at a family practice clinic in the ski-haven town of Vail, Colorado. His questions posed during a patient's first office visit may prompt a few double takes: How are you sleeping? What's your energy and stress level? How is your digestion and what's your exercise regime? How are your relationships and do you enjoy your job? He's not being nosy, he's working. "I'm really trying to understand the entirety of a person's life," he says.

And yes, naturopathic doctors are real doctors. They complete rigorous training with four- and five-year doctorate programs, including two years of clinical rotations. NDs are currently licensed to practice primary care medicine in sixteen states. "While this does not exclude practicing in the other thirty-four states, it does limit our ability to practice to the full scope of our training in these unlicensed states, like the ability to prescribe certain pharmaceutical medications and antibiotics if necessary," Nick explains.

Naturopathic doctors emphasize prevention versus the traditional "fix-it" perspective of medical doctors. "Rather than relying on medications and surgery to cover up symptoms, we try to find and treat the root cause of disease, thereby allowing the body to heal itself," he says from his office, a five-minute drive from the ski lifts. The philosophy is rooted in six principles:

1. Do no harm
2. Identify and treat the root cause of disease
3. Treat the whole person
4. Promote the healing power of nature
5. Uphold doctor as teacher
6. Advocate prevention and wellness.

Consider the case of a forty-five-year-old female patient with a lifelong history of migraine headaches that strike once a month around the time of her period. She's been taking standard migraine medication for decades, plus birth control pills, to try to minimize the excruciating pain. Every four weeks begins a countdown to the dreaded few days when life is consumed by the splitting headaches.

Only after seeing numerous medical doctors and trying several medications without success did she schedule an appointment with Nick.

"I can cure that," he told her. The first thing Nick did was analyze her lifestyle. Diagnosis: over-stressed, under-exercised, over-caffeinated and under-nourished. She drank coffee all day, interspersed with chocolate fixes.

"The crux of her case was to fundamentally change how she was living," Nick explains. He replaced her birth control with a combination of botanical medicines and high doses of magnesium, ordered a food allergy test, performed frequent cranio-sacral therapy sessions, and sent her to her first yoga class.

The test results showed she was allergic to coffee and chocolate—two vices she was dependent on. "She cried when I gave her the news, but she had suffered for so long that she was ready to try anything to feel better." She quit cold turkey and embraced Nick's treatment plan. The following month was the first she did not experience a migraine in ten years.

Instead of prescribing a medley of pills, Nick recommends natural remedies and nontoxic therapies. And he follows a "medicine of opposites" school of thought, a naturopathic term emphasizing the "energetic qualities" of medicine. For instance, St. John's Wort, a plant harvested from the yellow flowers of a small bush, is a commonly prescribed remedy for mild to moderate depression. But it's also a "cooling herb," meaning for a fifty-five-year-old patient who has poor circulation and is often cold, St. John's Wort may exacerbate her condition. Instead, Nick's solution would be an "uplifting and warming" medicine, such as ginseng and specific B vitamins. "It's important to match the treatment to the needs of the individual patient."

Nick didn't vacillate about which career field to pursue. "I knew

I wanted to be a healer from a very young age," he says. At twelve, he fell from a tree and hurt his lower back. For an active little boy who loved to play basketball, the injury was like a death sentence. "At that age you think you're invincible, but I remember having the sense, for the first time, that I was mortal."

He endured chronic back pain, but tried to go on "as though nothing had happened, only to find myself in pain every night after any physical activity. I took massive doses of Advil and simply ignored the symptoms the best I could, until they inevitably returned. I remember thinking, 'I don't want to be in this much pain forever. How can I be healthier?'"

Nick's parents took him on the rounds in search for help. The medical doctors' imaging tests couldn't pinpoint anything, and the chiropractor provided only minimal relief. Finally, nearly out of hope, his mother booked an appointment with an acupuncturist. "It was eye-opening," Nick recalls. "He asked me about foods and gave me herbs—I never heard that from an MD. I got the most prolonged relief."

From there it was a tunnel-vision focus on living a healthy lifestyle, including adding yoga to his regime in college—a practice he credits with ultimately eliminating his back pain. He graduated with a dual bachelor's degree in human biology and cognitive neuroscience from the University of Denver and wasted not a moment before applying to medical school. At some point while researching schools, he stumbled upon the naturopathic specialty. "I never knew that such a profession even existed, or that it was a viable option for a lifelong career."

Other doctors he sought for advice scoffed. "You want to study nature-what?" they asked. The brush-offs didn't dissuade him. "I was always inclined to eat a healthy diet, to use botanicals in place of pharmaceuticals, to experiment with acupuncture, to practice yoga. I think I just intuitively knew that this was how I wanted to practice medicine."

He enrolled at Bastyr University in Seattle, Washington, one of four naturopathic medical schools in the country. The first two years at Bastyr were like any other medical school—grueling. They "were extremely challenging. I often questioned if I had what it takes to carry on. I wasn't sleeping enough, eating well, spending time with friends, or acing my exams."

He took time off between the basic science years and moved to the south of India for several months to work in a school-hospital specializing in Panchakarma treatment, an extreme detoxification process created in India. Patients come from all over the world to participate in intense twenty-eight- to forty-two-day detox sessions. "With diet, oil massages, steam baths, laxatives, enemas, vomiting and leech therapy (to remove toxic blood), patients are able to release years of built-up toxins. It's as deep as it gets. It's not one of those quick diet fixes or three-day fad fasts," Nick says. "Afterward, patients feel light and buoyant and mentally clear. And they notice that their chronic health problems are significantly improved, or in some cases, cured all together."

Next Nick moved to Maui, where he worked on an organic fruit farm and spent his free time hiking, camping, and surfing with the other twentysomethings participating in the program.

Feeling refreshed and with rejuvenated focus (and toxin free), he returned to Seattle to complete his courses, but this time not losing sight of why he was there. "I released my grip on perfection. I made a conscious choice to shift my emphasis from textbooks to 'living' the medicine. I realized that medicine, as a field, is a lifelong endeavor, and not something I had to grasp all at once."

Practicing what he preaches, Nick's morning routine is serene: up with the sun and a short yoga practice; followed by meditation; a breakfast of oats, nuts, and organic fruits; plus a combination of vitamins, usually consisting of fish oil and vitamin D.

The extra effort helps keep him calm when reluctant patients refuse well-meaning advice, as can be the case with some parents. For example, when a mom comes in with her child who has eczema. "From a naturopathic viewpoint, eczema is often caused by food intolerances or digestive issues, and is simply the expression of toxins coming to the surface." Nick will examine the child's diet and suggest removing foods that may be aggravating the condition. Maybe milk? "The parents freak out. Perhaps they're skeptical about the treatment, or maybe they're stuck in their patterns. Whatever the reason, it can be challenging to get people to participate fully in their own healthcare, even for their kid."

Overall, Nick is hopeful that skeptical patients are on the wane and that attitudes are shifting, albeit slowly. "As it stands, the current healthcare system in America is extremely resistant to any kind of change," Nick says. "But people are hungry for this medicine, and I'm convinced that change is coming."

Postscript from Nick . . .

If I had to do it all over again, I would . . . Have put less of an emphasis on getting straight A's and more of an emphasis on becoming a better human being.

If I knew then what I know now, I would . . . Have traveled more before starting medical school. Or perhaps I would have spent more time in India or farming in Hawaii.

Three characteristics or personality traits you need to do this job:

1. Compassion
2. A curious and inquiring mind
3. Love and respect for nature

Don't even try this if . . . You're not willing to make this your life's work.

CHRISSY SEELAUS
Genetic Counselor
Chicago, Illinois
Age: 28

Five to ten minutes. That's about how long Chrissy Seelaus, a cancer genetic counselor, has to give a crash course in genetics to new patients before their attention evaporates.

It's a short amount of time to explain a complicated subject, but patients have reason to be distracted. They've been referred to Chrissy after their regular doctor raised a red flag based on answers to routine family medical history questions regarding cancer—young age of diagnosis, multiple generations with cancer, history of more than one cancer.

But before Chrissy can address the bigger issues, she starts with the basics. Holding her handmade illustrated flipbook as a prop, she points to the pictures: This spiral staircase–looking thing is called DNA. Sections of DNA are called genes, which determine everything about how a person grows and develops—short, tall, black hair, blond hair.

She flips the page and continues the tutorial: Genes protect against cancer. But, occasionally, a gene has a mutation and it can't do its job like it normally would.

Taking cues from their quizzical looks or knowing nods, Chrissy will either stop and repeat a step or press on: Most cancer is sporadic; only 5–10 percent is hereditary. Your doctor wanted us to meet to discuss the hereditary kind, specifically a gene that increases a woman's risk for breast and ovarian cancer.

For many of Chrissy's patients, primarily a low-income and minority population, this is the first they're hearing science jargon—DNA, genes, mutations. Many have competing immediate health issues, as well as social and financial burdens, that take priority over the futuristic-type notion of genetic testing for a cancer that may or may not occur.

For others, though, when not knowing becomes worse than knowing, they make an appointment at the city hospital in downtown Chicago where Chrissy has her office. Which is how Chrissy met Nancy.*

Nancy had been referred to the clinic after surviving two diagnoses of breast cancer (red flag No. 1), both before the age of fifty (red flag No. 2). She was concerned that her daughter, Julie, would be at a high risk for the cancer, even at her young age of twenty-five.

Before the appointment, Chrissy spoke to Nancy by phone to collect the family's detailed history for computer input. Software then ingests that information and creates a pedigree diagram. To the untrained eye, the diagram looks like a colorful jumble of squares (representing men) and circles (representing women), but for a genetic counselor, it's a road map illustrating how cancer has been transferred through the family's generations. Based on Chrissy's interpretation, she'll conclude if a cancer-causing syndrome is likely and a genetic test necessary.

Having a detailed family chart is a best-case scenario in this stage of the counseling, but often, there's little information to mine. Families don't always know who has had cancer or how far back it goes, or, especially with Chrissy's patient population, people can be ashamed and choose to keep it to themselves. "Basically, our whole risk assessment relies on what they can tell us," she says. "Getting medical records or death certificates can be helpful, but sometimes these aren't even an option if a family member had an illness a long time ago or in another country."

For this mom and daughter, it was Nancy who was the best candidate for testing since she was the affected person. A subsequent step is to assess family members' risk. "Just because there's someone in your

---

*Patients' names have been changed.

family who has breast cancer doesn't mean you should run out and get tested," Chrissy explains. If Nancy tests positive, her daughter has a 50 percent chance of having the mutation. Chrissy offers Nancy the genetic test, which costs approximately $3,000. Most of the patients are uninsured and seek financial assistance from outside sources.

But first, before any tests took place, Chrissy briefed the two women about the test's benefits and limitations. The benefit, she explained, is that "if we know someone is at high risk, we can do something about it." On the safest side, patients can choose a prophylactic mastectomy operation—removing both breasts—that reduces the risk of getting cancer by 90 to 95 percent. On the less aggressive side, routine mammograms and breast MRIs are available in hopes of catching any cancer early.

The major limitation, and frustration for patients, is that the test can be inconclusive. If the results come back negative for one gene mutation, it does not ensure a cancer-free future. There are twenty-five thousand genes in the body, and one test cannot catch everything.

Nancy took the test, and the results were positive. The daughter then was tested and she, too, lost the coin toss: she had the mutation.

Delivering bad news is part of the job; but how counselors help a patient cope is the bigger challenge. Translating science terminology and explaining what that terminology actually means is a constant juggling act.

The range of reactions runs the gamut. "They're all over the board—fear, denial, guilt. Some insist on running the test again. You get a lot of tears when giving bad news, and people are very concerned about their families," she says. "I try to balance the information without overwhelming them." Chrissy has learned over the years when to speak and when to be quiet. "Silence is a counseling technique. Instead of throwing more information at them, I let them process it and react. If someone's clearly upset, I help them work through it, or if someone needs a moment, I'll step outside."

Away from the office, the job title is still mostly unknown.

"Nobody understands what a genetic counselor is," she says in good humor. "I'm actually shocked if I tell someone what I do and they've heard of the profession before!" The blank stares and "What's that?" questions don't bother her. "Sometimes it's fun to let people struggle with it a bit and guess before I explain."

Besides, Chrissy didn't know what the title meant until her senior year of college. She studied animal science at the University of Connecticut with the intention of becoming a farm animal vet—a dream she cooked up from a childhood spent riding horses.

That plan lost steam and segued to one that would revolve around people instead. She loved genetics but thought it meant "playing with test tubes in a lab." She stumbled accidentally upon the "counseling" aspect online.

After graduating, Chrissy made an extended East Coast–West Coast roundtrip closing in on a career in the field: Los Angeles to work as the coordinator of the prenatal program at a free clinic, where she also shadowed genetic counselors—one year. Back to her parents' home near Philadelphia to take prerequisite classes for graduate school and work setting up veterans with disability evaluations—one year. Washington, D.C., to intern at an umbrella genetics advocacy organization—six months. And final destination: Chicago, Illinois, to earn a dual master's degree—genetic counseling and medical humanities and bioethics—two years.

Now, with a few years of professional genetic counseling experience under her belt, she recommends curious hopefuls to have some type of patient interaction, like working for a crisis hotline or in a genetics lab.

Being a part of such difficult life-changing decisions can weigh heavily on a genetic counselor whose job pays, on average, $63K a year. "Yes, there's compassion fatigue and burnout. I've been overwhelmed before and have learned not to do that," Chrissy says. To step away, she joins her running group once or twice a week and meets friends for dinner or happy hour.

"One of the challenges in my profession is that it's still fairly new, and we are still collectively working to gain recognition and respect," she says, estimating that there are fewer than five thousand genetic counselors nationwide, most of whom are Caucasian females in their twenties and thirties. "Many states have gained licensure for genetic counselors, which helps to ensure that only qualified professionals are doing genetic counseling," but such issues as getting proper billing and reimbursement for services remain unresolved.

In addition to the office and counseling duties, part of the job is keeping up with the rapidly changing literature: "New genes are discovered all the time. We constantly are integrating new research discoveries into the clinical setting," Chrissy says. To stay on top of it, she reads medical journals, attends conferences and follows an emailed Listserv with other genetic counselors around the country.

But when it comes to talking to her patients, the ones whose lives are at stake, she keeps the technology and medical jargon simple. The DNA lesson booklet she handmade may be one of her best tools after all.

Postscript from Chrissy . . .

If I had to do it all over again, I would . . . Not change a thing! To be honest, I wanted to know what I wanted to do right after college and jump right into grad school to get there. In retrospect, living in different cities and doing many different volunteer, shadow, intern, and job opportunities were some of the best life experiences, and made me feel even more prepared to enter my profession when I did. When I went to grad school three years after graduating college, I was confident that it was the profession for me.

If I knew then what I know now, I would . . . Have investigated this profession sooner. I felt lost career-wise in college because I didn't really know what was out there or where to even begin looking.

Three characteristics or personality traits you need to do this job:

1. The field of genetics changes constantly—you need a strong desire to keep learning
2. Good people skills and a caring manner
3. Flexibility in your job responsibilities

Don't even try this if . . . You want a job where every day is the same and you know what to expect when walking in the door.

Mentor's Insights: *Dr. Sidney Wolfe*

COURTESY THE HEALTH RESEARCH GROUP

Why You Should Listen Up—(a Selection of) Your Mentor's Resumé Stats:

- Founder and director of Public Citizen's Health Research Group, a consumer nonprofit advocacy group based in Washington, D.C.
- Expert on issues of drug safety, healthcare policy, Food and Drug Administration and hospital oversight, medical devices, Medicare and Medicaid and doctor discipline
- Member of the FDA's Drug Safety and Risk Management Committee
- Researcher at the National Institutes of Health specializing in aspects of blood-clotting and alcoholism
- Adjunct professor of internal medicine at Case Western Reserve University School of Medicine, Cleveland, Ohio
- Go-to public health safety expert for mainstream television and print media outlets; also regularly called to testify before Congress on health issues
- Undergraduate studies at Cornell University; medical degree from Case Western Medical School

Healthcare regulators are responsible for overseeing the industry. But who's overseeing the regulators?

Dr. Wolfe started Public Citizen's Health Research Group, a non-profit watchdog, to do just that. Since opening its doors in the early 1970s, the group has issued more than 1,900 reports and studies taking on all aspects of the business of healthcare: drugs, food, occupational safety, medical devices, as well as the regulation of doctors by state medical boards. In addition to the staff at the Health Research Group, Public Citizen also employs ten full-time lawyers who do "nothing but sue the government," Dr. Wolfe says with pride.

Some victories include partnering with the Natural Resources Defense Council to force the Consumer Product Safety Commission to remove hazardous children's products from store shelves. The Group had a hand in requiring New York City to publish calorie information on the menus at certain fast-food restaurant chains. Another accomplishment was to initiate successful efforts to get some drugs or medical devices banned or subject to much stronger warnings.

Needless to say, he's not the most popular guy with pharmaceutical companies or the Food and Drug Administration, but the regulators' regulator isn't supposed to be.

Burns on the Job

Why did I go into medicine? I chose to go into chemical engineering. I had an uncle that was an engineer, and I was fascinated and still am with chemistry. I applied to two schools—Ohio State (since I was an Ohio resident, if I got in there, it was essentially free), and Cornell (because they had a superb chemical engineering school). I said I would go there if I got some sort of scholarship, which I did.

I was physically driven out of chemical engineering because of horrible workplace exposures. You had to spend summers working in the industry.

One summer between my second and third year I worked in a chemical plant in Cleveland and was exposed daily to hydrofluoric acid. HF is used to etch glass, and it's also very irritating to the skin. I would come home with first-degree burns—like sunburns—every day.

This is 1957. There was no occupational health regulation at all at any level—no federal, no state, nothing. OSHA (Occupational Health and Safety Administration) passed in 1970, so it was way before that. I literally left chemical engineering because it was just too dangerous.

So, that's why I went into medicine. It was not the original intention. I went in thinking I wanted to do research, and I have spent most of my time doing traditional research—all through medical school, all through my residency, and while I was at NIH (National Institutes of Health).

One Phone Call and an Abrupt Change of Plans

It was my fourth or fifth year at NIH, and I got a phone call one day from a colleague who had been a resident in internal medicine with me in Cleveland. He was an Epidemiological Intelligence Service Officer at the Centers for Disease Control (CDC) and he said, "Do you realize that half of the intravenous fluids in the United States are contaminated with bacteria?" I said, "Yes, I knew that. I'm sure they are going to be recalled because there is no other option." He said, "That's why I'm calling you. The company has convinced the government not to recall the fluids."

The joint announcement by the FDA, the CDC and Abbott laboratories, manufacturer of the contaminated intravenous fluid, came on March 13, 1971. It basically said, "We are not recalling these because there will be a bigger health problem if there is a shortage of IV fluid." When he first read this to me, I said, "I can't believe anyone would say this. It's one of the worst statements I've ever heard." Essentially, use infected IV fluid, put them in the veins of people, and only *after* they get an infection should you stop using them? He asked, "Is there anything you can do about it?"

Ralph Nader, author and political activist, and I decided to insist, loudly, vocally, to get these off the market as soon as possible, and so we wrote a letter to the FDA commissioner saying there is clear unequivocal evidence of a serious public health problem.

So we sent this letter on March 23 to the FDA and released it to the media. Ralph and I were on all the evening news that day, and the next day the story was on the front page or toward the front of most U.S. newspapers. The following day, contrary to what the FDA/CDC/Abbott troika had said about the need to leave them on the market, the Abbott intravenous fluids were recalled. It was an extraordinary thing. I had no idea that it would have an impact like that—to stop it immediately. Right after that I started getting all kinds of phone calls from people in the government and elsewhere saying, "Good work on that, here is another problem, here's another problem, here's another problem."

Ultimately, there were a hundred deaths from septicemia (blood infections from the contaminated intravenous fluids) and thousands of cases of blood infection when all were counted up. The CDC later said that this was "the largest and most lethal known outbreak of nosocomial infection (caused by the healthcare system) associated with widespread distribution of a contaminated medical product in the United States."

The common denominator is that the government is not using its authority to do something about serious health problems. That characterizes probably five hundred or more initiatives we've undertaken in the last thirty-eight years. Ralph provided funding for this work, and I wound down my NIH research in the next few months. Public Citizen's Health Research Group was officially started in November 1971.

Delayed Career Decisions—Often a Good Thing

One of my daughters is a physician. Because her parents were physicians, she wanted to hold that off for a while, so she spent six years working in the health research and policy area, but not going to medical school. She did not start medical school until she was twenty-eight or twenty-nine. There are a lot of people who do that. The medical school I went to, Case Western Reserve, has what is called "bent arrows"—they almost discriminate against someone who goes into medical school right out of college. They would rather have someone who has done something else who says, "I did it, I didn't like it, I really want to do this."

When I was in medical school, we had a classmate who had a master's degree in Far Eastern studies. He had already been teaching and started medical school at thirty-five. My lab partner was a woman who finished college at thirty-eight. She decided she wanted to go to medical school, did pre-med in one year, started medical school at age thirty-nine and became a pediatric neurologist and practiced for twenty or thirty years. It was great being with people like that, because they were much more interesting than the wet-behind-the-ears people coming right out of college. I think that is a healthy kind of trend.

Mentors' Influences

In medical school, one of my mentors was Dr. Spock, Benjamin Spock, not the one in *Star Trek*. He was a psychiatrist, as well as a pediatrician, which isn't generally known. He was one of my teachers and had huge repercussions on what I eventually decided to do. He said, "It isn't enough for a doctor to take care of their own patients. They have a duty to the rest of society." He was a great role model for, in addition to what you were being trained to do, thinking of larger public health issues.

I belonged to an organization called Medical Committee for Human Rights, which provided all the medical care for the anti-war demonstrations in 1968. We also did free health exams for kids in Head Start, which didn't have enough money to pay for things like that. I was doing all this on my own time, and my boss was very respectful of these efforts.

Popularity Is Overrated

Each year at Public Citizen it gets more encouraging and more satisfying because we've been around for so long that people wind up having to take us more seriously, whether they like to or not. The satisfaction of successful efforts to improve the public health at large is just as satisfying—or more—as helping to diagnose and treat individual patients.

It is important to emphasize that this kind of work can't be done—this or any of a lot of other difficult, unpopular kinds of things—without huge personal support from your family and friends. And professional colleagues. I can call on lots of people who were at NIH when I was there, (and) who are still at NIH. I will ask them, concerning something we are investigating and about to take a stand on, "What do you think about this? I want to make sure that we're right about this." These people know why I'm calling, what the reason for the question is.

2

Entertainment Gigs

Show Business, 360 Degrees

INTRODUCTION

Of all the careers young people dream of pursuing, I'd wager entertainment might be one of the most popular. Why shouldn't it be? On the surface, it's a sexy business: movie stars are beautiful, films can be powerful, and everyone wants an audience.

Peel back the skin and the entrails expose an operation that is built on the back of a tireless work ethic and the ability to span white- and blue-collar people (or above and below the line in movie speak), with a little luck thrown in.

The priorities are different for entertainment gigs. Although education counts, it's not the calling card it is in other fields. No one cares where you went to school or what your parents do—unless they're in entertainment, too, in which case you are driven to "make it" on your own. The Hollywood boss cares about if you can show up on time and get the job done. Are you pleasant to be around? Because you're going to be pulling long hours with each other, often in stressful circumstances and tight production set surroundings. No one wants a whiner, as in, err, "When's lunch?" Or, "Are we done yet?"

If you can keep your ego in check, entertainment jobs can provide unparalleled access to the most creative minds in show business. Television and film sets might be the only places where electricians spend twelve hours a day with movie stars. The totem pole collapses, and tattooed grips and walkie-talkie–equipped production assistants graze the same boundless and free catering as the producers, director, and stars.

Not all entertainment gigs are restricted to Los Angeles, nor are they confined to television and film production. A film's credit crawl will scroll through hundreds of people involved in getting a picture on the screen. The same massive efforts can be applied to the creation of music, literature, theater, art, and many more right-brained pursuits.

Your twentysomething peers here provide a sample of a common theme that links entertainment gigs: getting a break. Each one jumped at his or her break when it presented itself with as much gusto as if they'd never get another one.

Before arriving in Tinseltown, Erica Helwick was a semi-recent college grad living in Chicago. She had no idea what she wanted to "be" when she "grew up," but she was certain it should be doing something exciting. "I knew I wouldn't be happy, say, selling insurance. It was important to me that my job be high-energy, fairly corporate—I don't think I'm a 'start-up' kinda gal—and also have a little flash, a little pizzazz," Erica says, her quick-tempo sentences punctuated with lively hand gestures.

Her break came a few weeks after touching down in LA, when she landed a job as the assistant—make that second assistant—at a top talent agency. Her boss represented A-list actors, directors and screenwriters (and occasionally required star treatment himself). For those wishing to follow in her footsteps, caution: bosses will yell at you and throw apoplectic temper tantrums, but don't take it personally. It is not about you. Repeat, not-about-you. Not in a bad way, it's just the Hollywood way.

Sometimes a break takes a while to pay off. Lane Shadgett was plucked from Harvard University obscurity by an Academy Award–winning screenwriter to be his assistant in Los Angeles. Lane had never thought of pursuing screenwriting, but when the golden opportunity appeared to shadow one of Hollywood's finest, he grabbed it.

Unfortunately, connections can only get you so far. Although Lane's access to his boss was unmatched, it didn't much help his screenwriting career get off the ground. Lane fled LA, only to ricochet back after a two-year hiatus, finally in the state of mind to attack a screenwriting career head-on. "The hardest part about following your dreams is figuring out exactly what they are," he says. The stranger's generous invitation and job offer got him to LA, for which Lane is grateful. But it would take his own initiative to make the break worthwhile.

Just as Lane is closing his laptop for a coffee break, about two thousand miles away, in Nashville, Tennessee, Kathryn Williams is probably still in her pajamas, punching away at hers. No red carpets to speak of here, and that suits her just fine.

Kathryn is an author of female teenage-themed novels, a career that originally seemed farfetched. In college, her courses in creative writing didn't count toward her English major. If the school didn't consider the curriculum a serious enough area of study, why should the students? "Kind of a mixed message," she says. But she figured out how to become a "creative writer" anyway, boosted by a Hollywood-esque tale of being "discovered."

Kathryn's first book deal came through a series of missed connections: A literary editor read her freelance article in a magazine and emailed her at the address given in the byline—she liked what she had read and wanted to see more. Kathryn never received the note, though, and the editor gave up. It was only a few weeks later that a random mutual friend of both made the link—bingo, a direct connect.

Serendipity also made a cameo for Colin Campbell and how he was hooked up with one of his entertainment gigs. The story dates back to an unremarkable $5/hour job he had in college manning the security desk at a dorm. It was an easy job that allowed him extra cash for art supplies and quiet time to sketch.

Colin made such an impression on his boss that, years later, the boss recommended him for a job as an illustrator for an archaeological-themed reality TV show. "You never know when a door will open for you," he says, still grateful for the lucky break. Colin was hired as the show's illustrator and then, lightning struck. Again.

Film, publishing, video games—they're all ways to tell a story and hopefully entertain an audience in the process. Christina Norman, the entertainment mentor and CEO of OWN: The Oprah Winfrey Network, knows a thing or two about entertaining audiences. In fact, you likely know her work quite well. Before being tapped to the top post of Oprah's new cable network, she ran MTV. She gives no-nonsense advice about working in show business. I suggest you take notes.

ERICA HELWICK
Talent Agent's Assistant
Los Angeles, California
Age: 27

Erica Helwick was perfectly content. She had all the makings of a twentysomething happy existence: recently graduated from college and living in a great city (Chicago), working at a stable job (in public relations), and surrounded by good friends. Even the winter was tolerable—when inside a bar watching football, as she and her friends often were on weekends.

But satisfaction can be boring, and if there was ever a time to throw caution to the wind, it's in your twenties, right? Something more adventuresome beckoned her, and the pull, it seemed, was coming from the West Coast—Los Angeles, specifically. "I had always been a bit star-struck and enchanted by the idea of a glamorous and glitzy Hollywood life," she says. "I would love to say I've seen every movie made and that it's been my passion to work in film since I learned to talk, but the shallow truth is I really wanted to do something, and be somewhere exciting."

In hindsight, star-studded Los Angeles was always in her destiny. Growing up in New Orleans, Erica oozed "cool." Boys wanted to date her; girls wanted to be her friend; teachers wanted to help her succeed. She gravitated toward high-energy people, like herself, and wanted to be where the action was. Only the epicenter would do. Destination: Hollywood.

She moved into a furnished sublet and immediately tapped the networking angle. Nearly everyone she knew, and everyone they knew, was fair game for a cold call, email query, or coffee date introduction.

Meanwhile, she signed up with a temp agency specializing in entertainment positions, a well-known way to nudge a foot in the door, and completed the rudimentary requirements like a few typing tests and a screening interview. The agency also handed her a lucky break: the No. 1 talent agency representing A-list actors, directors, and producers had an opening, and they could see her that afternoon.

She shot out the door and raced to the appointment, nervous as hell. "I felt really unprepared and scared out of my mind," she recalls. The loud sound from her heels click-clacking on the polished marble floor of the high-rise tower seemed to keep pace with the pounding in her chest.

It would be one of numerous interviews for the assistant position that she had over the next several weeks. Human resources explained the nitty-gritty: an assistant's base salary is about $28K. With overtime, which is all the time, the position can earn about $40K a year. With their reality checks and job description, Erica realized that, "all of my perceptions about what I would be doing as an assistant were completely wrong."

Undeterred, she pressed on, each interview inching closer to the agent's office: a meeting with the assistant she would be replacing, followed by an interview with the one staying, both of whom were close to Erica's age. She impressed them enough to get a face-to-face with the boss. "The first thing that shocked me was that he was a good four inches shorter than me," she says, remembering how she towered over him in her designer heels. "I instantly felt awkward when I had to bend down to shake his hand. He was very formal, wearing a fancy navy suit, and sat behind an imposing mahogany desk that dwarfed him even more than I did."

Erica passed muster and was invited for yet another follow-up interview, which almost ended on a bad note. "He told me, 'I shouldn't hire you. I'm worried you're too hyper for the position,'" she mimics. Retorting quickly, she convinced him it was just nerves and that she'd relax.

She got the job, but never delivered on the promise to calm down. This was a good thing, because she'd need every bit of her energy starting on day one.

The agency "would make your typical emergency room seem like a library," she says. It was nonstop commotion: assistants dashing in and out of the boss's office, the din of ringing phones and shrieks of "left word!" or "Brian Grazer on line two!" echoed down the corridor. The preferred mode of communication was yelling, and every question or request was "urgent!!!"

Based on her previous entertainment-related experience—a summer internship reading scripts and writing "coverage" for a film financing company—she assumed the assistant duties would be similar. "Wrong!" she clarifies for the record. "While a big perk of the job was that I had access to reading almost any script I wanted, I was kidding myself if I thought my opinion would be solicited. Big agencies have entire story departments dedicated to 'covering' scripts. That was one duty that was clearly out of my jurisdiction."

For months, she played catch-up at full speed. "The days fly by and your adrenaline is always pumping," she says of the hectic schedule. Twelve-hour-day workweeks and coming in most weekends never seemed like enough. On her limited discretionary time, she schooled herself in learning the town's major players: heads of studios, competing agents and their client rosters of producers, directors, and actors.

As "second assistant," Erica knew her place on the totem pole—the bottom. Her responsibilities were to schedule meetings and follow up on clients' payments and contracts. Booking and organizing travel was a constant headache. Not only was she at the mercy of airline schedules, street traffic conditions kept her up at night. Her boss insisted on printed directions everywhere he went, "with maybe the exception of the bathroom."

And the only thing he hated more than being late was being early. At one point, she made the mistake of estimating a thirty-minute commute to a client meeting. Traffic happened to be light that day, and he arrived in twenty minutes. "I'm early," he hissed to her through his cell phone.

Then there were the duties HR warned her about—personal errands and outlandish expectations. About once a week, the boss would email his infamous "Miscellaneous Lists," with the tacit instruction to complete not "when you have the time," but "make the time." The two assistants divvied up the laundry list of to-do's: find out why his home sprinkler system was drenching one side of the driveway while leaving the other side dry—Was there a problem with the rotation?—or call a major frozen fruit distributor to locate local supermarkets that carried his favorite Popsicle. Maintaining his social calendar sucked hours of her workday as she vigilantly organized his monthly "wine dinners" and ensured no two guests brought the same '82 Chateau Lafite.

On the other hand, interspersed with the high-maintenance assignments that might send others fleeing for a drama-free 9 to 5, Erica got what she came for. All these meetings and phone calls, after all, revolved around movie stars. On a daily basis, the elevator would *ding!* and voilà!—Brad Pitt, George Clooney, Julia Roberts—emerged, working the halls like a red carpet. "Cue star-struck LA-newbie running to the bathroom stall to call Mom with a full report," Erica says, who still gets goose bumps remembering shaking hands with film icons Cameron Crowe and Sydney Pollack.

Through the suck-it-up-and-do-it hazing, she also made a tight group of friends—other assistants who could commiserate with their own horror stories. "It became somewhat of a ritual for us to go to the hotel bar around the corner and bond over a glass of wine," she says.

Being privy to uncensored, semi-private conversations of Hollywood bigwigs intrigued her as "an endlessly fascinating sociological experiment of sorts," Erica says, recalling the lessons she learned while listening in on phone calls, an assistant requirement. She never tired of watching the boss negotiate, like when he convinced a studio head not to fire a film's director—that is, his client—or like when he was on the phone praising a screenwriter client's script—"Brilliant! Love it!"—and then hung up, turned to a colleague, and ripped it apart.

The best days were days when she simply felt, "I *get* it." "Days when you felt like you are part of a well-oiled operation, two steps ahead of the boss, and just 'on it.'" The boss must have noticed. He invited his two assistants to a celebratory holiday lunch and told them to book the primo table at a five-star restaurant. Ah, at last, some validation. Recognition. Appreciation. It'd be a heart-to-heart to discuss her growth in the company, some projects she'd been brainstorming, her feedback on how things were going. "I had my speech prepared," she says.

As the waiter poured the wine, Erica cleared her throat to begin. At the same time, the boss raised his glass, as if to toast, but instead to signal a pause. Swirling the red wine, he inhaled deeply, then exhaled into a breathless monologue about the vino's vintage year and the wine-making process. "It was interesting at first, but then as the salad course bled into the main course, and as I downed more wine, my eyes started glazing over." His wine-induced reverie was only interrupted when the waiter brought the check an hour later. "That was the day I learned a fundamental lesson about a lot of Hollywood bosses: when it comes to you, they probably don't care. It sounds harsh, and there are certainly exceptions, but if you are looking to have your hand held and life lessons imparted, you may have chosen the wrong industry, or at least the wrong boss."

Despite all the antics, Erica loved the job. It taught her to be resourceful and detail oriented—almost to a neurotic level. When she takes personal travel days, she instinctively drafts an itinerary, complete with contact names, emergency numbers, addresses, and yes, road traffic conditions.

"It kicked my ass and may have broken me down at times, but I met so many amazing people, read so many incredible scripts, learned so much. And, it has been a hell of a lot of fun."

Postscript from Erica . . .

If I knew then what I know now, I would . . . Honestly, I don't think I would do anything differently. I didn't go to the agency wanting to be an agent. I wanted to get experience, to make connections, to get my foot in the door, and to make friends, and my job there made all those things possible.

> **Three characteristics or personality traits you need to do this job:**
>
> 1 .Thick-skinned
> 2. Detail-oriented
> 3. Positive, proactive attitude
>
> **Don't even try this if . . .** You're not willing to swallow your pride and dignity and devote twelve-hour days to tasks that could most likely be completed by a fourth grader . . . or in some cases, a hamster.

LANE SHADGETT
Screenwriter
Los Angeles, California
Age: 29

Don't ask him to quote a line from his favorite movie, *All That Jazz,* because he probably can't recite one. Rather, ask him to compare its plot and screenplay structure to other films, and you'll get him talking.

Lane Shadgett had many career dreams as a kid growing up in Pittsburgh, Pennsylvania. Making a living as a screenwriter was never one of them. "I had always loved movies and watched them as a kid at, what my parents believed, was an unhealthy rate," he says. His dream gig growing up constantly changed—astronaut, professional soccer player, even a ballet dancer. But writer? Not a chance.

Cut to senior year of college, and writing still wasn't on his radar. Lane, a music and sociology major at Harvard University, envisioned himself entrenched in the opera world. Directing maybe.

He never got the chance—fate intervened and it came in the form of an Academy Award–winning screenwriter arriving on campus to research a script set at an Ivy League school. Lane volunteered to play tour guide. When the visitor returned to LA to begin writing, he emailed Lane follow-up questions about details—the layout of the dining hall or the cutthroat rigors of corporate recruiting on campus. "I'd reply with these carefully worded responses, composed over several drafts to achieve exactly the right mix of insightfulness and effortlessness, like they were just tossed off the cuff," he recalls.

It proved to be an impressive writing sample. He received a two-paragraph reply: the screenwriter had dropped his name to a renowned opera director, and he lobbed a compliment about Lane's writing before inviting him to Los Angeles to work with him as a protégé.

After thinking it over for several days, Lane put his opera career on temporary hold and headed to the West Coast. Ten days after graduation, he started working for the screenwriter in his beachside Malibu bungalow.

For the next two-plus years, Lane paid his dues—think dog-duty 24/7 and gopher runs restocking Perrier, lunch salads, and office supplies. The life of a personal assistant is never glamorous, and the indignities were many.

Still, there were major perks—traveling to Montreal for a four-month movie shoot and the boss's honest critiques of Lane's screenplay ideas. The feedback was usually harsh. Blood-red X's and "try again" were scribbled in margins on draft after draft.

Finally, Lane finished a screenplay he liked, but found, when trying to distribute it, that he couldn't get producers or agents on the phone. Frustration was mounting, and the assistant gig was getting old. "I got very discouraged, because along with the many super-talented people in Hollywood, there were always a couple of idiots, too. Instead of accepting this fact, I got angry at the industry. It wasn't a healthy place; my writing and morale suffered."

So, Lane bailed. He packed up, moved to Washington, D.C., and got a "real" job as a management consultant. He wore a suit to work, gave PowerPoint presentations, and made a hefty salary. "For the first year, I actually loved it. I felt like I was accomplishing something each day. I didn't care about the content, but I found it challenging, and for a while, that was enough."

Until it wasn't. Screenwriting still tugged, so he boxed up his life and moved back across the country to give it *one more try*. "It's so much different to uproot your life at twenty-eight than right after college. This was a serious choice involving real sacrifices. I was going back to try something that hadn't worked out the first time, and so I had a real fear that it was some kind of regression," he says.

Turns out, his two-year Hollywood hiatus helped his writing career in some unexpected ways. "Consulting is sales. Half of screenwriting is sales. The training I picked up at that D.C. job— learning to network, collecting business cards, chasing opportunities— served me well my second time around. My approach was totally different."

Lane networked nonstop, handing out business cards to any willing taker. "I wrote another screenplay and was absolutely ruthless about distributing it to anybody I could, then following up," he says, his efforts tracked via an Excel spreadsheet of contacts.

And then he got a break: an independent producer at a small production company, whom he had coaxed into reading his kidnapping thriller script, got in touch. The producer didn't want that story but needed a serial killer script rewritten quickly and cheaply. Lane was given a month and $2,000 to make it happen. "Thank God they named the price first. If they had asked me, I probably would have said five hundred dollars. Or less. I was too ecstatic to negotiate higher."

Other projects followed. The first script he wrote from scratch, for a fee, was an adaptation of *Lunar Park,* the best-selling novel by Bret Easton Ellis. "When I turned it in, I was pretty nervous. I thought it was good, but I didn't know what to expect," Lane recalls. Within a day, the producer called him back, elated, and told him that he had nailed it. "It was such a relief and such a rush that I was in a good mood for a week."

A completed screenplay is one thing; a completed film is another. Years may pass between the two milestones, and some never get made at all. A year after Lane finished both scripts—the rewrite and the adaptation—both were churning about in various stages of preproduction.

Another fair-warning tip: even if a screenplay does survive "development hell" and is shot, the product on the screen may not resemble the product on the page. Lane experienced this reality check while penning a work-for-hire assignment (i.e., "you're writing somebody else's idea—they're your boss"). The job was to write a small-budget film based on a pitch for a psychological horror story. "At first it was great fun—horror people are their own special breed—but soon I realized that I had gone to work for people who wanted to make a very different kind of movie than I thought I had pitched," he says. The producers were focused on appealing to a lowest-denominator teenager demographic, and they were more interested in gore, sex, and campy irony than telling a coherent story. "The first time the director told me he didn't care about the characters because teenagers in Ohio don't care about the characters, I actually hung up on him in frustration. Not my most diplomatic moment."

In the end, Lane wrote a screenplay he was proud of. "I thought I could 'trick' them into making something good if I gave them the gore but also secretly did the character work. Unfortunately, the filmmakers on set didn't think the material that was most important to me was important at all, and so much of it got lost in the filmmaking."

The show must go on. Most mornings you can find Lane at a coffee shop with his wireless Internet disabled, typing away. Following a detailed outline, he'll start to fill in the holes with dialogue and scene descriptions, maybe a few words to describe a character's mood, habits, or appearance. After a first draft, he'll follow every writer's mantra—rewrite, rewrite, rewrite—until he's satisfied.

Typing FADE OUT at the end of a script that you've slaved over is a sweet moment. "It's an amazing privilege to create worlds in your head, to imagine movies into existence, to invent stuff rather than interpret," he says. "If you're wired for this job, it's the most fulfilling thing there is."

There are times, however, when the fingers freeze and the mind goes blank. No dialogue, no transition, no clever plot twist is gelling. Unlike other lines of work, where there's a neat and tidy checklist and progress is based on ticking the items off, some days a writer can work for hours and accomplish nothing. "Worse, you can move backward. And it's a momentum game, so just like a good day tends to lead to more good days, bad days can pile up, too."

For nonunion writers, there's no such thing as a pay scale. Some beginners will give away their script for the opportunity to have it produced. The goal, for most, is to get that first job with a certified producer and qualify to join the Writer's Guild, the union that sets industry pay standards for screenwriters. As long as a writer maintains good standing (landing one to two jobs a year), the union minimum is approximately between $30K and $40K per assignment, plus health coverage and a pension. A-list screenwriters—usually the ones with a couple of Academy Award nominations on their resumé—can pull in $250K a week.

Even Lane, who's in the union and has an agent working to sell his scripts, has to be cautious with finances. "I'm always keeping an eye on the bank account, worried about where next month's rent will come from," he says. "You never know when you'll hit a dry spell."

Until now, Lane has been working with independent producers. His first script's production budget—the litmus language of a film's perceived worth—was $1 million, and the second is about double. *Lunar Park,* he estimates, will be close to $10 million. Next, he'd like to land a project with a major studio attached—heavy hitters like Warner Bros., FOX, or DreamWorks. Bigger stakes and more collaborators bring new creative challenges, he concedes, but the studios have far larger budgets and the resources to shepherd projects through to completion.

All the while, if everything goes as planned, his credit will read "screenwriter." "There's not really any such thing as a 'promotion,'" he says. "As I have more success, my 'quote' should go up, and hopefully, I'll have more opportunities to pick and choose my projects. But I'll have exactly the same title forever. Or at least as long as I keep doing this."

Postscript from Lane . . .

If I had to do it all over again, I would . . . Have a little more structure, less procrastination, more time with friends and girlfriends might have been nice. It's easy to lose track of "real life" when you're writing.

If I knew then what I know now, I would . . . Have gotten business cards printed up first thing when I came to Hollywood. Networking is a huge part of the job. It's important to be able to hand people a card, and it's important to put your work out there. Nobody's going to step up and volunteer to read it on his own.

Don't even try this if . . . Structure is important to you or you get easily overwhelmed by big, nonspecific tasks; don't really love movies or have a great support system of people who are willing to listen to you during the "dark times."

KATHRYN WILLIAMS
Author
Nashville, Tennessee
Age: 27

It must be a school night because teenagers are nowhere to be found at this suburban strip mall on the outskirts of Nashville, Tennessee. The Barnes & Noble bookstore is quiet except for a book signing in progress toward the back corner. A blond woman reads from her newly released novel, *The Lost Summer,* a coming-of-age story about a teenage girl returning to camp as a counselor for the first time, and all the lost innocence that follows: "At camp no one knew what your dad did or if your boyfriend dumped you or that you'd won the sixth-grade spelling bee. If they did know, it didn't matter."

The narrator and author is Kathryn Williams, whose cherub features could help her pass as a high school student herself.

Kathryn is earnestly prepared for this reading. She spent the night before selecting and rehearsing book passages and hand-wrapping snacks for her anticipated turnout of giddy teens. Those six captivated fans in the audience? "Those would be my friends, plus the guy who coordinated the event. Typical," she jokes. "Let me tell you, book signings are underwhelming."

Kathryn is a jack of all writing trades—author, journalist, and editor. About half her income—$40K annually, give or take—comes from entertaining young adults with her natural teen-angst storytelling style. She has published nine books, six of which were junior novels associated with Disney movies and penned under a pseudonym (Lucy Ruggles: an homage to her "dearly departed" dog, Lucy, and the street where she grew up, Ruggles Place).

She inked a book deal when she was twenty-five—an impressive literary milestone. Reflecting on her own story arc, Kathryn still pinches herself. "It's a little surreal."

After college, an overly hopeful and slightly naïve Kathryn made her way to New York City seeking a career that would "make a difference." She wanted to be a reporter, and with two editorial internships already to her credit, she secured an über-competitive summer intern slot at the weekly newsmagazine *Newsweek.* She worked hard to impress the editors, and they asked her to stay through the following fall to help during the presidential election season.

Her responsibilities expanded, and she rotated around departments, assisting anywhere she was needed: fact-checking for the international edition, contributing reporting for the business section, researching charts for the graphics team, and shepherding copy between writers, editors, and production staff.

Kathryn managed to get a couple of scoops and bylines, but in the big picture, she began to think that maybe journalism wasn't for her. "I realized that I wouldn't be writing about Darfur, but, more likely, about hard-hitting things like the Westminster dog show. Or better yet, captions about the Westminster dog show."

It didn't help matters that she lacked the confrontation gene essential for reporting. "A call for someone's comment about a story is not always welcome. I decided I hated ruining people's days. I just didn't have the constitution for it."

The magazine didn't have the funds for her. They were hiring one intern as full-time staff, and it wasn't her. Continuing on a "temp" basis wasn't an option, either, due to union rules. "It was a very unceremonious exit, and it stung."

"I hit full panic mode. Depression city," she recalls. "I felt like I was never going to find a job and I'd have to go home with my tail between my legs and get a useless grad degree to buy some time while I figured things out."

And then things changed. Through a friend she arranged an informational interview with an editor at the *New York Observer*, a weekly newspaper. No, they weren't hiring, he said, but she could write an essay for their New Yorker's Diary section "on spec" (meaning she'd only be paid if the paper ran it). She submitted a story about being Southern in the city, an idea that easily resonated for the Richmond, Virginia, native, and it went viral. Friends emailed the story link to other friends who then forwarded it to dozens more.

This is where her luck turned five-carat: An assistant editor at a children's publishing house read the piece and thought her style was pitch-perfect for a young adult novel for which they were scouting author prospects. The only difference is they wanted the opposite arc: a girl from the North moves South.

And so her fiction career began. The pair met for lunch, along with an executive editor. Kathryn submitted a formal book proposal and sample chapters. The pub house accepted it and signed her for two young-adult novels. Fast-forward three years, and a relocation to Nashville, Tennessee, and Kathryn, who used to fill her pink Trapper Keeper notebook with short stories and poems, was holding a tangible book in her hands with her name on the cover.

Of course, there's more to the story than that. Namely, the thousands of hours spent writing and editing in between sealing the book deal and celebrating at the book release party. "People often ask me what the writing process actually looks like. I am not a terribly fast writer, but I'm not one of those people paralyzed by every word choice, either," she says, describing a home-based workday that usually starts, and occasionally continues and ends, in pajamas. A typical day has mornings spent on emails and busy work; afternoons and evenings on writing, with a break for errands and exercise squeezed in.

Channeling what her audience, primarily teen girls, would want to read is an exercise in imagination. "My biggest inspiration has been my own experiences and memories from being that age," she says. Her twentysomething hobbies sneak into the story line, too (spoiler alert), like her love of cooking competition reality shows.

It must be noted: Kathryn's story breaks many of the rules of publishing. Most writers court publishers, not vice versa. The normal protocol of getting a book deal begins with finding a literary agent. Research appropriate agents and learn what type of books they represent—nonfiction, sci-fi, young adult. Make the effort to find out how the agent likes to be pitched—an emailed one-page query or a hard copy detailed proposal? "And if they want to see more," Kathryn advises, "be ready to send it. You can't just pitch an idea, you have to have the writing to back it up."

The agent's job is to work with the author to flesh out the book proposal and sample chapters in preparation for shopping it to publishers. Be prepared to turn over a complete manuscript, Kathryn says, as it's becoming less and less common for publishers to buy a book based only on a proposal and sample chapters.

Depending on which stage the book contract starts—proposal versus manuscript—the process generally includes months of writing and then several back-and-forth edit "passes" until both author and editor are happy. "Or somewhat happy; there are always compromises," Kathryn warns. Then the text is laid out by a designer, copyedited, proofread, and sent to the printer ("or OTP'd in publishing lingo—'off to production'").

Back on the writing side, the schedule isn't so formulaic. "Some authors will tell you they write every day. I'm not questioning the veracity of those statements—okay, maybe I am just a little—but I do not write every day. I can't mentally or emotionally, and I can't business-wise." Her versatile writing styles help her land other freelance writing and editing assignments and photo research gigs. "At this stage of my life at least, it is a very piecemeal career."

Part of the job is also marketing and self-promotion. "Books don't sell themselves, people!" she cracks. To get the word out she writes guest blogs, updates her website, and is resolved to join Twitter as soon as she can find the time.

Her followers are anxiously waiting. "I cannot describe how good it feels to have someone tell you they've read and enjoyed your work," she says, adding she makes the time to respond to every email from readers. "It makes all the blood, sweat, and tears (oh, God, the tears) worth it," she says of her most cherished job perk—interacting with fans.

But back to the tears for a moment. Hear this: writing a book is hard. "It's not like I wake up and think, 'Let's see, maybe I'll jot down some thoughts today and then get a scone and check my email,'" she says, riled at the notion. "I work my tail off."

The job comes with an enormous amount of pressure. "In any creative field, I think there is a huge, perhaps healthy, fear of failure. The truth is, I have no idea if I will ever sell another book. I like to think I will, but there are no guarantees."

And the last time she felt in over her head? "Um, yesterday? Every day? I keep saying I'll ride this gravy train as far as it will take me, but I can't ever take it for granted. While I most definitely would like writing to be a lifelong career, I am also aware that I am not a best seller (at least not yet). I know the survival of my career depends on me selling myself (and surrounding myself with smart people to do the same)."

She's certainly on the right track. She's selecting passages to read for her next book signing, which happens to be in Richmond. "I'm hoping for a bigger turnout, as I have a hometown advantage."

Postscript from Kathryn . . .

If I had to do it all over again, I would . . . Do it just the same. Except I would have taken a year off after college before rushing into the "real" world.

If I knew then what I know now, I would . . . Have weenied out.

Three characteristics or personality traits you need to do this job:

   1. A high pain threshold when it comes to rejection and criticism
   2. Confidence in the face of chaos. Writing and editing is a messy, messy process
   3. Good observational skills

Don't even try this if . . . You're "a math person."

Colin Campbell
Video Game Illustrator and TV Host
Baltimore, Maryland
Age: 28

Who says bleeding-heart artists can't make a living in entertainment?

Colin Campbell has carved out not one, but two career paths stemming from his passion for art: as an illustrator at a video game company and as an artist-turned-TV-host.

In the spirit of the fantasy sci-fi games Colin helps create, treat yourself to role-playing a day in his life: 9:00 a.m., enter the high-rise building at the back of the conventional business park in a suburb outside Baltimore, Maryland.

Nod to the security guard on your way to the elevator.

Flash your palm on the scanner (keys are so 2005), and exit the fifth floor.

Enter your workplace: the frenetic zone of mostly twenty and thirtysomethings collaborating to produce a fantasy game coming to an Xbox near you.

On the way to your office, pass by the "combat pit" where a half-dozen guys pantomime fight sequences that will morph into game maneuvers to outsmart villains.

Down the hall, poke into the motion capture experts' den where they tinker with computer software and key-frames to mimic movements available to the gamer, like falling off a horse or swinging a sword.

Meanwhile, next door, eavesdrop on audio guys pulling from a library of sound effects—cannons and horses galloping—to punch up the fight sequences.

Double back to the environmental artist's pit, where you, err, Colin, sits sandwiched between two 21-inch computer monitors. Today's priority is to complete the landscape of a quest (game-speak for mini-adventures), written by the narrative designer. A very simple example of a quest: help a prince save a maiden from an evil witch.

"I'll rough out the basic terrain and rocks and trees, usually with the quest designer right there with me. We'll play through it and see if it works, then start to polish," he explains. Frame by arduous frame, Colin paints in grass, fine-tunes specific textures, and tweaks the hues to match the mood (witch, dark and spooky; prince's castle, bright and happy).

The narrative designer and Colin go back and forth like this for weeks, sometimes months, until the quest illustration is complete.

It's art for entertainment sake. Yours, dear gamer. It certainly wasn't the kind Colin or his older sister were used to growing up in Athens, Georgia. Their dad supported the family as an artist specializing in tranquil, serene settings. He'd travel to distant corners of the world—Africa, Costa Rica, the Galapagos Islands—returning weeks later with oil paintings of indigenous wildlife or sweeping landscapes. As a teenager, Colin believed the pursuit of art to be a solitary one, and not for him.

Despite his resistance, by college, art was his second language. He attended Maryland Institute College of Art where he was bombarded by art media—painting, sculpture, photography, animation. Choosing just one proved difficult, but one requirement was essential: collaboration.

The end of college came and went, without the ah-ha moment some anticipate. "I thought graduation would be a milestone, but I break my life into life pre–Antartica trip and life post–Antartica trip," he says.

A few weeks after Colin received his diploma, father and son took off to the frozen continent on a ten-week artists' grant. Temperatures dropped below zero and daylight was fleeting. They traversed the barren landscape, sometimes staying in town, sometimes camping, to paint and photograph the natural environment around them—glaciers, icebergs, penguins, and seals.

"I grew as an artist in many different ways," Colin recalls of the life-defining trip. "I learned what it was like to work out on my own, outside of school, pursuing my own artistic interests. Antarctica is an incredible example of how difficult art creation can be sometimes—nothing is easy in Antarctica—but it also showed me what kind of growth and creation can come from that kind of effort."

While capturing the same subject, father and son's different approaches to art bubbled to the top. Colin favored quick, broad strokes; Dad labored over details with a pinhead-sized brush. Colin painted with gusto; Dad put forth sustained efforts.

Back from the proverbial mountaintop, Colin drop-kicked into the frenetic motion of the video game company, arguably the exact opposite of Antarctica's austere environment. He started as a paid intern and over five years, climbed the ranks to full-time environmental artist where he earns about $50K–$60K.

Crazy luck landed him the second gig as the TV show host and taught him a valuable lesson: never assume your past is behind you.

A former boss during Colin's college years called Colin out of the blue to say he had recommended him to a producer looking for an illustrator for a reality TV show. Taking a five-week leave of absence from the video game job, Colin joined the twenty-person TV crew.

The show is an archaeologically themed *Antiques Road Show*–esque production, where the crew descends on a dig already in progress. "Many digs go on for years and years," he explains. "We come in for three days to answer one specific question and dig in a very focused area."

For the pilot episodes, they dropped in on five digs across the country. In New Philadelphia, Illinois, known as the first town founded by an African American man before the Civil War, the team used tools to determine if a school building was buried beneath them. Southeast of Salt Lake City, Utah, the team caravanned for four hours up a switchback dirt road until they reached Range Creek, home to the Native American Freemont Indians more than one thousand years ago. Their mission: to uncover the story of this remote canyon and the Native Americans who lived there, and who knows, maybe "uncover clues about why they mysteriously disappeared."

Originally, Colin was hired as the show's illustrator—to sketch the tools or potential unearthed treasures that the team suspected existed below the ground. Then the producers, on their own hunt for a host, noticed his ease asking questions to the experts and tapped him to also be the program's host, a gig that paid $500 per production day.

"It's my job to be everywhere, asking questions as artifacts come out of the ground and walking the viewers through the events of the day," Colin says of the new gig's responsibilities. "Not having an archaeological degree helps a great deal—I'm generally asking the same questions a regular viewer would."

Adjusting to work in front of the camera took some getting used to for Colin, as TV host and illustrator, but also for the rest of the archaeological crew who are interviewed for dig-in-progress updates. Once Colin found his "on-air" voice, the crew hit a rhythm, requiring fewer and fewer takes. "We were ourselves in front of the cameras. It was a very nice feeling—not only because we were doing our jobs and gelling as a team, but because otherwise it's very stressful to get things wrong with so many people watching."

In his spare time, when not at work or on set, he's still usually involved in art. Come holiday time or a birthday celebration, Colin always hand-makes gifts. For the recipients, he jokes, it may be getting a little old. "I think they wish I'd just get them something from The Gap."

Colin also teaches a Photoshop class once a week at his old college (and gave the commencement speech for a recent graduating class). Most of the students, 75 percent of whom are female, want to go into the gaming industry, he says. A promising sign of future game designers? "In the next ten years, I think we'll see an exponential change," he says.

For whoever's listening, game on.

Postscript from Colin . . .

If I had to do it all over again, I would . . . Have spent more time reading and less time sleeping. Reading good writing has only ever served me well. Sleeping has, at times, made me miss things.

If I knew then what I know now, I would . . . Have had more patience. I'm still young and have been very fortunate, but when I was even younger I expected things to come to me much more quickly than they did. Looking back, the times where there was a lot more uncertainty were actually some of the best times. Also, I would have taken better care of my brushes as a younger and more foolish artist. I'm still young and foolish, in fact, but at least I take care of my brushes.

Don't even try this if . . . You can't work very hard for extended periods of time. There have been months, between all the different things that I do, where being successful meant I worked at one job from 8:00 a.m. to midnight to finish a deadline, then would go home and paint or draw until 3:00 a.m. That schedule might repeat for a few weeks. My definition of personal success *is* doing all these things, though. A person needs to find his own definition of success, and it doesn't need to be fame or fortune. In fact, it almost certainly shouldn't be.

MENTOR'S INSIGHTS: *CHRISTINA NORMAN*

COURTESY OWN: THE OPRAH WINFREY NETWORK

Why You Should Listen Up—(a Selection of) Your Mentor's Resumé Stats:

- CEO of OWN: The Oprah Winfrey Network
- Ranked in the *Hollywood Reporter*'s "Power 100 Women in Entertainment"
- Eighteen-year career at MTV: Music Television, beginning as a production manager in the on-air promotions department and gradually ascending to MTV president (during her run there, she was also president of MTV's sister network, VH1)
- Pre-MTV, moved up through television production, first as a production assistant on music videos and commercials, then as production coordinator, production manager, and eventually line producer
- Graduated from Boston University with a degree in film production

A successful career in entertainment? This was actually the backup plan for Christina Norman, the CEO of OWN: The Oprah Winfrey Network. "My family doesn't do this. I'm not born to this in any way," she says from her office in Los Angeles. "My biggest association with this is that I probably watched far too much television as a child."

Too much TV, plus a serious knack for getting stuff done. Long before boasting a CEO job title, Christina's gig was a much less glamorous acronym: PA, as in production assistant, the lowest rung on the crew sheet. The scrappy Bronx, New York, native learned the ropes working on music videos during the 1980s, a heady time for the music entertainment industry. Each project strengthened her resourcefulness, "whether it's one day making a perfect cup of tea for someone, which is an art, or solving something a little bit more complex, like getting a llama into Manhattan."

Fetching tea or llamas, it was just a matter of time before she was calling the shots. "I do know that I'm incredibly bossy and that I need to be in charge of something," she says candidly. How does she know? "I have brothers."

Christina's Advice to Her Twentysomething Self (and You)

I would tell her to be patient, to listen more than you speak. The best piece of advice I ever had was "Read everything that came across my desk." Everything. If I was making a copy of something, you could either copy it or you could read it and copy it. Find whatever ways possible to immerse yourself in the world that you're in.

Most twentysomethings, and I definitely was like this, you're ready to get started and you just want it to hurry up and happen. I think sometimes you just have to, I hate to say it, wait it out. Patience doesn't mean complacency. It just means looking for your opportunity in your moment and be ready to go for it. Eyes open, ready to pounce.

Talking to your peers is just as important as talking to your boss. When I became the head of MTV, this woman who worked in our ad sales organization had to see me right away. She comes in and she says, "How can I be you? I want your job?" And I was like, "Dude, I just got here, I want my job first." I think that we have to be a little bit patient to learn, to grow, to evolve, and to make sure that you are open to every opportunity, because the one you think you want may not be the one that is right for you. And the one that you're not even thinking about could be your perfect fit.

Own Up to Your Mistakes

The biggest mistake people make, or I certainly made, was in trying to cover up mistakes. You don't want people to think that you don't have it together. You want to project this image of, "I got it. I know this." I still do this to a certain degree. You really want to project that confidence.

One of the first jobs I had was as a receptionist at a small production company. The specialty was mostly kids' toy commercials. One of them required some sort of a lizard in it. I don't even remember what kind of a lizard it was, but we had to get this lizard and, of course, there are animal wranglers that could have gotten one. It would have been very easy to do, but no, I went and I bought it. That was so dumb. So, now I've got this lizard in my house and I'm thinking, "What am I going to do with this thing?" But I just really wanted to show "I got it, I'm really responsible, I can take care of this."

When you make a mistake, it's a great opportunity to learn something. My mother would say this to me all the time—it drove me crazy. Something bad would happen and she would say, "Well, this is just a good learning experience." I don't want a learning experience. I will pretty much give myself any mistake once. After that, you have to figure out how not to do that again. And if you can't, then maybe you're not in the right place.

A "Net" of Mentors Versus One Mentor

I think I like "net" better than "mentor" in a lot of ways, because I think mentoring sounds very weighty and intimidating. It sounds like a full-time job. As much as it's appealing to look for a mentor, build a net, because everyone you encounter in one way or another can help you in ways that you might not even imagine.

A lot of my mentors are not even people I know. I think Andrea Jung, who runs Avon, is the coolest person ever. She runs a great, giant company and I don't know her. I've seen her speak a couple of times and I say that she is in my net, because every time you can read an interview where you glean something that you didn't have before—that's another piece of your net.

There are so many places in which I've looked for inspiration from other people whose careers and paths I admire and respect. I didn't know Oprah before a year and a half ago (when I joined OWN), and I would definitely have said that she was in my net, too, as somebody whose integrity I wanted to emulate.

When the Career Road Forks, How to Decide When to Go and When to Stay?

That's a great, great question. I wish I could be as articulate about it as I would like to be. You meet a lot of people who say, "In five years, I want to be here and in ten years I want to be there and in fifteen years . . ." What's really interesting in the people that I'm meeting in my career right now are people who are going into their second and third acts. People who are really embracing the notion of, "That was great, I did that thing, but now I'm doing this other new thing and it's really exciting to me."

So, what I would say to twentysomethings is no act is forever. When you look at a new opportunity and you weigh the pros and cons, whatever your method and process is—if you make the list on two sides of a piece of paper "pros" and "cons," or you need to talk to everybody in the world and get their opinion before you decide what you should do—you can leap into something and, if it's not right, you can jump out. You can reinvent yourself. You see these amazing paths that people have taken— why can't that be you?

Explore New Career Opportunities . . . but Don't Make a Career of It

When the path forks you might want to take a peek over there and think, "Hey, maybe, why not? If it's the wrong fork, I can always come back and go the other way."

In my early days at MTV there was a lot of boomeranging—people who left only to come back and say, "It was better here. I liked it better here." And we would say, "Yea, come back, we're glad you're back." Or, that fork takes you to yet another fork that may end up being the right path for you. So, it's not necessarily always about retreating as much as it is about continuing to move forward, but taking your own path.

There's a difference between being a serial job-leaver and someone who is looking for opportunity. I'm sure that you've been at those parties where you run into somebody who you haven't seen in a while and they're talking to you, but their eyes are scanning the room behind you to see if there's somebody better to talk to—you don't want to be that person. You want to be the person that absolutely embraces an opportunity and makes the most of it while continuing to look for what could be on the horizon for you.

The Right Amount of Ambition

Not being prepared is probably my biggest pet peeve (by the way, I also hate being Googled, so that's just one of those contradictions). If you're coming for an interview, really, can you read just the last five things that have been on the Internet about this company? Know something about what you're coming in to, the job that you should be doing. Ambition is amazing; a bold, blind ambition is a turnoff. Someone who is aggressive and assertive and is willing to work hard is great, but like the person who came and sat in my office and said, "How can I have your job?" after I'd just had it for two days—that was kind of a turnoff.

Here's the one thing that people will never turn down: "How can I help you? How can I help you be successful?" Okay, let's think of some ways that you can help me, and they're going to help you, too.

Team Player . . . When Appropriate

It's important to be supportive of your team, but it's also okay to have your own ambitions independent of that.

When I first worked at MTV, there was a group of us that had been pro-moted. When I got the offer to go to VH1 it meant splintering off from the group. I was being singled out to do something a little bit different, and it meant that my relationships with them in some ways had to change. That was hard in some ways because, you know, you're not equal with them anymore, but it was also my opportunity.

I think that's another big mistake that younger people make—when you get into that first role where you are managing people who used to be your colleagues and now you are their boss, and you still want to be their friend. It's okay to treat people fairly, but at the end of the day our relation-ship is going to change, and maybe that's going to be hard for both of us. I have an old assistant, who I absolutely worship, and her line was, "It's show-biz, not show-friends."

Parting Words: Say "Hello"

Be kind and fair to everyone you encounter. One of my other little pet peeves was when people would be mean to my assistant on the phone and they would think somehow I wasn't going to find out. Be a jerk to her and then expect to talk to me? It doesn't work that way. Having been the receptionist, I remembered everyone who was nice to me. There were definitely people whose messages got lost, I will not deny. Everyone de-serves to have you say "Hello" to them. Everyone deserves your kindness in some way, and it will be returned to you a thousand-fold.

3

Do-Good Gigs

It's Cool to Do Good

INTRODUCTION

What *is* a "do-good gig" anyway?

It's anything you want it to be, as long as it's, well, doing some good. These days, you can tailor a job that combines your specific interests—whether it is sports or teaching or social change—and your altruistic ambitions. If traveling abroad to a third world country sounds a little too exotic, and not in a good way, that's all right. Plenty of opportunities exist in your hometown, if not down the block.

Philanthropy in the United States goes way back. In 1643, Harvard University initiated the first recorded scholarship fund and fund-raising campaign, which volunteers called "begging." In 1887, religious leaders established the Charity Organizations Society, better known today as the United Way.

Modern-day Americans have remained charitable, consistently investing money, time, and energy into do-good endeavors. Twenty-somethings, who don't have the bankroll to write checks, have also found ways to give back, usually through variations of public service.

Young people came out in droves to support Barack Obama during his campaign for president, proving they had a visceral response to his "Yes We Can!" message. A staggering 61 percent of voters under age thirty sided with the Democratic candidate, helping to propel him to the world's most powerful office.

Do-good gigs were injected with a second wind when the economy began to nose-dive. Unemployed young adults with time to kill started to reevaluate what kind of work they wanted to do, and it invariably tilted toward making a difference. With the career landscape changing drastically, so were twentysomethings' attitudes toward work—they wanted fulfillment, and not the kind that only comes with zeros at the end of a paycheck.

The application numbers for the nonprofit Teach for America illustrate the do-good trend. In 2007, when the economy was strong, approximately 18,000 people applied; three years later in 2010, on the tail of a recession, more than 46,000 people applied. Of those, 4,500 graduates were accepted. The program is competitive, but it's not an aspiring teacher's only course of action, as you'll read in this chapter.

In addition to flocking to established nonprofit organizations, young adults are getting creative.

Take Drew Chafetz. A soccer nut since childhood, he was obsessed with the sport. He played in high school and college, but didn't have the on-the-field skills to ratchet his game up to professional level. Game over? Not quite. Also an avid traveler, Drew was backpacking abroad when he came across kids playing soccer in a needle-infested, glass-littered alley. He couldn't shake the image. "I saw a problem and actually thought I could do something about it." He rushed back to the United States and started an organization from scratch that builds soccer fields in Guatemala.

Speaking of trips abroad, Laura Somel had "always, always, always" wanted to join the Peace Corps. To prepare, she majored in Third World Studies at a small liberal arts university in southern Tennessee. A year after graduating, she applied and landed a world away, in a tiny village in Morocco, the first Peace Corps volunteer assigned there. Hers was a more traditional do-good avenue, but as you'll read, she had a totally untraditional experience.

Leslie Feingerts tried what she thought was the most direct route to become a teacher: the über-popular Teach for America Program. She was turned down after round one. Understandably discouraged, she gave up—but only temporarily. Now she's a powerhouse teacher, instructing the bright minds of tomorrow from a classroom in New Orleans. "Teaching takes tremendous energy," she says. "When the kids are at school, you have to be on. If a child melts down or your class explodes, be ready."

Ben Rattray believed he was more than ready for a cushy job in finance. The Stanford University graduate thought he had it all figured out—become an investment banker, make gobs of money, and retire after fifteen years to do what he really wanted to do (make an impact in the world). But this do-gooder pulled the plug at the last minute on his Wall Street career ambitions, opting to put all his energy into a start-up website focused on social change.

The ultimate do-gooder, Jeffrey Sachs, is this chapter's mentor. If you haven't heard about him, shame on you, because the man is everywhere. His illustrious professional career in economics started early, when, as a twentysomething himself, he became one of the youngest tenured professors at Harvard University. Since then, the numbers guru has been busy: serving as an economic advisor to governments in Latin America, Eastern Europe, and the former Soviet Union; and co-founding the Millennium Promise Alliance, a massive endeavor that aims to eliminate extreme poverty in sub-Saharan African nations. Columbia University recruited him to start the Earth Institute, a mega–think tank battling to solve mega-problems.

My interview with Sachs took six months to secure. Each time I called to follow up, he was traveling from continent to continent— speaking in Denmark one week, presenting to the United Nations the next. Finally, his assistant found one slot in his schedule—his last availability for six months, she told me. When we started to roll tape for the interview, the recorder wouldn't work. Sensing my panic and embarrassment, Sachs simply switched the audio cables to their correct ports. "There's usually a solution," he said—as good an explanation as any for why he still gives a damn after all these years.

Because, pssst, if you haven't picked up on it already, here's the new secret: it's cool to do good.

DREW CHAFETZ
Founder of a Nonprofit
Washington, D.C.
Age: 26

Drew Chafetz has always been a bit of a nomad. By the time he was twelve, he had visited six continents. His parents were voracious travelers, toting along Drew and his younger sister and encouraging them to see destinations as more than simply tourist attractions. "I saw kids in difficult circumstances. It's not common to have that degree of exposure at such a young age," Drew says now, reminiscing about the family's monthlong excursions to Brazil, Kenya, and Tibet.

During most of those trips, Drew would finagle a way to get in a game of soccer. He was a fanatic about the sport, and anytime he saw kids playing a pickup game nearby, he'd rush to join in. His was an innocent motive—he merely wanted to kick around a ball with the boys—but, unbeknownst to him at the time, something bigger was percolating: he was crossing the threshold from idle tourist to participating player. "Soccer allowed me to be a part of cultures very different from mine," he remembers.

Years later, while in Europe and on a break from a semester abroad, he came upon a familiar scene echoing his childhood—local kids playing soccer. But this time, Drew was struck by the reality of their improvised field—playing barefoot in a grim, trash-strewn back alley. "There was a deep canal running through the alley. I watched them jump back and forth over it while trying to play," Drew recalls. Cue lightbulb. "It hit me that they didn't have anywhere else to go. The kids were struggling to play soccer—a very simple game—but nothing about this was simple." Drew remembers saying to himself, "There is something fundamentally wrong here."

His mind racing, Drew reboarded the tour bus and immediately started to scribble notes—documenting where he was, what the kids were doing, how their situation could be improved, who might be interested in helping. Drew didn't realize it at the time, but this impromptu brainstorm session, bumping down pothole-riddled streets, would be the blueprint for his business plan.

It's not uncommon for passionate ideas to lose steam when folks return to their day job settings—the out-of-sight, out-of-mind syndrome. Not so for Drew. "I was possessed," he says. He had a semester left of school and immediately enrolled in classes where he could weave his idea into the curriculum and assignments. "It was totally undefined, but I started talking more and more about it—to friends, professors." An old college buddy and fellow soccer teammate agreed to partner up, and they started breaking ground on the concept that summer.

Without funds for an office or a concrete idea of how to launch a nonprofit, they transformed Drew's parents' basement into a pseudo-office. It seemed like a logical—and free—starting point. After all, as Drew is the first to admit, his work history to that point was devoid of nonprofit experience: a finance internship during college, some restaurant waiter gigs, and a ski bum stint in a boot rental shop.

The idea began to evolve, and the do-gooders gave their project a name, love.fútbol. The duo was adamant about keeping their mission

straightforward and their vision vast. The love.fútbol organization
would "empower under-served communities worldwide to build
safe soccer fields for youth." The two twentysomethings started a research phase, immersing themselves in books about theories for social
change and speaking with professionals in the industry. Drew credits
the book *How to Change the World* by David Bornstein as having an
especially strong influence. They compiled some basic literature and
their small website, at first a mere one-page PDF document, grew to
include blogs and their aims for the project.

Meanwhile, they got the technicalities out of the way. Drew's
father, a lawyer, coached him on how to apply for 501(c)(3) status as
a tax-exempt nonprofit organization. With a polished draft of love.
fútbol's mission, vision, and goals, Drew and his business partner approached potential advisory board members and recruited a motley crew of acquaintances who expressed support for the nonprofit
startup.

With the research, nonprofit stamp, and the advisory committee
in place, the partners turned to another essential component: money.
Friends and family kicked in for a one-night fund-raiser at a local bar.
The effort raised $600—seed money that would help fund an initial
exploratory adventure to Guatemala, the country chosen for the pilot
project.

All the pieces were finally in place, but Drew wrestled with
one gnawing question: will this idea fly? While in Guatemala for
twenty-one days, he met with a range of local contacts and soaked in
the culture, scouting potential project sites, weighing community interest, and meeting with prospective partnering organizations, including
the Guatemalan government's Department of Physical Education—a
business relationship that remains significant to love.fútbol.

When he returned to the States, he was confident and energized,
still buzzing from the local communities' feedback. The answer to the
question—Is this a good idea?—was a resounding "Yes." "When we
came back, we were able to speak more intelligently about our idea.

We had photos and anecdotes and evidence about the exact problem we wanted to address. We came back with fire-power." Drew got to work building a better website and securing more advisory members.

Armed with real faces, places, and strategy, Drew felt empowered to approach soccer icons for support. A major coup involved tracking down the former head of the U.S. Soccer Federation. "I'm not confident in a lot of areas, and I have a very limited skill set, but when it comes to love.fútbol, I am fearless," he says with characteristic self-effacing wit. There have been many great days, like the classic ones watching a kid's face light up on inauguration day of a soccer field. But landing a "name" is a thrill. "It means we've got a shot at reaching that many more kids. I'm always thinking about the future," he says, grinning at his nervy aggressive strategies.

A subsequent multi-city fund-raising blitz enabled Drew to finance a return trip to Guatemala for a live-in comprehensive follow-up. Make no mistake, this was not an excursion gallivanting around Central America. "It was an intense seven-month business trip," he says sternly. "We were up at dawn most days, and had responsibilities. People had donated their money, and we took it seriously."

In the two years since its launch, love.fútbol has financed five soccer fields in five regions of Guatemala. The organization provides financing for raw materials. From there, it's up to the communities to organize themselves, and donate the land and labor. "We are completely dependent on the communities to take charge of their own project. The locals are the most critical piece of our developmental model."

Drew orchestrates the next step from the same headquarters where the nonprofit had its humble beginnings—Mom and Dad's basement. And while he is his own boss, he's the first to expose the downsides of autonomy. "It's easy to look at what I do and think it's for you. A lot of people want to find alignment between their interests and passion and skills, but it's important for them to know that this is painful at times." Running your own business can be isolating, and it demands sacrifices. On Tuesday nights, the one evening Drew grants himself to meet up with friends, he's hard-pressed to leave love.fútbol at home, finding himself still talking business after hours. "It can be difficult for me to get out of my love.fútbol mentality," he confides. "I feel like I understand what new parents mean when they say they have no time anymore to themselves because of a newborn. This is my baby. It's a living, breathing thing."

Postscript from Drew . . .

Three characteristics or personality traits you need to do this job:

1. Passion. I felt some sort of obligation and that I could do something about this inequality.
2. Resilience. Be able and ready to fail a million times.
3. Be principled. When you start a venture, some well-intentioned supporters might try to dilute your core mission by injecting their own views as to how the project should progress. Sometimes that's necessary, but you need to stick with your own moral compass of the project.

If I had to do it all over, I would . . . Have taken some more time to live my own life before I took this venture on. I'd love to go to graduate school, to live abroad. But, it's hard to imagine stopping the momentum.

LAURA SOMEL
Peace Corps Volunteer
Morocco
Age: 23

When Laura "Lo" Somel signed up for the Peace Corps, she was ready to dedicate the next two years of her life to civic service, with one minor caveat: anywhere except Eastern Europe or Asia, a part of the world she considered too austere. As luck would have it, her assignment? Moldova, a country smooshed between Romania and Ukraine, and about as desolate as they come.

Instead of panicking or canceling, she diplomatically asked for an alternative placement. She envisioned the former USSR state as cold, gray, and landlocked. "I wasn't strong enough for that setting. I still don't think I would be," Lo says. The organization complied and offered her a Small Business Development Volunteer slot with women artisans in Morocco. "Waaay better," she says, laughing now.

Lo is a gangly young woman who fits the profile you'd envision of Peace Corps volunteers: calm, introspective, affable, patient. When her long brown hair isn't in a ponytail, it sits wavy on her shoulders. The bottoms of her corduroy pants are torn from years of dragging on the ground.

The Peace Corps had "always, always, always" been her dream. After college, and with that mantra in mind, she worked for one year in public relations to bolster her work experience before packing a few belongings and embarking on her do-good journey.

Her destination: Ain Chaib, an Arab village with a population of 1,300 located in southwestern Morocco, a far cry from her hometown of Washington, D.C. Two dusty corner stores stocked basic supplies—soda, chips, gas. Most of the women in town worked at the orange and clementine factory, shuttling the fruit through a heating process to loosen the peels and brighten their color. "We were kind of the Florida of Morocco," Lo says. The majority of men walked forty-five minutes to the closest town for work as mechanics or produce distributors.

After a three-month training period in the host country, Peace Corps volunteers typically are placed with local families in their assigned posts until moving into solo housing. Lo's host family was a lively group of six, spanning three generations: a grandmother (who didn't know her age), her two sons, one daughter-in-law, one grand-child, and one unmarried daughter. The close-knit, conservative Arab family and their American guest, who they treated as a daughter and sister, shared a one-story mud house in the middle of town. At first, the communication at family meals was challenging—Lo had only a few months' worth of Arabic lessons, and the family did not speak English. "I had to get creative. We'd act out a lot of what we were say-ing to each other," she says.

The household embraced her immediately. The rest of the villag-ers, however, were skeptical of the new foreigner. Lo was, after all, the first Peace Corps volunteer in Ain Chaib. For many, she was also the first American they had ever met. The acclimation period was difficult. "In the beginning, the most frustrating part was not know-ing if my every action was culturally acceptable or offensive. I got really stressed about that aspect, because being culturally appropriate was the most important thing for success," Lo recalls. Having never considered herself a feminist, the gender inequalities she witnessed every day convinced her otherwise. "I saw injustice and sexism and experienced what it means to be a secondary person. I had to learn to look down and not to argue when I spoke to men. I had to learn that it was not my job to change the culture."

A few weeks into the assignment, Lo had a reality check of just how different American and Arab cultures were. "I was accused of be-ing a prostitute, because I had supposedly been to a café with a man." In the small town, women who visit cafés were considered prostitutes. The women made up rumors about Lo because she was foreign, and with nothing to do all day, gossiping was a main activity. "I got really upset, because I was trying so hard to be culturally appropriate, and I did not know the language well enough to articulate myself."

The obstacles seemed endless, and most days Lo felt in over her head. In the village's languid, slow-motion pace, a twenty-four-hour day felt like an eternity. A few of those hours were spent at the

Women's Center, Lo's formal working assignment. The center was open from 2:00 p.m. to 6:00 p.m. every weekday, with the first hour spent on literacy class and the last three hours devoted to artisanal skills like needlepoint and cross-stitch. The center also served as a meeting point where women could gather to spend time outside the house. Making money from their craftwork was never an original goal, but as Lo's influence and trust grew in the group, the Arab women eventually learned to market and sell their goods.

Having only a few hours of work each day at the center left plenty of downtime—a struggle for the busy-bee American who was used to ticking off a lengthy to-do list. "I would break my day up into hour slots, reassuring myself that, if I got through an hour, I only had a certain number to go until I could go to sleep," Lo says.

One of those hour slots was dedicated to exercise, a perfectly normal activity in any American town, but not in this conservative community. Lo soon realized that for a woman to jog by herself was socially unacceptable. Her adopted brother insisted he chaperone her runs in the field. Once she ratcheted up her regime to daily runs, he bowed out. "He finally said, 'Forget this, go by yourself,'" she quips. She did, and with time, it became a way to demonstrate healthier living practices, eventually inspiring the locals to start a walking club. "We'd meet at six a.m. and do a half-hour power walk. Soon enough, we had ten people meeting. We'd also do simple yoga and an aerobics class twice a week."

After the second month, the young American felt she had developed trust within the village and the Women's Center, and made the decision to stay with her host family (as opposed to living on her own—another socially unacceptable thing for a female to do). "I became more confident and fluent with my Arabic. The decision to stay with my family was crucial to helping me integrate into the community and to learning the language."

Lo had found her footing, but she was still careful never to force her American work ethic on the women. "My work in the village started out with a small project to build trust and demonstrate that as a random girl who showed up one day with no actual skill in crochet, needlepoint, and knitting, I could be useful." She helped three girls design a souvenir that the group eventually marketed to a high-end tourist hotel. The success did not go unnoticed. "Once the other women saw these three girls with their payday earnings, I had officially proven myself worthy of being there."

The locals and the Peace Corps volunteer formed an unlikely team—the women with their sewing skills, the American with her encouraging business direction. "I wasn't going to tell them what to do. My job was to help them realize their potential and to take ownership," she says. "Credibility doesn't come from your mouth, it comes from your hands."

The wealth of becoming a Peace Corps volunteer is rewarded in experiences, not the paychecks. Lo's salary was $200 a month (plus health benefits), which was converted into Moroccan dirham. But the real dividends came from watching the women embrace their newly acquired business skills. "I will always remember traveling with the women and girls who had never left the village before or been away from their families, or seen a big city or the ocean. I have priceless images of seeing their eyes grow so large and their smiles break across their veil-framed faces in sheer excitement for their new reality." Lo recognized how far she had come, too, remembering those isolating days when she endured silent knitting sessions and skeptical looks from the women she was meant to help.

Looking back on the experience—the ecstatic highs and the despairing lows—Lo wouldn't change a thing. "I learned how to fail and be broken and put myself back together. I learned how to communicate without words and to re-assess what being 'busy' and what 'getting a lot accomplished' meant."

In a full-circle irony, the end of Lo's Peace Corps stint brought as much pain as the beginning. "The day I left was another terrible,

terrible day. I was so sad. I have never cried so hard," she says. "I never knew how I could let my Moroccan family and community know how much I loved them."

Postscript from Lo . . .

Three characteristics or personality traits you'll need to do this job:

1. Flexibility. Almost everything will NOT happen like you think it will. When you are left waiting for hours on the side of the road for the one bus to come by, and some kid comes up and tells you that bus broke down, you need to be able to figure something else out and not give up.
2. Go into everything with NO expectations. In the Peace Corps, you might not know what will be asked or expected of you, but if you go in with an open mind and a willingness to try, more opportunities will come your way.
3. Don't stress out. It's never worth it. I found that everything I went through was a profound learning experience, no matter how challenging or disastrous it might have seemed.

If I knew then what I know now, I would . . . Not be so hard on myself. I did really well and overcame a lot of obstacles. I didn't realize how life changing it was going to be.

LESLIE FEINGERTS
Public School Teacher
New Orleans, Louisiana
Age: 27

Wearing a worn set of paisley pajamas, Leslie Feingerts clears her throat, cocks her hand on her tiny waist, and mimics a Valley Girl voice: "Like, the answer is *totally* on the page, guys. *Totally,* no reason to miss it, so just *totally* underline the evidence, Yah!"

The students erupt in laughter. "Ms. Feingerts, quit bein' silly!"

ten-year-old David* chuckles from the back row, snuggled into his frayed cartoon pajamas. The kids quiet down and soon all Leslie sees are the tops of little heads, faces buried in their notebooks.

The pajamas "get-up" and the Valley girl character are a couple of go-to personas Leslie plays in an effort to engage students. Gimmicks aside, the important takeaway here is that the kids are *learning*.

Leslie's journey to this classroom was a circuitous one. Beginning and ending in New Orleans, she took pit stops in Dallas and New York City within the span of five years. What eventually brought Leslie back to New Orleans was an opportunity to teach in her hometown. But it wasn't just any teaching gig—it was teaching at a public charter school opening for the first time post-Katrina, the 2005 hurricane that ravaged the city. As one of a ten-person staff, Leslie was recruited by a new charter school system committed to rebuilding the city's public education program. The hurricane leveled life as most New Orleanians knew it; its wake left a golden opportunity to redesign a school system that had been plagued by poor performance for years. To get the job done would take innovative thinkers who welcomed an experimental undertaking.

The twentysomething teachers were given a daunting assignment: launch an academic program for one hundred low-income fourth and fifth graders. Teach them to understand basic math and reading skills (for those who were behind in their education), as well as more advanced lessons (for those who were caught up). Do this not in a designated existing schoolhouse, but on the third floor of an aging high school shared with rambunctious teenagers in the busy crosshairs of midcity New Orleans. The end goal: get these kids on track to graduate from high school and college.

For Leslie, a teacher with only one year's experience, the odds

*Students' names have been changed.

of creating a high-performing school from the ground up were intimidating. More immediate concerns—ensuring students showed up, maintaining a modicum of control during class—were the petite 5-foot 2-inch, 95-pound teacher's priorities.

The newbie teachers, facing the onslaught of ten-year-olds, looked to each other for guidance and morale boosts. "Starting a school is like nothing you could imagine," she recalls. "We worked eighteen-hour days. We barely knew one another at first, but the energy was so high. We became each other's support team. I'd bring a coworker lunch every day; he'd bring me coffee. It was emotionally and physically exhausting."

Propelled by determination, the staff—and students—plowed through the first year (the ten teachers lost a combined one hundred pounds). The following term, the program quadrupled in size when the school became K–6, increasing the student body to 440 students. To keep up, thirty additional teachers came on board, and plans were approved to break ground on a new campus. But the yearlong construction phase meant that in the interim, prefabricated modular buildings served as makeshift classrooms.

The annual benchmark of standardized testing was especially challenging. Preparation could be dreadfully monotonous. "The kids hate test prep. It can get brutal," Leslie admits. To keep them on track, the self-described goofy gal needed to spice up the lesson plans and raise the bar on her approach.

Enter: Judge Moody.

Leslie walks into the classroom as Ms. Feingerts, the stern but sensitive reading teacher, to take attendance. She exits a few minutes later and returns as "Judge Moody," a crotchety character with a gray wig and black robe, who is partial to the sound of her pounding gavel. "The honorable Judge Moody has entered the courtroom," she says, impersonating an imaginary court clerk in a terse and menacing deep voice. "All rise." The kids scramble to their feet. The classroom, now a mock courtroom, is a forum for the mini-lawyers, presenting "evidence" to support their answers to reading comprehension questions. The strategy aims to familiarize the kids with typical standardized test questions—"What conclusion can be drawn from the reading passage?" or "What is the author's purpose?" Come test time, drawing on the exercises in class, they'll be able to defend their answer. "I'm being absolutely ridiculous as Judge Moody, but the kids are having fun with it."

Not every day is a mock courtroom production. "To execute something like that is exhausting," Leslie says of the off-the-wall teaching roles she's invented.

The Dartmouth College graduate and high school track star always had an interest in education. Her hopes to join Teach for America were sidelined when she was rejected after the interview and teaching demonstration. "I think my confidence was lacking," she reflects. Looking more like a teenager, the twentysomething woman's stature might have led the interviewers to think she couldn't handle the rough inner-city school environment.

Feeling stalled out, she dabbled in politics, coordinating local volunteer efforts for a political campaign in New Orleans. Once the campaign ended, she set her sights on New York, a city she had always dreamed of tackling. Landing in the Big Apple, she was elated and hit the interview circuit with energy. No jobs were panning out, and the English major soon realized that it was time to compromise. "I was sick of saying I was unemployed, so I took a job I knew was wrong for me—media planning and advertising." The work itself, assisting clients to decide where to place their digital ads, proved lackluster, and the day's tasks would often be completed long before 5:00 p.m. hit.

Having extra time turned into an advantage, and it allowed her to reflect that the Teach for America rebuff didn't have to be a permanent derailment from her first love: teaching. Soon Leslie was spending that free time productively, applying to teaching fellowships both domestically and abroad. Texas Teaching Fellows, located in Dallas, accepted her, and she once more prepared for a cross-country move.

An intense summer training session prefaced a year of teaching seventh graders. While driving to work one day, a news radio piece about a shortage of teachers in post-Katrina New Orleans piqued her interest. "I loved my kids in Texas and hadn't intended to go back home, but how could I not?" Leslie felt compelled to join the rebuilding effort. An added motivation was the city's signing incentive: approximately $12,000, including moving costs and bonus, boosting the salary to around $60K.

But, as any teacher knows, these classroom do-gooders aren't in it for the money.

They're not in it for the temper tantrums, either, but meltdowns come with the territory. One day that sticks out to Leslie as among the worst was the day she let herself engage in a power struggle with a twelve-year-old—in front of the class. The young man had been talking out-of-turn and Leslie, annoyed, took her authoritative teacher tone with him. "He started screaming back in my face," she remembers. "He stands and starts bucking up—puffing up his chest, spreading out his arms, challenging me. I lost complete control of the class." The kids started to throw wads of paper at each other and shouting across the room. In an attempt to regain control, Leslie started yelling, too. When that nightmare of a day finally ended, there was one surprise still awaiting her: the boy had stolen money from her purse. "I knew it was going to be hard, but you never know how hard until you're in the throes of it."

Leslie admits she broke down—and cried on the phone to her mom—a lot that first year. But, she realized, the upping-the-volume strategy doesn't capture the kids' attention no matter how strong your vocal chords. She learned to run a well-managed classroom, with organized routines the kids could anticipate. She discovered an even-keel approach was most effective for creating student–teacher moments that made the battles and tears worth it.

One especially talented troublemaker, Gretchen, is the perfect example.

"Gretchen would roll her eyes, talk back, refuse to do any work, and was failing at the end of first quarter," Leslie recalls. She could throw the entire class off track with one well-timed, smart-ass comment. Despite Leslie's repeated attempts to connect outside of class or engage the parents, she was getting nowhere. "Right before Christmas break, I was standing at the front of the classroom and when I turned around to write on the board, she wrote on my shirt. I stayed calm. 'That's okay,' I said." A school rule prohibits kids from wearing jewelry, and Leslie had confiscated Gretchen's earrings earlier that morning, which now became barter material. "I'll use your earrings to pay the dry cleaning bill," she told the student.

While taking a tough stance—"You have to be firm while they test you to see what you're made of"—Leslie continued to engage Gretchen, giving her positive incentives and setting measurable goals.

Eventually, the "ah-ha" moment: Gretchen gave up and gave in. "She realized it wasn't worth it," Leslie says. After Christmas break, Leslie returned to find an apology note resting on her desk that read, "I'm sorry. The real me is here," and enclosed was $10 for the dry cleaning. "I had a different student for the second half of the year."

Postscript from Leslie . . .

If I had to do it all over again, I would . . . Read *Setting Limits in the Classroom* and *Teaching with Love and Logic* before I ever started teaching.

If I knew then what I know now, I would . . . Observe more teachers my first year.

> **Three characteristics or personality traits you need to do this job:**
>
> 1. The ability to form relationships (connecting with kids)
> 2. Perseverance
> 3. The desire to reflect and constantly learn
>
> **Don't even try this if . . .** You don't think every child can learn, you don't have patience, and you don't have a sense of humor.

BENJAMIN RATTRAY
Social Entrepreneur
San Francisco, California
Age: 28

When Ben Rattray was a kid growing up in plush Santa Barbara, California, he dreamed of one day becoming a flashy investment banker. "I grew up in the 1980s watching movies like *Wall Street.* It was such a decadent time, people making tons of money. I was barely ten, but I loved the idea of wearing double-breasted suits," he remembers.

Years later, a simple question dislodged Ben from that money-induced reverie. While enrolled at Stanford University, and admittedly overconfident of his smarts, Ben recited his life plan to one of his professors: "I'm going to work in investment banking until age forty, at which point I'll have enough money to retire and do what I really want to do," he said. She had seen his type pass through before and challenged his game plan. "What if you got a job you never wanted to retire from?" she asked simply. "That set me on the right path," Ben says.

Eventually. It would take several years and a couple of detours for Ben to earn his current do-good title: CEO and founder of

www.change.org—an online media network site that raises awareness about social issues and connects well-meaning people with like-
minded nonprofits. He doesn't wear double-breasted suits. Jeans and
T-shirts are the anti-office dress code, and his workplace isn't in a steel
and glass high-rise, but in a town house he shares with three roommates in San Francisco.

How does a banker wannabe wind up in the nonprofit Internet
start-up world? By finally giving credence to the social change ideas
he had shooed away for so long.

Back in college, Ben and his buddies debated social issues for hours
in their musty dorm rooms. They floated lofty ideas—ending poverty,
spreading education—while sipping cheap domestic beers from the
mini-fridge. The intent was genuine, but no one ever mobilized to
the actual doing-something-about-it stage.

Everyone moved on. Ben earned his master's in political and economic theory at the London School of Economics. From there, he
relocated to Washington, D.C., to work as a consultant, and eventually to help launch a software company. The start-up's mission—to
help nonprofits apply for federal grants—provided a platform for Ben
to hone his Internet start-up chops. The software venture ultimately
failed, but Ben made sure he wouldn't repeat first-timer mistakes. "I
learned what not to do. While we were great at the talking part—selling our vision and convincing people to come on board—we lacked
action. I learned that whatever product or service you're promoting,
it must match the vision."

By this point Ben's vision was circling back to his earlier social change ambitions. But still unsure of how best to execute his
ideas, he figured law school would provide a better launching pad to
get involved. At the very least, it would provide a refuge for three
years until he could figure out the next step. He dutifully went
through the motions—LSATs, applications, transcripts—and when
New York University offered him a spot, he promptly sent in his

deposit. Relief set in—the next three years were accounted for, or so he thought.

Six weeks before orientation, Ben changed his mind. His idea for a social change Internet website that he had been silently dismissing suddenly became an urgent priority, especially given that he'd be holed up in law school for the next three years. It was now or never.

"I gave myself seven days to write the business plan and twelve hours into it, I knew I was onto something special. I almost turned manic," Ben remembers. "I think I slept two hours a night for a week and just wrote and wrote. I wrote about ideas and thoughts, explorations about giving and social issues online."

That brainstorming binge became the blueprint for www.change. org. Now the site has over a dozen broad categories aggregating information on a slew of critical issues—from animal rights to human trafficking to peace in the Middle East. "We want to be the starting point for social action online," Ben says.

The job of CEO in an Internet start-up means you do a little of everything. "This is exciting and gives you exposure to an enormous number of people, ideas, and experiences, but it also means you're pulled in many different directions and have to do a number of things you don't like much—in my case, finances, legal, and general operations unrelated to management."

Ben breaks down his typical day in hourlong blocks of time devoted to such items as conversing with potential nonprofit partners on upcoming projects or campaigns; conferencing on new product features or improvements; meeting with team members to get updates on their work and provide feedback; strategizing about future projects and preparing supporting marketing materials; and the dreaded hours of general operational tasks—paying bills, wading through legal documents, and managing finances.

Ben works sixteen-hour days during the week and five to ten hours a day on the weekends. Forget a social life. "I have no time to date someone seriously. I tried it once, but I had to say, 'I can't hang out during the week at all, and only during part of the weekends.' I watch zero television, see nearly zero movies. I don't take vacations—maybe a weekend trip, but no real vacations." Ben used to jog in college, but now he only exercises when he can justify it. "When I'm finishing up a conference call, I'll put on my running shoes to go the half a mile to the burrito stand, where I go five times a week for lunch, so that I can run back and eat it at home."

The most popular Internet sites can eventually make millions of dollars (err, make that a "b" as in "billion"—Facebook has been valued at several billion dollars). Early start-ups, however, aren't nearly as lucrative and many never break even. Change.org originally took 1 percent of all donations, but recently eliminated that charge from their revenue model. To make money now, the website charges a flat fee based on the size of a nonprofit's campaign. It took several years, but the site is almost profitable, Ben says, relieved.

And Ben's salary? "This is going to sound funny, but I actually don't know what I pay myself. I basically take as much money as I need every month, ranging from three thousand to four thousand dollars, and no more. This isn't because I'm entirely selfless—the compensation for founders of companies comes in potential equity returns, not in salary."

A couple of tips for those wishing to follow in Ben's footsteps: First order of business—get help. Ben trolled the business networking website LinkedIn for successful individuals with like-minded, do-good experiences as potential board advisors. After reaching out to dozens of leads, two solid prospects agreed to meet with him and ultimately referred him to other potential supporters. Slowly, Ben was able to recruit a board of advisors. "They don't devote a ton of time overall, but we're grateful for their guidance," he says.

With a support team loosely in place, Ben reached out to any nonprofit organization that would agree to a meeting. "Cold-calling a hundred people a day was never something I had a problem with," he says. Neither was showing up for a face-to-face: "I met with a hundred nonprofits in a month—in person. I flew into New York City and had nine meetings in one day, starting at eight a.m., ending at seven p.m. I was extremely aggressive."

Change.org officially launched in 2007. In its first month, Ben estimates the site logged five hundred thousand visitors, a respectable debut. Fours years later, they're averaging 1.5 million hits per month. By comparison, the most popular websites have millions of visitors per *day*.

Numbers aside, the site is making an impact. After Barack Obama was elected president, Change.org ran a competition calling for new policy ideas for his administration. The site received more than 7,500 submissions and 650,000 votes. The top ten ideas were formally presented to the administration at a National Press Club event in Washington, D.C., just before the inauguration.

The large house he shares with his roommates in San Francisco serves as a quasi-decompression chamber. "It's what keeps me sane. It's huge and beautiful, with lots of light. I can pace from one side of the house to the other while on the phone." On the other end of the line is often his second-in-command, who lives twenty blocks away. "I talk to my CTO (chief technology officer) maybe ten times a day, but actually see him once every three weeks." The average staffer is twenty-eight years old and works virtually from various places in the country, like Los Angeles and Washington, D.C. "We're calling and instant-messaging each other. Reading each other's Tweets. There's a collective presence, but we're all miles away from each other."

The life of this do-good Internet start-up CEO is frenetic, and the sacrifices have been high. "In my case, I've given up most everything," Ben reflects, "but it's never been a question in my mind. I think it's going to be a very special thing. It already is a very special thing."

Postscript from Ben . . .

If I had to do it all over again, I would . . . Have started a company earlier in life. Seriously—I wish I hadn't waited until age twenty-five. It sounds funny, but at twenty-eight I'm now relatively old among first-time Internet entrepreneurs and sometimes feel behind.

If I knew then what I know now, I would . . . Have sought out peer mentors sooner. When it comes to the social web and social entrepreneurship, successful thirtysomething entrepreneurs have more relevant experience than older and more established professionals.

Three characteristics or personality traits you need to do this job:

1. Determination
2. Flexibility in the face of rapidly changing circumstances/responsibilities
3. Ability to convince/sell/motivate people

Don't even try this if . . . You're not willing to sacrifice just about everything else in your life to make your company/organization a success.

MENTOR'S INSIGHTS: *JEFFREY SACHS*

COURTESY THE EARTH INSTITUTE

Why You Should Listen Up—(a Selection of) Your Mentor's Resumé Stats:

- Director of the Earth Institute at Columbia University
- Special advisor to United Nations Secretary-General Ban Ki-moon
- Director of the UN Millennium Project, which set goals to reduce extreme poverty, disease, and hunger by 2015
- Prolific author, including two *New York Times* best-selling books, *The End of Poverty* and *Common Wealth*
- Named one of *Time* magazine's "100 Most Influential People in the World"
- Go-to do-good confidant for celebrities and politicians, such as Angelina Jolie, Bono, and Bill Clinton

By profession, Sachs is an economist—his three degrees from Harvard, B.A., M.A., and Ph.D., can attest to that. So can the fact that by his late twenties he was a tenured economics professor there. But more than a numbers guru, he's an economist doing wildly cool things to make a difference. An entire wall of Sachs's office is filled floor to ceiling with framed photos of him with esteemed dignitaries like Pope John Paul II and President Obama. Here, Sachs reflects about catching the do-good bug early in life, after visiting a pen pal in Germany. The trip abroad galvanized him, setting him on a one-way course determined to confront big-world problems with can-do solutions. Over the years, he's given countless public speeches—an event he once considered a me-talk-you-listen scenario. Not anymore. The message is that everyone has something to learn from the next person, even though that person beside you might not immediately seem so much like a lesson-in-waiting.

The Twentysomething Years

I was having the time of my life. I had already fallen for economics and was grappling with big questions that turned out to be questions I would continue to grapple with for the next thirty-five years.

At the end of high school, I was starting to realize that I didn't really understand enough about the world around me. I had visited a pen pal in East Germany, which was just one of many eye-opening experiences, so all of a sudden the questions of capitalism and socialism, which were certainly beyond anything I had thought about in high school, were in my head.

I was reading a lot of books, not spending too much time in pubs. Sounds pretty prosaic, but I had this idea of studying and understanding something as big and abstract and fascinating as the world economy, suddenly unfolding before my eyes, and I just loved the idea of it.

In my junior year (in college), I was reading two of the great philosophers at Harvard who were battling each other at the time—John Rawls and Robert Nozick. John Rawls had made his great contribution, *A Theory of Justice,* and Robert Nozick had made his great contribution completely different, called *Anarchy, State, and Utopia.* One was from the left and one was from what we would call the right, and here I was a young person in the middle watching this great intellectual battle unfold in local territory and I just found it exhilarating.

Any Regrets?

I don't feel a deep regret of having gone one way or that I should have gone another way. But, I do feel endlessly, it's trying to understand where to take the next step. And certainly, realizing down the road that there were other ways to do things or other things I should have understood. That's a constant experience.

I can't say it was a huge set of setbacks, or failures, or perseverance and I finally made it. It was nothing like that. It was just a very supportive environment. I worked hard and was rewarded academically and felt the exhilaration of early accomplishment. I had a life-changing experience when I began to leave the classroom and to do the things that have really captivated me for the last twenty-five years.

I think that is part of my good fortune—I came into a career, a profession, and a lifelong activity based on something that I was deeply interested in and curious about for a long time. Work on things you're interested in because that's the ultimate source of satisfaction. Having a compass of why you're doing the things you're doing has been the key for me.

Secret to Success (and Setbacks)

You draw satisfaction from your successes. If it were all setbacks, and it often is setbacks, they get pretty exhausting and believe me, I pound the table, scream a bit, get very frustrated at lots of things, so it is not all peace and light. But I think there is certainly a mix of inner drive that I personally really like what I'm doing. I take meaning from it and that is the No. 1 point. And when I say "I," I actually mean "we" because it is a family endeavor. Without my wife, who supports every aspect of this at every turn, it would actually be more grueling than probably I'd accept.

Sometimes you succeed in what you are trying to do, and that can carry you a very long way. The taste of accomplishment is really sweet. When I first saw that "something" that I knew in theory actually worked in practice to help stop inflation, or "something" that I had read in a history book was actually helping to solve a problem, the feeling was amazing.

Maybe in other professions that feeling comes regularly. If you are a doctor you learn something and then you see your patients get well. As an economist, it's a little bit less straightforward.

In 1985, when I watched a hyperinflation end (in Bolivia) and I watched another idea make a breakthrough on helping Bolivia to cancel its crushing debts, I was really hooked. By 1986, I had been at it pretty much around the clock since coming in as a freshman in college for the previous fourteen years and I thought, "Gee, that's why I wanted to do this. It actually was right, the idea that you could learn something and be useful." That was a great, great motivator. There have been enough of those experiences to give me the energy and the satisfaction to do my best, to keep doing it.

But believe me, it's not a world where there is any guarantee of justice, any guarantee of right reward. Innocent people pay terrible prices all the time. Stupid people come to power. Vicious people have capacity to do great damage. Being engaged in seeing some of that day-in day-out has its constant edge as well.

Mentors—A Father to Emulate

I had wonderful feelings from books that I read—obviously not direct mentorship, but feeling a connection with things that people had thought in other contexts and circumstances and feeling that, "Gee, there really is a connection in all of this."

I had the inspiration of my dad who was the most important figure for me in teaching me something about a sense of justice. A paragon of professionalism, he was a labor lawyer and a Civil Rights activist. He had the most natural sense of justice and equality and instinctive desire to help solve problems. For me, he was a completely vivid and powerful demonstration of what it means to be a professional in all the best senses—a person of exquisite ethics, mastery of a subject, and a commitment to serving others. That is really a very good start to have. In fact, how much more do you need?

Straightforward Advice

I start from a simple point that is very trite, perhaps, but we have one life, and making it meaningful is the essence of a good life well lived. Find meaning in what you are doing. Meaning comes in a lot of different ways, so there is no one approach. I think that the standard one should feel is that a life well lived and well examined not only gives the obvious comforts, but also gives a sense that fulfillment is the greatest thing that one can have. This world is very tough. It's very easy to get lost and confused, and keeping that inner conviction is vital.

Ever Get Nervous?

Nope, actually not. But there is something that I have learned, which I find important for me—maybe it's a very specific thing, but I give a lot of public speeches pretty relentlessly. Something finally dawned on me a while ago about it. For a while, a public speech was prepared—do a good job and don't make a fool of yourself. Okay, after a while you master that.

And then, for a while, you know you're going to do a pretty good job. Make it interesting and informative and feel the satisfaction almost like a performance.

Then something many years ago really struck me, which is that this is a chance for you to have a real conversation with a group who you might not see again. Everything changed for me in speaking. Whether it's a public speech or we are meeting, it's an exchange that is worth having and worth taking seriously. It's not a performance. It is actually an opportunity to have a meeting of the minds.

Don't think that you are standing on a stage and you are giving a performance and your voice might crack or something. It is nothing to do with that. You know something. They are there because they want to hear your thoughts, so tell them. Honor them with the respect to do a good job on that.

Anyway, it may sound silly, but it puts issues like nervousness into a completely different category. It's remained in that sweet spot for a long time and I like it very, very much.

When people tell me, "Oh I'm so nervous about tomorrow and so on," I really try to explain why that's the wrong emotion completely. It has nothing to do with nerves. It has to do with this great opportunity you are going to have and take advantage of it. Make sure that you are in the zone as it were—really communicating all these wonderful things.

People have things to add to other people's lives, and that's presumably why you happen to be on the stage today and in an audience the next time. It's a very interactive, powerful phenomenon—but actually, what else is there? That's society.

4

Green Gigs

One Earth, Billions of Footprints

INTRODUCTION

The millennial generation is serious about being green.

Increasing numbers of college students are deciding to major in environmentally focused disciplines, like energy and climate change, and educators are adjusting their curriculum to keep up. At Stony Brook Southampton in New York, sustainability is woven into all coursework, whether it is in literature, economics, or architecture classes. At Arizona State University's School of Sustainability, undergraduate and graduate degree programs feature a variety of green disciplines.

Outside the classroom and inside the dorms, green is the theme, too. The EcoDorm at Warren Wilson College in Swannanoa, North Carolina is a nine-thousand-square-foot sustainable, idyllic green dwelling. Surrounded by 770 forested acres, the students plant fruits and vegetables in their permaculture garden and then prepare the produce in one of two kitchens partially built with recycled fence posts. At Oberlin College in upstate Ohio, eight students convinced the school's administrators to purchase an off-campus, 1800s-era, two-story house as a green-living pilot project. In order to cut their carbon footprint, the undergraduates get creative—timing their showers, composting their food scraps, and collecting rainwater for their garden.

Sustainable living habits? Check. Environmental-specific degrees? Check. Next focus for the footprint-conscious twentysomethings: green jobs. Wise decision since it's an exploding field, buoyed in part by the 2009 $790 billion economic stimulus plan, $60 billion of which was designated for environmental initiatives.

And as with any growing industry, disagreement exists about what will be the "next big thing." In fact, two of the young adults profiled here come from conflicting schools of thought regarding whether homes producing their own energy is a short-term or long-term option.

Brian Perusse earned his M.B.A. from Georgetown University with the intent of working in renewable energy. He got a job in "business development" with a company that designs tractor-trailer-size batteries that work as energy storage warehouses. When we started the interview process, I asked what that job description actually meant. His response: "My company develops large-scale energy storage projects that provide regulation services for the electricity market (balancing supply and demand fluctuations)." My response: huh? Thankfully, Brian dumbed down in layman's terms what his gig means.

The education portion of Mariana Arcaya's resumé is loaded— B.A., M.S., and a Sc.D. to come. As a data analyst and urban planner in Boston, Mariana's gig encompasses numerous green initiatives. She's not the one physically planting new trees or separating recyclables (although she does do that at home); she's the one deciding where the parks should go and what methods of recycling are most effective.

The one actually doing the planting would be Benjamin Shute, an organic farmer in upstate New York. His is a more down-to-earth perspective, literally. The job isn't as old-fashioned as it sounds. As people start to pay more attention to their environmental impact, an analysis of what they eat, and where the food is coming from, is inevitable. Folks are more cognizant of nutritional labels and what exactly those long, complicated, hard-to-pronounce ingredients are. Less really is more when it comes to fresh food. I found Ben, where else, on the farm where he was happy to share his story once the day's chores were completed and the tractor put away.

Where does green living start if not in the home? Dan Kartzman would like you to subscribe to this theory. The New Jersey native spent a few years in San Francisco learning the tricks of the "home performance" trade. The industry, which calls for homes to perform to energy standards just as cars must, is in its nascent stage. The market uncertainty hasn't fazed Dan, a take-it-or-leave-it young man who returned to the East Coast full-bore to start his own home performance business.

When it came time to invite a green gigs mentor, a mentor of mine suggested the president of the Natural Resources Defense Council, Frances Beinecke. I read her bio online and, impressed, decided to conduct an impromptu Facebook poll: Have young people heard of the NRDC or its president, Frances Beinecke? Nearly everyone responded "No." Disappointed, I thought to pass and go for a celebrity type but quickly changed my mind. Here was the woman at the helm of one of the largest environmental advocacy groups in the country and a stalwart defender of wildlife, land conservation, and all things green. We should get to know her. This was an opportunity not to be missed.

BRIAN PERUSSE
Renewable Energy, Business Development
Washington, D.C.
Age: 29

Happy hour for Brian Perusse is different from yours and mine. The two-for-one drink specials and half-priced appetizers, yes, but the conversation is not your average wind-down chat. Each month, when the "Renewable Energy Group" meets at a different bar around Washington, D.C., you're likely to hear name dropping with a mouthful of tongue-twisting energy jargon: frequency regulation, photovoltaics, certified emission reduction. The group—sometimes one-hundred strong—is a mix of "cap and trade guys," lawyers, clean-tech aficionados and, of course, one of the co-founders himself, Brian.

He's the person you'll want to meet first. Buy him a beer and he'll patiently explain what the renewable energy fuss is all about and why he's hitching his career to an oversized battery. "Some great things are happening," he says with hushed enthusiasm. His optimism about the "green" industry and his own career swivels have been a work in progress. "I didn't know what I wanted to do, I had an interest in everything. Now I have a laser focus."

First, a quick tutorial: energy demand fluctuates by the hour. Demand rises in the mornings (hair dryers, coffeemakers), peaks in the early evening (televisions, microwaves), and drops off at night. The aggregate hourly "load-curve" is fairly predictable, and supply, provided by power plants, can be scheduled more than twenty-four hours in advanced.

The "intra" hour estimates, however, are more complicated. The electricity grid, which reads the second-to-second pulse of power needs, is truly a just-in-time system that must synchronize the supply to match demand or outages can occur.

The moment-to-moment supply component is the tricky part. It's also the fun part. Cheers to you, Brian.

Brian works for a company that develops enormous batteries— take a deep breath—to provide the balancing services required to instantaneously match supply and demand. In locations such as Pennsylvania and California, where energy storage technology is in the pioneering stage, huge batteries—fifty-three-foot-long shipping container lookalikes—are literally parked nearby U-Haul style, wired to its operating grid. When the power plants produce too much electricity and the demand falls quickly, the excess energy is absorbed by the battery, where it's stored until needed. Conversely, when the energy demand surges too quickly, the electric grid instantly taps into the battery for a boost. Think of the battery as a shock absorber for the power grid.

"The job of the battery is to take away a job that's being done by a power plant," Brian explains. Inside the trailer, a wizardry portal of eighty thousand batteries resembling oversized, squatty Duracell-C batteries are lined up in trays and stacked cheek-to-jowl.

Because power plants pollute around the clock—2.5 billion tons of CO_2 a year, by some estimates—the point of the batteries is to make a significant dent in the emissions through the efficient use of energy.

Cha-ching. Everyone wins, and saves—the utility companies and the consumers (not to mention Mother Nature). "If a utility doesn't have to spend money on wasted fuel or system upgrades, it can keep prices low," Brian says. Just as large infrastructure expenses trickle down to customers, so can savings.

Behind the scenes, on the eleventh floor of an ordinary office building in the Washington, D.C., area, Brian manages up to a dozen of these projects simultaneously. On his speed dial are several internal team members and outside sources to nudge the projects along: the power plant managers, tax and real estate attorneys, and battery manufacturers. For his work, which routinely tallies fifty-hours-plus weeks, he's compensated around $100K a year, not including health benefits. He'd prefer to dress in jeans and flip-flops than the ho-hum business casual dress code, but the frenetic pace of the industry suits his restless nature. One of his must-haves at the workplace is headphones with which he can stay tuned to loud music—preferably Trance or anything Hip-Hop.

A six-figure salary, data sheets, and conference calls are a white-collar leap from his post-college playgrounds. He didn't know what he wanted to do for a career so after graduating, he tried on for size soccer coach, ski instructor, bartender, and airport baggage handler. Dad's reaction: "Get serious." (What? Logging 160 ski days in a season isn't serious?) Brian returned home to help the family's catalog mail-order craft supplies business build its Internet presence. The business had been in the family for generations, and he always assumed that he'd be tapped to take over one day.

Brian stuck it out for two years. On a whim, he applied to the Peace Corps (after getting over the idea that it was a place "for a bunch of hippies"). During his two-year volunteer stint in North Africa, he saw communities use the abundant sunshine for solar hot water heating. Simple-looking devices—big tanks with glass collector plates—sat atop roofs and heated homes' water supplies. Why was something so simple not used in the United States, he wondered.

With a curious interest in renewable energy, Brian returned to the United States after completing his service. Awaiting him were the green industry's latest buzzwords—wind and solar power. Perfect, he thought, where to begin? To get his feet wet, he worked for a year selling renewable energy products to especially adept do-it-yourselfers who installed their own solar devices. Ironically, this firsthand experience with the solar gear and logistics ended up pivoting him in a different direction. Wind and solar may have the potential to become major energy resources, Brian believed, but the industry is still in its infancy, and those options need to work out a few kinks before being accepted on a grand consumer scale.

"Residential solar, though idealistic, is not going to be the major area of growth in the new clean economy in the short to medium term," he says. Why? Because, right now, it's too expensive. "You have to design around the roofs, put people on the roofs, wire the house," Brian explains. "The costs just don't make it economical for homes." Among the first signs, he predicts, will be solar-outfitting on large commercial buildings, like office towers and shopping malls. Individual residences with solar and wind capabilities may follow.

The marketplace reality check convinced Brian that in order to have a better sense of the finance side and a grasp of the emerging industry as a whole, a graduate business degree was in order. He enrolled at Georgetown University to immerse himself in finance, international studies, and energy-focused classes. But the school fell short on energy classes that were available to business school students. To fill in the vacuum, he took matters into his own hands. He spent hours outside the classroom doing part-time work and projects for renewable energy companies in D.C. The initiative was a move well played—his current employer signed him as a consultant once he graduated.

Designing academic programs around a field that is changing so rapidly is a challenge for any graduate institution. It's also a hurdle for the businesses themselves. The blink-and-you'll-miss-it pace means very few market reports are up-to-date. More than a hundred suppliers of battery technology are in the marketplace; roughly 75 percent of them are in either a start-up or growth phase, Brian says. The best way to learn the breaking news is to talk to others in the field. "It is one area where I wish I had more time to devote."

What little extra time he does have, he pours right back into staying on top of the research. "I often feel way in over my head. When I get home from work, I usually read industry news reports or related books, like Earth2tech.com or EnergyBiz, for one or two hours each night just to get caught up." Aware that the concepts can be quite dense, he picked up the book *Made to Stick*, written by Chip and Dan Heath, about how to explain complicated concepts in simple terms so people will understand them. "I feel I am often treading water with just enough energy left to stay afloat, but never enough to accelerate. I go to work every day trying to learn new concepts and ideas and know that I can ask for help when I am really lost."

Brian's one-hundred-plus happy hour pals come in handy for that, too.

Postscript from Brian . . .

If I had to do it all over again, I would . . . Have started earlier in the field and learned more about electrical engineering, chemistry, and physics.

If I knew then what I know now, I would . . . Never have wasted time trying to do something I couldn't become passionate about.

Three characteristics or personality traits you need to do this job:

1. Passion
2. Analytical mind for numbers and basic engineering concepts
3. Hard work ethic

Don't even try this if . . . Yon can't deal with uncertainty or have the patience to sit in front of a computer screen for a long time.

MARIANA ARCAYA
Urban Planner
Boston, Massachusetts
Age: 28

Mariana Arcaya's awareness of green issues started when she was a preteen embarking on her seventh-grade camping trip. Her science teacher–guide confiscated all artifacts from the civilized world—watches, disposable cameras (no cell phones in those days). He taught the kids how to start a fire without matches and impressed upon them the importance of conservation. "I remember being alarmed, thinking, 'What if we did lose all of the rain forest?' He really had a way of bringing home the threats even out of the wilderness."

Fifteen years later, she is still grappling with "what-if" green scenarios.

Her journey for answers is twofold—part professional, part academic. As a data analyst for the Metropolitan Area Planning Council in Boston, Massachusetts, she shuttles between her downtown office and Harvard University, where she is pursuing a doctorate of science in social epidemiology.

From her sixth-floor perch at work, huge windows look across rooftops of low-rise buildings and skyscrapers in the distance. Down below, joggers cut through Boston's shopping district. Those windows also serve as a screen through which she can check the oncoming weather with colleagues and wonder, "Can we beat the rain?" Being able to anticipate rain, sleet, and snow is no minor consideration for Mariana given that she logs fifteen miles a day on a bike shuttling from one place to another. She doesn't own a car or a washing machine, and she diligently composts her food scraps.

Tacked to the walls surrounding her cluttered desk, four-by-five-foot maps tell stories of a half dozen projects. Many depict how Boston and its surrounding areas are faring on environmentally focused initiatives and land use decisions.

Recycling, for instance. A handful of municipalities in the Boston region adopted a controversial policy called "Pay as You Throw," under which residents were charged a small fee to toss trash. To see if the policy improved residents' recycling habits, Mariana culled data from the Department of Environmental Protection, ran statistical tests, and designed a map to illustrate the results: the incentive to recycle (or disincentive not to) works. The findings were reported to the region through MAPC's annual calendar, which then balanced the pros and cons of implementing the policy for other municipalities to consider.

Some projects allow Mariana to step away from the computer-generated data analysis and talk to folks in person. For a project in Chinatown, she works with community partners to help the mostly foreign-born, low-income residents prepare for when catalytic development projects come to the area. Mariana's job is to provide technical support to the Chinatown agencies to ensure the local population benefits from new developments rather than becoming displaced victims. If it's a large housing project, will there be green space and affordable housing? Are maintenance jobs available in the new building, and is the local job training curriculum preparing adult education students to take those jobs? The goal is to reverse the traditional model, which occurs, Mariana says, when "neighborhood changes happen all of a sudden, and it's too late for local residents to take full advantage of it."

Another strategy to track Chinatown's environmental future comes in the unconventional format of a video game. With academic and local partners, Mariana's team is designing a 3D animated version of Chinatown, recreating the historic neighborhood in virtual space, and enlisting residents in the planning process. Players choose characters and are assigned a mission—find an apartment to rent or locate a medical care facility—then asked to give feedback on their success or trouble spots. "The idea is to spark conversation and prompt residents to think through tradeoffs in their neighborhood. We ask, 'What do you want your city to be and how can we get there?'"

Equally important to Mariana's career game plan is her academic push. While studying environmental science as an undergraduate at Duke University, she was exposed to a laundry list of issues—water, conservation, wildlife—that she felt warranted attention. The hard part was deciding which deserved her long-term attention. "Over time, I came to realize the ways we build our housing, our streets, our parks make a huge impact on how much energy we use and on our health," she says.

She plowed through classes so quickly that come senior year, she had the option to graduate a semester early. She declined her professor's invitation to stick around campus to do research in favor of traveling solo to New Zealand and Australia until it was time to graduate with her class. "From a career perspective, it wasn't a smart move. Others were getting their names on publications," she reflects. "Publications are like currency in academia." But that epiphany would take a couple more years to set in. First, she'd spend two years after college at an environmental consulting firm to gain work experience. Surrendering to the pull of a peripatetic lifestyle once more, she quit that job and took off traveling for ten months, volunteering at an animal conservation preserve in Kenya and surviving a mild bout of malaria.

Eventually, ready to pursue higher education, Mariana returned home, carefully plotting her next step. "I kept narrowing my interests, finally deciding that my green contribution was going to be through smarter planning." With that goal in mind, she earned a master's in city planning at Massachusetts Institute of Technology, then leaped onto her current Ivy League campus for yet another degree.

For the most part, she's a star student and employee but concedes a chink in her armor. "I'll be honest, I've always gotten good work reviews. But I might be a candidate for a less than stellar work *habits* review." She hates time sheets so much that she forgets to submit them. "My boss jokes that the payroll manager is always angry at me because I'm so delinquent at turning them in. I'm not very good at keeping up with housekeeping tasks at work."

At school, with other members of her doctoral group, water-cooler chats invariably turn to parents. "Someone will mention that her mother sent her an article on healthcare. We say 'Oh, that's really sweet, but that's not really what we do.'" Mariana's mom, however, is an aberration and could tell you tit-for-tat about her daughter's gig. "My mother understands better what I do than anyone else's mother I know of. She constantly wants to know what I'm reading, and I'm always amazed she reads those journals, too, and follows up on the journals' references." Dad isn't so up-to-date. "He'll ask, 'Oh, why did you decide to switch fields?' when I haven't switched at all, it's just one long continuum. He wants to hear about milestones, while my mom, who is the most intellectually curious person I've ever met, is into the minutia of what I do."

To track that minutia, Mariana aims for fluency in Excel and other data programs. "To work in this field, yes, you have to be quantitative and not be afraid of technology," she warns prospective planners. "On a regular basis, I have to get comfortable with software programs I've never heard of. We'll be on a conference call with the video game developers and they'll spit out programming software titles. I have to make notes so that I can Google them later."

The more trying realities of the gig are those Mariana has no control over: decision making and financing. "We are not a zoning board or the redevelopment authority. All we can do is make recommendations; we don't make the decisions about what is built and what isn't." And in difficult economic times, funding is tenuous. "Development plans in the city are constantly changing, and lately, being put on hold," she says. "Even large foundations that support our work are losing their endowments and making funding cuts. It's frustrating."

Balancing the two tracks makes for a hectic schedule. "Every day I have so many places to be—at class five days a week on three different campuses, work, two soccer leagues, meetings for a nonprofit research group I started. Just getting to where I'm supposed to be takes considerable planning," she says, taking a deep breath.

But the way she's wired, she wouldn't have it any other way. "I'm a little claustrophobic," she confesses—a condition possibly brought on by a fear of being hemmed in professionally. "I'm interested in a wide range of things and think of myself as cross-disciplinary. I like to feel that opportunity is wide open."

Postscript from Mariana . . .

If I had to do it all over again, I would . . . Have spent one year less at the consulting firm and started my graduate studies earlier. I'm starting to bump into real life. I'm twenty-eight and will be done with my degree probably at thirty or thirty-one. I'm working alongside people in their early twenties already putting money into retirement. It's easy to feel behind.

Three characteristics or personality traits you need to do this job:

1. Collaborative. Your ideas are not always right; others will have better ones that you didn't think of. I've noticed that planners are generally okay with this concept. For others, their training is more oriented toward quantitative and tying statistics up in a nice little bow.
2. Flexible. It's not a good field to go into if you're going to freak out when the rug is pulled out from beneath you.
3. Like technology and numbers. I think that's where the field is going. MAPC uses keypads during public meetings to get feedback on ideas and proposals; they allow us to see the results on the screen immediately.

BENJAMIN SHUTE
Organic Farmer
Tivoli, New York
Age: 29

The window flower boxes and rooftop plants weren't cutting it for Ben Shute.

Trading in his khaki pants and tweed jacket for overalls and a wide-brimmed hat, the city slicker decamped from Manhattan's affluent Upper East Side to put down roots—literally and figuratively—in a more bucolic setting. He now runs his own thirty-acre organic farm in New York State's Hudson River Valley, producing seasonal vegetables sold at farmers' markets and to local restaurants.

The evolution of Hearty Roots Community Farm—the culmination of his journey from chockablock high-rises and yellow city cabs to tractor trailers and seed plows—wasn't what Ben had envisioned growing up. "I never planned to get into farming," he says in a soft-spoken voice, belying the tough tone needed for his day job.

In college, he was interested in food politics and food justice—the notion that food is a right, not a privilege. Taking that mission statement to the streets while working for a nonprofit, he cajoled pedestrians into signing petitions for local food action, like nudging grocery stores into accepting food stamps. When a coworker mentioned a Connecticut nonprofit that operated a farm program for young adults considering giving farm life a test run, he wanted to check it out.

"I started helping out one day a week at the farm to get a taste of where food came from. I didn't learn much about how to farm—what I learned was how much there is to know about sustainable agriculture, and what a rich and intellectually challenging pursuit it is." The test run was a home run, combining his conviction for food justice and his love of living off the earth. "I realized that one of the key things for giving communities better access to food was making sure farmland was preserved and well farmed."

That experiment piqued Ben's interest enough to dig deeper and challenge his green thumb for a season in the Pacific Northwest. He landed in Oregon, where he worked as a farmhand from April to December.

Back on the East Coast, he brainstormed how to start his own farm. A chance meeting with another aspiring farmer during a food justice conference prompted the two to team up. She knew a land-owner in the Hudson River Valley—a retired dairy farming couple in their eighties willing to rent the duo an acre of land and loan them some used equipment in return for their help around the property. Score one for Ben—what he thought was going to be a major obstacle was actually doable. "Depending on where you are, land is expensive to buy. Renting is cheap, about fifty to a hundred dollars per acre per year. It's so cheap because a lot of people who own land, but don't want to farm it themselves, receive a tax exemption if they rent it."

Even with the lucky property break, the beginning was rough. Ben was commuting two hours every weekend from a stable city job he kept while feeling out his farming gig. His business partner, meanwhile, was on site, holding down day-to-day operations. When they started, "the scariest part was looking at the seedlings and not knowing if they were going to grow." Broccoli and onions—both "finicky" vegetables, but able to tolerate cold temperatures—were the pilot veggies.

Those early days may also have given the landlord reason to be concerned about Ben's farm aptitude. "I was driving the tractor in front of an eighty-eight-year-old lifetime farmer and I ripped the entire door off the barn." Unfazed by the destruction, the affable farmer-owner-mentor shrugged. "I needed to fix that door anyway. Guess I'll get to it now."

As season two approached, Ben had enough confidence to quit his job in the city and move to an apartment three miles from his stake in the ground. The team grew to a staff of ten and an inventory of five tractors. "Every year we've bought what we could afford." It's a motley crew of folks, male and female, all under thirty-five. Some are students from the local colleges, others are young people curious about a career in farming. "You can thrive here with a bunch of different skills. Just be ready to work when it's hot or cold, rain or snow."

And as the farming results showed promise, so did the finances. "In the six years that I have been running my own farm, I have gone from making less than minimum wage to making about twenty dollars an hour." Ben pays his team members between $9 and $12, and now that he's the boss, he feels strongly about offering subsidized health insurance for all employees. "When I worked on farms at which healthcare wasn't offered, I felt taken advantage of; it's dangerous work."

The daily routine of a farmer depends on the season. The ticking clock on the wall is the sun in the sky. Here's a year-in-the-life crib calendar:

Spring. The ground is thawing as the growing season begins. Ben's to-do list: plant seedlings in the greenhouse, irrigate the land, scout for pests and disease in the field, create planting schedules and modify them on-the-fly as weather changes. What to show for it on the dinner table? Broccoli, beets, and kale.

Summer. "The day length gets longer as the solstice approaches in June, which means that weeds and plants are growing exponentially faster by the day." Growing the produce means choreographing a war against bugs and a balance of water and fertilizers. The fruits of the labor: basil, bell peppers, eggplant, and watermelon.

Fall. Bring in the harvest before it gets super cold. Ben welcomes the slight reprieve from the backbreaking manual labor required during the first half of the year. "It is a true relief once the first frost comes in October, killing off many of our sensitive crops and eliminating some of our workload." Seasonal treats: leeks, onions, turnips, and pumpkins.

Year-round. Maintaining all fronts. "Running a farm is a bit like two full-time jobs"—one outside, one inside. Among the administrative chores: bookkeeping, hiring, taxes, purchasing supplies and equipment, marketing, customer relations, collecting money and paying bills, managing coworkers.

The trick is balancing the two gigs. "Once the produce starts growing in the field, the farm shifts from it being on my schedule to me being on its schedule. I do my best to keep up, but there is no down time and no time for slow reflection on how things are going."

All this work behind the scenes culminates in a rainbow of fresh produce, which Ben shuttles to six markets within a ninety-mile radius. Customers become co-op members for a $400 to $600 fee covering a twenty-two-week season. The farm invests the proceeds into the next growing season. "We know exactly how many customers we have. We grow exactly how much we need to grow and how much we'll sell." In return, members pick up their vegetables each week from their neighborhood designated markets—five to twenty pounds typically, enough to feed a two- to three-person household.

Among his best customers are his parents, now converts to his career path. "My parents were skeptical at first, but now have more understanding between the connection of farming and politics of food. When I first started, my grandmother was freaked out by the idea of voluntarily working on other peoples' farms."

Despite the demanding lifestyle, Ben is fielding frequent queries from folks curious about his seemingly utopian career. "Lately, we've had a lot of interest from investment bankers who have lost their jobs." Even Ben's recent bride is a recruit of the grow-it-yourself mantra, flexing her farming muscle with a small field of fresh-grown flowers. "I'm pretty sure she wouldn't be a farmer if it weren't for me," Ben jokes.

Not every season is a success. One day early in his venture, "I realized a whole bunch of spring crops, that were already pre-sold to customers, were not going to grow to size and were basically a failure." What can you do about it, or any other regrets? Not much. "You've got to move ahead. No time to dwell on it. The weeds are growing."

Now in season six, Ben's green thumb is legit. The farm operates debt-free and Ben owns half the equipment. The once accident-prone farmer has found what makes him happy. "I love the variety of tasks that keep things interesting, and thinking creatively to make all of the various systems of the farm working together smoothly. Getting to work outdoors with great people on my own terms keeps me in good spirits. And being proud of what I am doing is very fulfilling in the long term."

The best day so far? "I imagine the best day on the farm would be one in which everything went according to plan, no equipment caused problems, all the plants were healthy, and the weather was perfect. It hasn't happened yet."

Postscript from Ben . . .

If I had to do it all over again, I would . . . Have farmed for the two years that I spent working in an office in my early twenties.

If I knew then what I know now, I would . . . Have irrigated that bed of broccoli seedlings earlier in April 2005.

Three characteristics or personality traits you need to do this job:

1. Big picture thinker
2. Creative problem solver
3. Focused hardworker

Don't even try this if . . . You can't deal with frustrations on a regular basis, or you don't like responsibility.

DAN KARTZMAN
Home Performance
Brooklyn, New York
Age: 28

Dan Kartzman doesn't consider himself much of a follower, but when it comes to energy efficiency, he's a loyal disciple. He has embarked on a one-man reverse migration from the West Coast, the supposed genesis of all good green start-ups, to the East Coast to spread the green gospel one home at a time.

The breakout "home performance" industry is ripe for the taking, and Dan plans on earning his slice. He may just be onto something. Consider a few stats reflecting industry trends, according to the Pew Center and Efficiency First, a nonprofit trade association:

- Residential buildings account for 21 percent of carbon dioxide emissions from fossil fuel combustion in the United States. (By comparison, passenger cars count for 11.5 percent.)
- The majority of America's 128 million homes do not operate efficiently and need large-scale retrofitting in order to do so.
- A 25 percent reduction in residential energy, one of the industry's goals by 2030, is equivalent to saving as much energy as the United States imports from Saudi Arabia every year.
- The industry will employ 1.25 million direct construction jobs.

Just as gas-guzzling vehicles have met with government scrutiny and consumer resistance, homes may be the next target for tough mandated environmental regulations. Dan is banking on this.

In San Francisco, Dan earned his green chops by working for a home performance company where he put in long hours learning the trade. Up until then, the only eco-experience he had was a college course studying the dynamics of peak oil. Now, a full-fledged believer in saving the earth, Dan is driven by equal parts humanitarian urge and an entrepreneur's rush to be the first. "There's an excitement and a financial payoff associated with being early on the wave that's always appealing to me," he says.

He became versed in the home performance inspection process: an average 2,500-square-foot home might have a problem with high heating bills. Homeowner calls for a low-cost consultation. A ghost-buster team is dispatched to the home to uncover symptoms. Using gizmos like a "blower door," the crew measures leaky windows and looks inside walls to detect inefficient air drafts and poor air circulation. Their subsequent report may recommend moderate up-grades that can reduce heating bills by 30 percent to 70 percent, Dan says. Another satisfied customer.

There are instances, however, necessitating a more drastic overhaul. If the process moves into reducing excessive energy waste from major systems like the air conditioner and furnace, remedial upgrades can require investments of $3,000 to $6,000 for part replacements, or even tens of thousands of dollars. Such was the case for a recent client whose expensive water heater energy-efficient upgrade repeatedly malfunctioned, each time leaving the family in the cold, quite literally. The culprit turned out to be a faulty thermostat, which Dan and his crew eventually remedied. "It was a disappointing and anxiety-ridden situation," Dan recalls with obvious angst. "I had connected with the homeowner, sold them the solution to their problem, and during the process of getting the job done right, put him through undo stress. I felt terrible."

Dan is mindful that the green industry is, well, green. Newcom-ers should know that it's not a "slam, bam, thank you, ma'am" type of field. "We consider ourselves lifetime consultants," he says, fully cognizant that bad publicity can sink a start-up, and follow-up is as important as landing a new customer. With his energy and hopes now invested in the New York–New Jersey launching pad, Dan is motivated by the seemingly few competitors nipping at his heels. "I figure I have several years before I need to worry about competition. The next few years are about market development and getting the business to the point where all homeowners know what home per-formance is," he says with the urgency of a preacher. From that pulpit, he'd be wise to keep an eye on the rearview mirror: government leg-islation is fueling the industry with pending bills offering consumer incentives—significant tax advantages and rebates—for investing in energy-saving steps. New green start-ups will inevitably follow.

As a kid, Dan was not about saving the planet. More of an athlete with a focus on basketball in grade school, he became a technology consultant after college. The computer-science major then took a year off to travel in South America, where he and a friend flirted with the idea to flip houses. As the housing industry went bust, his plans tanked, too. Always on the hunt for the "next best thing," Dan decided to bet on the prospects of home performance as a potential career and returned to the United States.

He staked his first claim in San Francisco, where he was raking in $100K per year with a $40K potential bonus. Now, as an entrepreneur in unchartered East Coast territory, he is starting from scratch. "I'm introducing myself into circles, offering to speak at green jobs conferences, and networking to find teammates to help build the business," he says.

Dan's aggressive "can-do" attitude is crucial to his strategy, but he concedes he is learning to tailor it to a variety of audiences. "I tend to be demanding at times, but I believe in what I do and speak with conviction and intensity. This can rub people the wrong way and be mistaken for arrogance and cockiness." How can he tell? "Oh, things have come up over time. When I see people's reaction, I inquire about it. My family certainly keeps me grounded."

The mix of tenacity and confidence is a logical reaction for a young man who realized that "boss" suits his personality more than "employee." Working for someone else, he found that the most frustrating part of the job was not having enough control over company strategy. "Sometimes you'll see something that doesn't make sense and raise a point about it, but, as a company, we continue to do it because it's ultimately the decision of whomever is in charge," he says. "It's hard to watch what you believe is wrong in an organization you care so much about. The only way I've figured out how to get around this is to become the person in charge."

Ever the businessman, Dan recalls an especially memorable day on the old job when the team landed a seven-figure investment.

Although prohibited from disclosing the exact amount, he revels in the score. "We had all been working so hard together for two years in a cramped shoe box of an office. We got word on a Friday afternoon, just before the banks closed, that the money was officially in the coffers." Ironically, the following Monday, Lehman Bros. collapsed and all investment went dark. The capital infusion was also a timely benchmark in the company's growth. "It symbolized the light at the end of the tunnel, or at least the light at the end of one tunnel and beginning of another," he recalls.

Admittedly strong minded, his relentless style seems to be mellowing. "I won't fail at something for lack of effort. I may not be the smartest person, but I work for it." In this phase of a start-up in the green arena, he plans to put to work a few hard-earned lessons. "Now that I'm in a leadership position, I've learned that it's not about 'my idea' getting done, but instead to create ways for people to be passionate. That means that my idea might have to wait. Nothing is happening so fast that there won't be time to try something else."

Postscript from Dan . . .

If I had to do it all over again, I would . . . Have talked less. Everyone you work with has a unique perspective to offer. In the long term it's in your best interest if you can understand their positions and make decisions with as much information as possible. If you're talking all the time, you will not be making informed decisions.

If I knew then what I know now, I would . . . Have been better to myself. I was constantly pushing myself to the limit, and as a result, I spent Thanksgiving, Christmas, Memorial Day, and Labor Day sick. Things get done over time; it's best for my business if I'm operating at my highest rate of effectiveness.

***Three characteristics or personality traits you need
to do this job:***

1. Curiosity
2. Tenacity
3. Business sense

Don't even try this if . . . You're not willing to do whatever it takes
to get the job done. In a start-up environment, very little happens
unless you do it yourself. That doesn't mean the big decisions or
strategic partnerships, either—I mean buying the printer, setting up
the phone system, all the little things a business needs, but are not
glamorous.

MENTOR'S INSIGHTS: *FRANCES BEINECKE*

MATT GREENSLADE

**Why You Should Listen Up—(a Selection of) Your
Mentor's Resumé Stats:**

- President, Natural Resources Defense Council
- Named to the ranks of *Fortune* magazine's "5 in power positions"
- Board member on a slate of green coalitions: World Resources Institute, the Energy Future Coalition, and Conservation International's Center for Environmental Leadership in Business
- Recipient of various green awards: Rachel Carson Award from the National Audubon Society, the Annual Conservation Award from the Adirondack Council, and the Robert Marshall Award from the Wilderness Society
- Graduate of Yale College and Yale School of Forestry and Environmental Studies.

The Natural Resources Defense Council is often the unsung hero in environmental causes worldwide. Founded in 1970, the non-profit environmental advocacy group has stayed true to its powerful mission: to protect wildlife and wild places and to ensure a healthy environment for all life on earth. It might sound like a quixotic goal, except that the organization actually does *do* these things. Employing some of the nation's top experts on environmental law and science, NRDC has been attached to almost every significant global warming, energy, land conservation, wildlife and ocean protection policy in the country. Some victories you may have heard of (helping to place the polar bear under the protection of the Endangered Species Act); some you may not (saving thousands of acres of Utah's Redrock country from oil and gas drilling), but all have been in vigorous defense of our earth.

The Manhattan-based headquarters exudes a serious "We-Can-Do-This" attitude while keeping the mood light. Goofy Polaroid pictures of the staff are taped to the kitchen wall. A mural of larger-than-life-size animals and vegetables in the lobby reminds folks why they're there. The infectious energy permeating throughout is no doubt set by its president, and your green gigs mentor, Frances Beinecke. Slender and fair skinned, but tough and direct, Beinecke is now in her third year as boss—having begun as an intern more than thirty years ago. She's proud of the group's accomplishments, but knows there's still plenty to do.

A Place in the Woods

When I was in my twenties, it was a time of great controversy, and a very active antiwar movement, but also the beginning of serious environmental concern. I was in college for Earth Day and young people were asking, "How can I make a difference in this world?" Things looked pretty bleak.

I was always thinking of the public sector and urban policy because that was right at the time a lot of cities were burning, as a result of the many riots and demonstrations. Then I became passionate about the environment and fell in love with the Adirondacks. Our family had bought some property, and here was this great six-million-acre wilderness that I had known nothing about. I was looking at this wonderful area and wondering, "What's a long-term protection plan?"

Hitchhiking in Africa

I was not one of these "I know what I want to do" people in college. I had no idea. Some people have a passion. But for most people, it's somebody or an experience that sets you down a path, and things develop step by step. I don't think everyone knows at the beginning or throughout college because you are exposed to so many things. You need something to unlock it.

After college, I went to eastern Africa—Ethiopia, the Congo, Rwanda, Tanzania, Kenya—for three or four months. Places that have gone through terrible crises of genocide, famine. The tensions of protecting natural systems, and the needs of humanity—jobs, well-being, security—they all came into play.

We went to Rwanda to see an old family friend, Roz Carr, who was an amazing woman. She lived in the Kibo region where all the genocide has been. She ran a plantation and grew flowers and had spent a lifetime there and was passionate about Africa. A very brave, single American woman living on a plantation in what was then a very remote place, she eeked out a living, and then after the genocide, she opened an orphanage for the kids who had lost their families.

I came back and I still didn't know what I wanted to do. I was interested in the environment, signed up for the Yale School of Forestry, but even then, I didn't know what avenue. I thought I'd go into land conservation. But by happenstance, I ended up coming to NRDC, and that unfolded an entire opportunity and career on the public policy side. As an intern you never know where you're going to end up—you may end up being the president, who knows?

What My Kids Think I Do . . .

My three daughters, now in their twenties, thought I was the "earth's great defender." I remember one "Take Your Daughters to Work Day" when they came into an NRDC conference room. They were young at the time, and said, "What does Mom do? Well, she goes to a lot of meetings. We thought she was protecting the earth when she actually goes to meetings."

A Young but Not So Diverse Movement

NRDC's staff is 60 percent women. John Adams, our founder, was fantastic in providing opportunity for women. I think the environmental movement provides a lot of opportunity because it's a young movement. It started in 1970. You weren't coming out of a long period of a movement with a lot of strong male domination and then trying to even that out.

But the environmental movement is not nearly diverse enough from an ethnicity or diverse background standpoint. It's something we really have to change. I went to an all-girls high school, then I went to a very dominated men's university, and I guess I am just used to it. It doesn't really faze me anymore, but I think a lot needs to happen to provide more leadership opportunities for women across all levels of society.

Environmental jobs cross all sectors now. When I was in graduate school you went to an environmental group. That was it. I don't think there were many other choices. Now every level of government, every company, every institution, whatever your job is, you have a responsibility toward your environmental footprint.

Every mayor, every city, every corporation is looking at this issue of sustainability and environmental footprint. Also, in the energy sector, there are just unbelievable opportunities for innovation and for creativity. Global warming and creating a clean energy economy dominate the business agenda. So many people who think they have the invention that is going to be cleaner, greener than anybody else want to create new ventures, new companies.

The number of environmental programs that have developed at universities is really vast now. People want to advance sustainability, greener lifestyle, green product lines, greener footprint across the board—there are just huge opportunities to do that. It's out there for the taking.

Best Way to Deal with Failures and Regrets?

That's a hard one because it's much more convenient to forget.

One thing about failure is you must get over it. The worst thing you can do is not try. Trying a lot of different things and seeing what works is the important thing to do. Being comfortable with the tried-and-true strategy because it works may result in incremental advancement, but it might not result in the dramatic change that you seek.

My job, as the president of NRDC, and previously when I was executive director, is really a support job. We have this huge, talented staff. I want to be sure they have the support they need to be creative and try things and see where those things go. So, it's not so much what I do, but it's really providing the environment that allows people to try, and fail, and succeed. As long as success outweighs failure, as long as failure doesn't put the institution at risk, you ought to be out there trying everything you can think of.

One thing I've learned, and it's even more true today, is that it's very important to understand what will motivate others. You know what motivates you, but what motivates you doesn't necessarily motivate those people you are trying to reach. You've got to have an ability to hear the other side. That was a very hard lesson learned. When you come in with a passion and a mission, you basically are convinced you are right and you want to convince other people you are right and they're wrong. Well, that's not necessarily the most persuasive thing to do. Part of being persuasive is understanding the other side.

Besides Hard Work, What Does It Take?

A couple of things: I had a great mentor who was our founder, John Adams, a very passionate, charismatic guy who gave opportunity to young people. When I was first at NRDC, he recommended that I join boards like the Adirondack Council, the Wilderness Society—these were huge opportunities.

Somebody has to give you an opportunity, and mentors are incredibly important. Finding somebody who is going to see that it's to their advantage to put people forward and give them experiences that they wouldn't otherwise have.

Another thing: In the early years of a career you don't know necessarily what your skills are. You know you're trained in something, but you don't know what your instinctual skills are. So as you develop, you begin to see what they are. You have to be self-reflective—what are you good at and what are you not good at?

I like to work with people and to manage. I like making NRDC strong with all these pieces. I worked on land use, I worked on coastal zone management, and I worked on offshore oil and gas leasing. But what I became more interested in was, what makes the whole thing work? I had opportunities to then become the program director. To me, the management style here is one of support and leadership—more of the coach than the captain.

You spend a lot more time at work than you spend doing anything else, so you better be with a group of people and in an environment you really enjoy. You want to know that you spent your time doing something you really loved, that you cared about not only the issue, but also the work environment and the relationship you have with people. It's the combination that really makes the difference.

5

News Gigs

All the News That's Fit to . . . Print, Televise, and Blog

INTRODUCTION

L et's get the bad news out of the way—journalism is in trouble. Newspapers like the *Rocky Mountain News* and *Kentucky Post* have disappeared entirely. Others are experimenting with a hybrid model: some slashing home delivery to three times a week and many moving the bulk of their content online.

Weekly and monthly magazines aren't faring much better. *Portfolio,* CondeNast's *Vanity Fair-meets-Forbes,* folded after just two years of publication. Even *Playboy* is feeling the pain. By 2010, the circulation of the infamous men's magazine had dropped precipitously to 1.5 million from a peak of 7.2 million in 1972. So much for sexy pubs being recession-proof.

Broadcast news isn't a shining star anymore, either. The major networks' news broadcasts once dominated the 6:00 p.m. television slots. Remember hearing about Walter Cronkite, "The Most Trusted Man in America"? The days of iconic anchors are over, as audiences drift to other platforms like cable, the Internet, even phones. Twenty-six percent of Americans now access news on their cell phones, according to the State of the Media, a website that tracks media trends.

The statistics beg the question: Why have a news gig chapter in the first place?

Simple: because solid journalism is not disposable, and there are still jobs out there. Our generation may not be consuming news the way our parents do, but that doesn't mean we're not paying attention. We're sensible enough to know that we can get the news on our terms—when and where we want it, whether on our laptops, on our phones, or from our friends' social networking links.

In this chapter you'll meet four of your peers helping to deliver the news to you via a variety of formats.

Asa Eslocker, a midwest fraternity boy turned NYC-savvy television associate producer, knows how important it is to be versed in all new media formats. "If you know how to shoot, edit, and publish on the web, that'll make you a valuable hire," he observes, now that he has a 360-degree perspective from inside the trenches of the newsroom. Scheduling my interview time with Asa was difficult. On more than one occasion, he had to cut the conversation short because he was in the middle of staking out a suspected terrorist in Denver or en route to Dublin, Ireland, for a location shoot—footage slated for an upcoming broadcast, and undoubtedly, a web link and blog post, too.

Newspaper journalist Caleb Hannan was perfectly happy indulging a failure-to-launch lifestyle after college graduation. He and his "super senior" friends stuck around campus, working odd jobs and pretending they were still in school (the social parts at least). A tragic family accident brought that blasé attitude to an abrupt end and Caleb faced the "What Do I Want to Do with My Life?" question head on. He chose to pursue newspaper reporting and started off on a rocky journey, moving three times in eighteen months because of layoffs or newspaper closings. Why not choose a safer career?

The matter-of-fact reporter deadpans, "Oh, Jesus. In lieu of some nifty quote or story, I'll just say this: You can put on a smile for a day, or a week, but if you know someone who's truly following his dreams, then you know what it looks like when someone's not faking."

Local broadcast reporter Maggie Crane is blond and bubbly, with a face for television. Her winsome appearance, however, belies her fighting nature. The cancer survivor (the makings of a separate book entirely) tells us about the rise of a midwestern gal to Los Angeles entertainment journalist, and explains why leaving Hollywood behind was not a tough decision. From her post in southern Florida, she reports the local news—anything from fatal car accidents and hurricanes to beekeepers and circus clowns. The variety now holds her attention.

And perhaps the coolest job on the planet—an intern at the Food Network (hey, not all careers start with salaried positions). How do you get a gig working with food anyway? Kelly Senyei had several internships at major news networks that plumped up her resumé, but it was her obsession—and I do mean obsession—with cooking that inspired her to start a food blog while attending graduate school in journalism. Her culinary passion and inventive website posts helped her wedge her foot in the door as an intern. I caught up with Kelly when she was visiting her mom at home in San Diego, an appropriate spot to dish about her back story since Mom's kitchen is where her cooking craze began more than a decade ago.

A 20/20 perspective as mentor for this news gig chapter comes from Nicholas Lemann. Landing his first assignment while still in high school in New Orleans, Lemann's trajectory included stints at the nation's most esteemed publications—the *Washington Post* and the *New Yorker,* among others. Currently dean of the Columbia University Graduate School of Journalism in New York City, he has a unique vantage point on an evolving industry—a foothold in both the real working news world and in an institution training aspiring journalists.

ASA ESLOCKER
Associate Producer
New York, New York
Age: 28

It was hour No. 3 of a stakeout on a drizzly day deep in West Virginia's coal country. Asa Eslocker, associate producer for ABC's Investigative Unit with Brian Ross, had flown down from New York City, equipped with a video camera, to get answers. The subject of the story he was working—a CEO of a major coal company who was allegedly bribing members of the state's Supreme Court—was not returning calls for comment, and the story was set to run on an upcoming *Nightline* broadcast. "No comment" means no story; no story is never an option.

The rental car was inconspicuously parked in front of the mining company's headquarters, far enough away to not raise suspicion, yet close enough to make a positive ID. Finally, the CEO pulled up and Asa pounced to confront him, camera rolling. The coal titan did not appreciate the uninvited guest. "He basically assaulted me, broke part of my camera, and pushed me fifty feet while threatening me," Asa remembers.

By the time Asa hustled back to New York City that afternoon, the coal company's attorneys were already calling the network, threatening the young producer for assaulting The Boss. "I showed the tape to my managers and dealt with our lawyers and the senior vice presidents," Asa says. "The tape showed I had done my job correctly. I was vindicated."

Asa and his team later won an Investigative News/Business Emmy for that story.

Welcome to the world of television news production. Not every story will require such wily tactics. The job of an associate producer, especially one on an investigation unit, is to get what needs to be done, done. And it all begins with the story.

An ABC investigative team of twelve, which contributes to ABC

news programs *World News, 20/20,* and *Good Morning America,* depends on a variety of insider sources for investigation-worthy story
leads. They are also tuned into mainstream news media—newspapers,
competing TV networks, National Public Radio—tracking who's
covering what and how well. Most stories are assigned to producers
by seasoned managers with a keen sense of what stories make com-
pelling news. Once an idea moves to the front burner, after a variety
of approvals through the show's chain of command, the story is cata-
pulted into production—think dozens, even hundreds, of phone calls,
thorough online research, exhaustive travel, and logistical organization.

On most assignments, Asa can expect to travel to shoot locations,
set up interviews, or stake out a subject who "most likely does not
want to be found." The team has perfected the "accountability interview" (known as an "ambush" in some circles). When an interview
subject isn't cooperating or is ignoring them outright, they'll put a
producer on a plane to stage an intervention (with a ready and rolling
camera, of course). It makes for high drama, and even better television.

Asa first got a taste of the producer lifestyle while he was a college
student in the Midwest. ABC News had descended on the campus,
along with dozens of other media outlets, to cover a presidential debate. Asa seized the opportunity. "I weaseled my way into a runner
position and helped with all the aspects of their debate coverage,"
he recalls. He ran errands for producers, picked up food and drinks,
drove correspondents to and from their hotels, and duct-taped clocks
to the wall in the makeshift production office. When the crew needed
a stand-in so they could test their camera angles, Asa piped up and
leaped into position. He was hooked. "I could do this one day," he
says, recalling the note-to-self moment.

The ABC News fleet left as quickly as it had appeared, leaving a
buzzing Asa with a stack of business cards, inviting him to keep in
touch. He did, and when it came time to submit his application as an
intern at the network the following summer, the effort paid off. His

follow-up and networking helped him score a spot on the morning news show *Good Morning America.*

In the big city, he was humbled to learn that what he thought was a solid "foot in the door" was a sobering reality check: the other interns bustling around were producer wannabes, too. Chances were that they also would be applying for full-time jobs come graduation. Asa had to up his game.

Back on campus for his senior year, he pitched a novel idea: a college morning show for the university audience. When the administration's initial reaction was a dismissive, "It can't be done," Asa charged ahead. The school had a newspaper but no broadcast or journalism program. Yet, for some reason, it had a defunct media department with a few pieces of equipment that no one seemed to know about. Once Asa figured out the bureaucratic ropes to get a green light, production was still an uphill battle. "We were like bulls in a china shop, totally self-taught; trial-and-error all the way. Sometimes the show would air in black and white because we hadn't hooked the cables up properly. We had to teach each other how to work the cameras, edit—it was a mess."

But over the course of his senior year he, along with a crew of thirty student staffers who followed Asa pied-piper style into the production, had turned in a respectable body of work of half-hour news broadcasts four times a week. The semester's worth of shows won the university's coveted "best new student program" award.

When it came time to approach ABC News with job credentials, he had his trump card: a "reel," as they say in the biz, showcasing his award-winning work samples.

After six years with the national network, Asa may be more seasoned, but he still appreciates the power of initiative. "To start out and stand out in this business, you have to demonstrate many talents, such as managing staff and dealing with superiors. It's more than just getting good grades in college. You have to make something your own."

The job can be intense. With only few hours' notice, Asa may be boarding a plane to Ireland or Denver or wherever else the action is happening. This can get old. "I like traveling as much as anyone else, but it can certainly be aggravating when you've made plans and have to cancel at the last minute."

Speaking of job frustrations, as with most news gigs, many producers lament their pecking order on the pay scale. Asa's salary was about $30K per year when he started at an entry-level position. Because he worked so much overtime, he earned nearly double that. Now, as an associate producer, the pay is between $50 and $75K. The salary discrepancy is a bone of contention. "You could easily make more money per year at an entry-level position here with good overtime hours than an experienced associate producer who has worked at the company for four to six years."

And getting paid to tell stories, which is what journalists aim to do, sometimes means covering stories you'd rather not. One of the worst days of Asa's career so far came when he was still a newbie while on location near Philadelphia. An American civilian named Nick Berg had been kidnapped in Iraq by Islamic extremists. Asa was then working for the booking department at *GMA,* and like every media outlet, *GMA* wanted Berg's parents to spill their heart out on *their* show. "When I got to his parents' house, it was a media circus. There were rows of news vans and satellite trucks lined up and down their quaint suburban street. The family was completely overwhelmed." Reluctantly, Asa approached the front door and knocked. Like the many other members of the news media who tried before him, his queries were met with a barrage of verbal disdain from an angry family who considered the media intrusion reprehensible.

The fleet of reporters camped, waiting for the family to acquiesce. Then the news hit: Berg had been beheaded by his captors, on video. "I was numb, and I hated that this job had made me numb." But the horrific death only upped the ante for landing the family interview. Asa had no choice. "It was time to work."

For days, Asa attempted to secure the interview on behalf of *GMA*. The devastated family ignored any media requests. By the time relatives were willing to talk to reporters, Asa had been promoted to a different ABC News program.

In the big picture, even Asa is afflicted with wanderlust. "I still don't have any idea what I want to 'do.' When I was fifteen, I wanted to be a high school science teacher. When I was twenty, I wanted to be a lawyer or a politician. Last year, I wanted to do political reporting and get my pilot's license," he says. "Last month, I wanted to do environmental reporting and travel around the country in an RV run on vegetable oil. Yesterday I thought about buying land and starting a vineyard in Texas. I'm very proud of what I do for a living, and four out of five days, I truly love it."

Postscript from Asa . . .

If I had to do it all over again, I would . . . Travel the world before taking a real job.

If I knew then what I know now, I would . . . Have a lot of anxiety about how this job will mesh with raising a family. I love it now and it works great being a single guy in New York City with this job. I can travel, I can work late, I can be selfish toward my needs and my career's needs now. But will I feel unfulfilled with such a demanding, low-paying job in an expensive city when I decide to have a family? These are issues I've been grappling with since I took this job six years ago . . . and I still do not know the answers.

Three characteristics or personality traits you need to do this job:

1. Thick skin
2. Intellectual curiosity
3. Entrepreneurial spirit. (We don't make a lot of money. You can't do this job if you don't have an ingrained sense of social justice or prevailing ideal to help the common good.)

> ***Don't even try this if . . .*** You're afraid of conflict or asking tough
> questions or sometimes pushing people for answers. Or, if you have
> thin skin about conflict or worry about being yelled at.

CALEB HANNAN
Print Journalist
Nashville, Tennessee
Age: 26

Caleb Hannan grew up in an afternoon: the Wednesday a furniture
delivery truck ran a red light and slammed into the car his mother and
grandmother were in, killing them both.

That day Caleb was off from a job he admittedly despised—"driving
wealthy people around, trying to hammer them into buying condo
time-shares they probably didn't need," he says. The job was a joke, but
he was in no rush to become an adult, so what was the harm?

Then fate intervened.

When Caleb's father reached him on his cell phone to deliver the
horrible news, his world collapsed in an instant. "I broke down like
never before," he says.

Eight months earlier, he had graduated from college. Not ready
to tear himself away from the laissez-faire campus lifestyle, he stuck
around the Virginia resort town. Most nights, he and his "super senior" buddies sat around drinking cheap domestic beer. Caleb knew
his job was a bore, "but I made a decent amount of money and still
had enough time to get drunk five times a week."

After the tragedy, he quit the job and said good-bye to his friends.
His dad helped him move back to Washington, D.C., and into his
mom's condo that now belonged to him. "I'm an only child and my
parents were divorced. So there I was, in charge of my mom's estate
at twenty-two years old." The real world he had kept at bay was suddenly and unfairly all too real.

For the next several months, Caleb and his dad and uncles worked through the paperwork involved with his mother's finances and property. Emerging from that haze, Caleb struggled to plan the next step. He wasn't going back to the carefree campus life—that chapter was closed. Before he could move forward, he had to think back to what it was he had enjoyed doing for work. His stint writing for the college newspaper came to mind. He decided to give journalism a go.

Calling in a favor from a family friend, Caleb secured an internship at a lifestyle magazine in Washington, D.C. ("There is nothing wrong with nepotism, as long as you own up to it," he says frankly. "The worst thing you can do is pretend it didn't help you get a job when it did.") The magazine gig was an interesting experience but didn't engage him as much as he had hoped. The publication produced soft lifestyle pieces. For a guy who doesn't shave every day and who generally wears the same pair of skinny Levi's, it wasn't a good match.

What followed was a series of false starts and bad luck—more than two years of internships at various magazines that didn't pan out to full-time jobs; fellowships at papers that folded, forcing the staff to disperse for jobs elsewhere. In less than three years, the twenty-six-year-old traveled from D.C. to Chicago to Cleveland chasing writing gigs. Interspersed in there were a few self-discovery months, moving back home, traveling to Southeast Asia, and "failing miserably at pitching articles to larger publications."

After the Cleveland paper where he was working was bought out, the staff did what most do when they hear in the middle of the day that they've lost their jobs: they reconvened at the local bar. As folks commiserated by the jukebox, the editor tapped Caleb on the shoulder. "My boss, a guy I really didn't know that well, told me to come join him outside the bar for a smoke, then asked what I thought about Nashville."

Nashville? As in Tennessee? Sure, Caleb was game. The editor took Caleb under his wing and the two joined the editorial team of an alternative weekly newspaper that had been established twenty years earlier. At last, Caleb's byline would read "staff reporter."

With the new title comes new deadlines: Caleb is responsible for a major monthly feature-length article, an occasional one-thousand-word piece on a city official or human interest story, and two blog posts a day. "Most of the time I show up at the office a little before my boss (no matter how laid-back your boss is, it's still a good idea to get there before he or she arrives) and start making phone calls, checking e-mail, and writing posts."

Caleb de-mystifies what a reporter's job looks like: "I'd like to think the job of a staff writer has a little more variety than most—and certainly, compared to a toll booth operator it does—but for the most part that's what it looks like: a dude sitting at a desk typing away, occasionally picking up the phone and talking to someone, anyone, who knows a lot more about something than he does."

The newsroom atmosphere can be disarmingly relaxed—until deadline. Like the time Caleb was a day away from turning in a controversial exposé about a shady but powerful real estate developer. The developer had filed for bankruptcy in the past, and some people believed he'd surreptitiously moved assets around to smooth a comeback. Caleb had been working on the story for a month, and the piece was nearly done. All that remained was the customary legal vetting.

Except this time the lawyers had some concerns. "For an hour, the lawyer expertly poked holes in every argument I thought was rock solid and gave me an unwanted, but necessary, crash course on libel law. Basically, if the story had run how we had intended it, there was a very good chance I could have been sued," he says. The article was in the last stages of fact checking, a point at which writers are supposed to be able to breathe a little easier. Instead, Caleb spent the next six hours frantically scrambling around downtown Nashville, digging up additional paperwork to back up his reporting. Back in the office, his editor was meticulously deleting any quotes or assertions that might be misconstrued.

Young reporters like Caleb learn by the sink-or-swim method. For a cover story about Nashville's highly anticipated new convention center, Caleb found himself face-to-face with the mayor. Weeks of research had prepared him for this moment, and he braced for the rehearsed, politician-like responses. What he did not anticipate was the mayor's entourage—three press aides, each ready with talking points. "The cumulative effect of their tailored suits, spreadsheets, and utter certainty in their logic did make me feel like a grade-schooler sitting in on advanced calculus."

Depending on location and experience, a print reporter's starting salary hovers around the low $30Ks. With the news industry undergoing seismic changes and job security a thing of the past, Caleb, a newspaper loyalist, concedes it's time to invest in some camera and audio equipment to boost his value. But even with all the uncertainty and shuffling around to different towns, what makes it all worth it? "Getting paid to tell stories. And seeing my name in print—oops, not supposed to say that one out loud," he says, feigning embarrassment.

One story he's especially proud of is a profile he wrote about a young woman who attempted suicide for the third time after being rejected from a Christian-based counseling center for being gay. As a troubled gang member from the Bronx, she had been treated like a daughter by the group's founder but then harshly repudiated when she came out as homosexual.

"She had only recently gotten her life back on track when she agreed to talk to me," Caleb recalls. "Having her tell me her story felt like a scoop, but it also felt like a sacred trust, i.e., don't fuck over the woman who's already been fucked over numerous times in her life." The day the story appeared, she called the office. "Caleb, I think I love you," she said. "She was only kidding, of course. But still, that was a good day."

Despite the logistical merry-go-round Caleb has ridden in the pursuit of his career, the young journalist is not jaded. He's in this field for the long run. But in a floundering industry, does he ever think he'll fail? He answers with typical self-deprecating honesty: "I'm the guy who once had a last-ditch story-pitch about a homeless guy who lived in the basement of my apartment building. Try *have failed* and *will fail again*."

Postscript from Caleb . . .

If I had to do it all over again, I would . . . Be here.

If I knew then what I know now, I would . . . Be wealthier.

Three characteristics or personality traits you need to do this job:

1. Patience
2. Thick skin
3. A dark sense of humor

Don't even try this if . . . You don't like talking to people.

MAGGIE CRANE
Broadcast News Reporter
Ft. Myers, Florida
Age: 27

Maggie Crane is riding shotgun in a white television news van with the station's call letters WINK stenciled on the outside. The cameraman, a young guy in his twenties, is at the wheel racing through yellow lights, deftly maneuvering around the traffic. Maggie reapplies her makeup and cradles a cell phone by her ear, listening to the assignment editor relay what little information he has: house fire, Lee County, one confirmed dead. It's nearly 4:00 p.m. and in less than one hour, Maggie will be broadcasting live from the scene.

And the scene is manic. Dozens of firefighters try to get the blaze under control. Police cordon off the area and wave curious onlookers away. Paramedics swarm the surroundings. The cameraman pops the curb, lurching to a stop. Maggie leaps out, canvassing the crowd for a familiar face—a police chief or fire official to grab the latest details. At the same time, she's keeping an eye out for a neighbor or witness who might be willing to talk. She needs to act fast: forty minutes to air time.

A fatal fire—this is a big deal for the local news team, and for Maggie. The newscast will open with her segment on location. On another day, it's more mundane lineups: an alligator's doctor visit or Halloween preparations. The fly-by-the-seat-of-your-pants stories are the ones Maggie thrives on. "I crave breaking news," she says proudly.

Four years earlier and about a thousand miles away, in St. Louis, she got bit by the news bug while interning at the local NBC affiliate. Late one night, the assignment editor—the position that dispatches reporters and camera teams to locations—had stepped away, and Maggie found herself manning the desk solo. She was monitoring the police scanners when a tipster called with information about a helicopter crash. He wouldn't give his name and was about to hang up when Maggie coaxed him for more information she knew she needed to grasp the story. "I remember the assignment manager coming back over to grill me on all the questions I had asked and the information I had gathered. He seemed so pleasantly surprised that I knew what I was doing (well, at least I pulled it off that way!) that it made me really consider the news industry."

Maggie juggled the demanding thirty-hour-per-week internship with a full slate of communications courses at St. Louis University. "I

was one of those kids who was kind of good at everything—always
made straight A's. After my professor in my first journalism class consistently read my papers as his favorite, I thought 'Hey, there might be
something to this.' "

She stacked her mornings with classes to free up her afternoons—
crucial, as her call time at the station was 1:00 p.m., followed by a
nine-hour-plus shift. From this post, she learned the behind-the-scenes
protocol for one-hour productions—fielding calls from public relations companies pitching their clients, helping the show's anchors prep
stories, rousing the audience gathered outside the floor-to-ceiling
windows each day. Picture the afternoon version of the *Today* show.

After graduating, she packed her bags for Los Angeles. The Academy of Television Arts & Science (the organization that produces
the *Emmys* award show) offers paid eight-week internships in a variety of television production placements. Maggie nabbed the coveted
spot at E! Entertainment Network, where she ran her share of gopher
errands, but also tagged along to red carpet events, interviewing celebrities like Bruce Willis and the cast from the HBO series, *Entourage*.
The excitement kept her in LA for a year, but soon Maggie found
herself bored by the superficiality of who and what she was covering.
"I didn't feel I was making an impact. I wanted to tell people about
things that would make a difference in their lives."

Before she turned her heels on the world's entertainment capital,
however, she plotted her next step. Pulling from a few celebrity interviews, she cobbled together a reel that used their sound bites for a
hard news angle about the importance of voting.

Maggie set her sights on an on-air job fully aware that only a small
town would take a chance on a novice reporter. News markets are organized in a hierarchy: New York City and Los Angeles ranking No. 1
and No. 2, respectively. St. Joseph, Missouri, market No. 201, offered
Maggie an on-air position, with a backwater salary to match, $20K.
Learning the ropes in a smaller market had its advantages, however.

"I wore every hat in the newsroom. I blundered my way through my first live shot, found my on-air 'reporter voice,' and learned to shoot, write, edit, produce, anchor, and manage."

One year later, she had strengthened her reel enough to bump up in market: Ft. Myers, Florida, No. 62.

Now, she's living her dream, or as close to it as possible. "I don't know that I ever knew what I wanted to do, but reporting lets me do it all, in a sense." There are the days she lives for, like the time her reporting helped get an unemployed mother of two her house back after a bank admitted miscalculating her mortgage rate.

And then there are the days she would rather not re-live—like the day she missed "slot." "Slot" is the designated time a story will air. "If it's scheduled to air at 11:02 p.m. in the newscast, you better have it in by 10:50 p.m." Maggie knew she was cutting it close, but both her cell phone and laptop clocks were slow, giving her the erroneous impression she had a few seconds' padding. "By the time I was ready to go live, we were already in the top of the newscast and my lead story wound up buried down a few slots. This made me mad because I worked my tail off for seven hours to turn in a two-minute story. It also really made the producer mad because I'd just gone and screwed up the flow of his show. There were some fireworks that night."

Not everyone is a fan. Instead of commenting on the story's content, a viewer once wrote an email critiquing Maggie's appearance. "He told me it looked like I fell asleep chewing gum, the gum fell out, got stuck in my hair, and I had to cut it out." Not exactly constructive feedback. "I can't help that he wouldn't know a cute, stacked bob if it bit him in the ass," she says. Ever the diplomat, she wrote an email in return "politely informing him that as a cancer survivor, I'm just thankful to have hair! He didn't respond."

After almost three years at the local station, Maggie feels she's ready for the next market jump. Her efforts are stymied, however, because as she's learning, the turnover in network news is very slow.

"Our anchors are well-seasoned veterans who aren't going anywhere. For me to move up, it means moving out of town to a different, bigger market."

She's also eyeing the day when her finances are a little more stable. "I know I could make more money reading water meters for a living, but I love what I do." Like newspapers and magazines, broadcast news is transforming. "I look at the way the industry is changing, how cuts are being made, why companies are going to one-man-bands. I question if this is the right job for me. I do want a house one day. And on the piddly salary I earn, I don't know how feasible that is at my age."

Whenever she thinks of jumping ship to safer pastures or career paths, she reminds herself of her father's missed opportunities. "My dad comes from a generation that believes jobs are doctors, lawyers, or teachers." Her father, a customer service representative, always daydreamed aloud about becoming a high school history teacher or a soccer coach. He never did it, and as he watches his daughter follow her dreams, "he sees how passionate I am about what I do. I think he might be a little jealous."

Postscript from Maggie . . .

If I had to do it all over again, I would . . . Have double-majored or went immediately for more education part-time. This industry is pretty unstable right now, and I wish I had had the foresight to choose something else as a backup . . . just in case.

Three characteristics or personality traits you need to do this job:

1. Curiosity
2. Integrity
3. Outgoing

Don't even try this if . . . You don't have a thick skin!

KELLY SENYEI
Food Network Intern and Food Blogger
New York, New York
Age: 23

When Kelly Senyei tells people she's an intern at the Food Network all small talk comes to a screeching halt, and the questions start flying: Have you met Rachael Ray? Is there food everywhere? I wish I had the guts to do that. How'd you get that job?! She'll be at a friend's BBQ, where the guests are mostly bankers or lawyers, "and as soon as my job comes up, people stop," Kelly says. "I know nothing about stocks and bonds, but everyone knows about food and can be included."

Growing up in San Diego, Kelly, her dad, and her siblings came home to a freshly prepared meal every night. Noni, the über-mom, made it look easy. "My mom would be driving carpool to a field hockey game and bring fresh apple turnovers with ice cream," she recalls.

Mom also made it look fun, encouraging young Kelly as a sous-chef. During a visit home recently, the two (while cooking, naturally) were trying to pinpoint the moment Kelly's love of food turned from a helping-in-the-kitchen hobby to a full-blown career aspiration. After all, her brother and sister were on the academic track—the older sister in her second year of law school, the brother finishing up Yale University undergrad and then heading to medical school. Everyone assumed Kelly would follow a cerebral career path, too.

And then the picture taking began.

"I started photographing things I cooked in high school, like giant chocolate cupcakes or cheese and meat platters. That got some strange looks," she says, laughing. "But to me, I wanted to immortalize it. To me, food wasn't just food. It became art."

Barely out of high school, Kelly was so keen to keep cooking that she pitched the idea to her parents to skip college and go straight to culinary school. Treading carefully, so as to not squash their daughter's passion outright, they encouraged Kelly to finish college first, and "if you still want to go to culinary school, fine," they said.

Kelly obliged and set off to Northwestern University in Chicago, where she seized every moment to be in the kitchen. "I hosted four-course dinner parties, catered weeknight TV get-togethers. You name it, I cooked it." The communication studies major dabbled in a few journalism classes and spent her summers interning at television affiliates in Chicago and New York. She loved food, but how sensible is a career in food? she reasoned.

When it came time to graduate and decide the next step, Kelly faced a dilemma. "I had already put down my deposit at culinary school when I heard I was accepted to graduate journalism school." She turned to her parents for advice. "Go to journalism school, and if you still want to go to culinary school afterward, fine" they said, echoing their response a year earlier. Kelly complied. Again.

As a way to decompress from j-school assignments covering unsolved murders and city hall, she cooked. One night, while preparing her mom's babyback ribs, she started typing the recipe to give to friends. Or should she post it online, she wondered later that night. Better yet, what about a blog? "It sounds so cliché but I literally got out of bed at three a.m. because I couldn't stop thinking about starting the blog. I had no time for it during the day, so I worked on it between two and five a.m. I felt like I was leading a double life— reporting on a sewer plant spill while trying to decide what would work better for a recipe, Parmesan or cheddar."

Ten months later, at the journalism school's annual career fair, the economy was in the tank. The get-a-job fair "turned into the j-school unpaid six-month-internship fair." Kelly met with thirteen media companies and invariably, the conversation turned to her food blog, prompting her interviewers to suddenly perk up. "It made me stand out, and it demonstrated a passion for something outside the norm. Everyone loves food."

No solid job leads came from the career fair, but a professor introduced her to a Food Network insider shortly thereafter. Kelly's blog
helped seal the deal, and she was asked to join the Network's digital
website team as an unpaid intern. Kelly had at last been paired with
her true love—food! Yes, it was unpaid, but it was a start.

The network headquarters in New York City is heaven for foodies.
Guests entering the lobby are bombarded with cooking shows playing on mounted television screens. Eggplant- and zucchini-shaped
pillows spruce up couches. For a young woman whose most cherished possessions are her grandmother's 120-year-old cookbooks and
a cake pan in the shape of a football stadium, work feels like home.
Four internships and a master's degree later, Kelly had arrived.

As an intern, Kelly's responsibilities range from the interesting to
the mundane. Demonstrating an affinity for caption writing, she soon
became the point person grinding out hundreds of catchy phrases to
accompany the food pictures. Sound painful? Not for Kelly. "I imagine
myself cooking and what I would pair the dish with or which wine
I would serve." Phrases like "quick and easy," "freezer friendly," and
"fresh ingredients" are among a dozen taglines that help jump-start
her brainstorming. Not that she needed much convincing: "I love all
things food. I love talking, writing, and describing food."

The tedious parts invariably surfaced when a fellow foodie hadn't
been fed. During a photo shoot in midsummer for the highly rated
Thanksgiving Day spread, the crew set up shop in a tiny rented apartment downtown. The food photographer was hungry and Kelly was
dispatched to locate gluten-free yogurt. "I about died of heat exhaus-
tion and just keep thinking, 'Oh, my God, I paid sixty thousand dollars for a graduate degree and I'm on the hunt for gluten-free yogurt.
Where did I go wrong?'"

Thankless errands come with the entry-level post. What really
bugs Kelly, though, are people who don't take food media seriously.
"It's not like there's breaking news when the Gruyere puff pastry
with fig jam recipe isn't uploaded to the website correctly," but it can

be stressful. And it is work. "Some people in the hard news industry think food journalism is fluffy and that anyone can write about a chef's latest take on Osso Bucco or a new gadget's arrival in the culinary market. It takes more than a passion for consuming calories to make food look and sound appetizing." Even at the junior level, after having written hundreds of captions, Kelly struggled to make each one stand out. "From the thirty million cakes I've tried, how am I going to make this one sound different?"

For inspiration, she might consider a quick field trip upstairs. Follow the chefs into the elevators with their carts of fresh food and exit on the "Test Kitchen" floor where six fully equipped kitchens are combined in one, presenting a sea of stainless steel ovens and cook tops. It's here where recipe developers, culinary producers, and recipe testers (*recipe testers!*) fuss over the "beauty plate" that will be hand-delivered to the networks' morning shows for their food segments. Come at the right time and Bobby Flay might be practicing his iconic flips.

The free food and recipe trade secrets aside, Kelly pursues food journalism for the interaction it inspires. "I love the sharing aspect. Getting people's take on different dishes, hearing about what ideas they associate with, hearing reactions—positive or negative. Not every chef is everyone's idol, but it starts a dialogue."

That dialogue ends, however, in Kelly's apartment, where she concedes she's better off living solo. The hall closet is filled not with extra shoes or linens, but with kitchen gadgets and cans of specialty foods. "Some girls lust for Prada. I lust for the latest food processor," she says. Good thing she doesn't have a roommate, not that there's space for one anyway. "I have to live by myself. I'm very territorial about my kitchen. If I had a roommate, it could get ugly."

Postscript from Kelly . . .

If I knew then what I know now, I would . . . Have started my blog my freshman year of college to have already built a following.

Three characteristics or personality traits you need to do this job:

1. Passion for food (and I'm not just talking about a love of eating)
2. Creative mind-set
3. Persistence to stand out among the crowd

Don't even try this if . . . You think food writing is an excuse for a "real job" or is all free meals and a never-ending glass of wine.

MENTOR'S INSIGHTS: *NICHOLAS LEMANN*

REBECCA CASTILLO

Why You Should Listen Up—(a Selection of) Your Mentor's Resumé Stats:

- Dean and professor at Columbia University, Graduate School of Journalism
- Author of five published books, most recently *Redemption: The Last Battle of the Civil War*
- Staff writer for *The New Yorker*; national correspondent for the *Atlantic Monthly*; national staff reporter for the *Washington Post*; managing editor of the *Washington Monthly*; staff writer for the *Texas Monthly*
- Contributing writer to the *New York Times,* the *New York Review of Books,* the *New Republic*, and *Slate*
- Worked in documentary television with *Frontline,* the Discovery Channel, and the BBC, among others
- Graduated magna cum laude from Harvard College with a concentration in American history and literature.

Veteran journalist Nicholas Lemann never battled the "What do I want to do with my life?" question head-on. The man was practically born with a reporter's notebook and pen in hand, but he understands today's generation is embroiled in it.

The imposing wooden desk in his corner office on Columbia University's campus seems more of a storage area piled with newspapers and drafts of working articles than an actual work surface. He usually prefers chatting while sitting on his gray leather couch, Mac computer on his lap, typing away—which is exactly where I found him when I approached him for this project. I had my spiel rehearsed, ready with additional talking points in case he wavered on participating. No need. "Of course, I'll do it," he responded with characteristic enthusiasm, perhaps inspired by having had a mentor or two himself long ago.

Here, Lemann tells you firsthand why focus is so important, and what it was like being one of the youngest staff writers ever at the *Washington Post*.

The Early Days

From the time I started working, or really before I started, I had a pretty clear idea of the niche I wanted to be in. When I was quite young, like fourteen or fifteen, I would go to the library and read magazines voraciously. So, I don't have a lot of experience myself with all these other parts of journalism. But what I take from my own experience is that it's useful to focus on exactly what you want to do. Try to be very clear in your mind about what you want to accomplish, what medium you want to work in, what subjects you want to write about, and then try to figure out how to train yourself to do it as well as possible, and how to find places where you can do it.

On the Road Again

I spent a lot of time traveling around Texas—this was at the height of the oil boom years. Texas was coming of age, becoming urban, so I was writing a lot about a generation of people who had grown up in the country and come to the cities and suburbs and were trying to invent urban Texas. That was a lot of fun. I spent a lot of time in those years just driving around Texas doing stories on this and that.

I was smoking cigarettes at the time, I hate to tell you. I was driving a Volkswagen and basically just lived on the road. I had a little apartment in Austin, a room above a garage, and I would leave Sunday night and be on the road all week and come back Friday night or Saturday morning and do the laundry and pay the bills. Then I'd go out on the road again.

Journalism Too Risky, Pick Again?

In the early going I was afraid that I just wouldn't be able to find a way to make it in journalism, and that I would have to stop and go to law school or something like that. My parents were very, very worried about journalism as a career for me, and they considered it too risky and inse-cure. That's the main thing I remember being worried about—whether I would be able to find my niche and be able to make a living doing this kind of work. Fortunately that worked out.

Do-Overs?

Oh, boy, there were a couple of times. I went to work for the *Washington Post*. I think I might have been the youngest person ever, even now, to have been part of the national staff. I was twenty-five and I was very green.

The management at the time had a theory they called "creative ten-sion." They would often assign two reporters to do the same story and then have them compete with each other to see who did it better, and that's the story they would run. It wasn't fun.

I was involved in an internal, somewhat bitter, office dispute and found it very upsetting. A senior reporter had done a story, and the managing editor felt she had not done it right. He had me do the same story again. It made the senior reporter very angry. I talked to a few friends about it, and one of the friends told another person. Even now, but certainly then, the

Washington Post was really in the spotlight, and so if there was any little scandal happening in the newsroom, it would get covered. Somebody tried to do a story about this little brouhaha I had been involved in, and I felt terrified that I would be in trouble with my bosses. I was very afraid and confessed to the managing editor, and he said never do it again, but it is okay this time. And the whole thing died down, but I remember really feeling that I had screwed up then. The lesson? Don't whine!

Mentors for Life

I had a series of mentors. Right after college I went to work for a little magazine called the *Washington Monthly* in Washington, which I am still very involved with. It's a very small, always-on-the-brink-of-extinction magazine, and the founding editor/owner, Charlie Peters, was definitely a mentor and still is, to some extent. I just had lunch with him yesterday. He would be at the top of the list. But I was fortunate to have a number of different mentors.

These people meant a lot to me. What would have happened if I hadn't encountered them? Would I have encountered another half dozen people? I don't want to go into the territory of saying I owe everything to these mentors and, if they hadn't plucked me out, I would be packing boxes for Amazon.com in their warehouse in Nebraska. I do think I was already a journalist and would have found a way to do it, but it's important to have people who believe in you and who can teach you things, and go to bat for you. This job at the *Washington Post,* for example, was completely engineered by Charlie Peters.

*

The Big Picture

Journalists tend to be trained in ways that are very self-referential to journalism. You're taught the norms of journalism—learning how to report, learning how to tell stories, but that's relatively easy to pick up just in the workplace. But what we are supposed to be doing in life is understanding things in a deeper way. That's harder to pick up inside a news organization and easier to pick up at a university. It took me a long time to understand how to interact with the body of knowledge about whatever I was writing about in a meaningful way, and that's a very important skill for a journalist.

I also think it's a mistake to choose jobs in any field, and certainly in journalism, because they are prestigious, because they are comfortable, because you like the location, because they'll impress your friends. When I moved to Texas, for example, which is still one of the things I'm most glad I did in life, I had been living in Washington, and all my friends thought I had lost my mind because, if you're a journalist writing about politics, you are never supposed to leave Washington to go to Texas. I did it because I was focused on this particular kind of work I wanted to do, not on where I lived or where I stood in the pecking order of Washington journalism.

Final Thoughts

Here at the university, we have prominent journalists who speak to our students, and they always say things like "go for it," "live your dream," "believe in yourself." All that is true. I'm not going to deny any of that. But I would say it's very helpful to try to focus on what it is you actually want to do. Think of yourself as somebody who has a craft or a skill or a profession, and then really try to master it.

6

Government Gigs

In and Around 1600 Pennsylvania Avenue

INTRODUCTION

"**J**ohn, we've got to make it cool again."

That's what President Barack Obama said to John Berry, the man he tapped to lead the Office of Personnel Management, essentially the federal government's human resources department, about working in government.

In an effort to recruit new blood into an arguably stale and stagnant job field, the Obama administration is turning its crosshairs to a new pool of prospects: twentysomethings.

"When Neil Armstrong walked on the moon the average age of the federal workers who were at Mission Control—the people who got him there safely and got him home—was in the late twenties," Berry said in a magazine interview in 2009. "We're not the first generation to try to involve young folks . . . the government did it very effectively in the sixties, and those people produced miracles."

Now they want those people to be you. The quagmire bureaucratic mind-set is out; new progressive, outside-the-box thinking is in.

To reach your generation, they're infiltrating social media platforms in which you're well versed.

They also have a lot of jobs to fill. The federal government is the nation's largest employer, according to the Bureau of Labor Statistics. It employs two million people, not including U.S. Postal Service personnel or employees who work at national security agencies, like the Central Intelligence Agency. And that's just federal—several million more jobs exist at state and local government levels.

What distinguishes the new blood from the old is that twenty-somethings will probably not stay at one job for decades, as opposed to government "lifers" who stake their claim and stay put. Ironically, change *is* built into the system. Every four years, the country is asked who should have a turn leading the nation. For the foreseeable future, here are four twentysomethings working for that change in "cool" government gigs—some inside the Beltway, some outside.

Don't be distracted by Yuh Wen Ling's official title: policy analyst in the Office of Economic and Strategic Analysis in the Office of the Assistant Secretary for Transportation Policy. It's a mouthful and she's the first one to admit it. Arriving at this job was quite an odyssey for the young woman who emigrated from Singapore to New Jersey when she was six years old. At heart, she's a travel-fanatic, which, in a way, is appropriate for a person working at the Department of Transportation.

Inside another government agency, Cara Schmidt studies "Classified" and "Top Secret" documents at the Department of Defense. All in a day's work for this intelligence analyst specializing in the Afghanistan-Pakistan region. She has a sensitive assignment that is rarely spoken about in public, and agreed to participate in this book on the condition that her profile be reviewed by the DOD's Public Affairs office.

Shifting gears to state government, Jerry Greenspan is a chief of staff for a U.S. representative in Houston, Texas. As an only child of blue-collar parents, he grew up about four hundred miles down the Gulf coast in Brownsville, where he never had trouble speaking his mind and pointing out inaccuracies. He likes to tell the story of when he was thirteen or fourteen and the city newspaper ran a letter he wrote critiquing what he believed to be mismanagement at a local golf course.

Government is in sharp focus for Andrew Snow, a D.C.-based freelance photographer. He doesn't work for a politician or have a bureaucratic title; his perch behind a camera lends him a different perspective of the Washington circuit players. He captures the theater that is politics and its bastard stepchild, war, with a camera. Before turning twenty-six, Andrew covered the Israel-Palestine conflict and Arizona senator John McCain's presidential campaign along with a few lower-profile events in between. Cobbling together assignments is the life of a freelancer.

Maybe the trick to staying "cool" is valuing youth—not so much in age, but in spirit. As a U.S. Congressman and mentor of this government gigs chapter, John Lewis is a prime example. The man recently entered his seventh decade, yet delights like a man one-quarter of his age when he speaks about work. He has been representing Georgia's fifth district since 1987 and prides himself as being a loyal public servant to his constituents, often pulling strength and vitality from his twentysomething days as a legendary Civil Rights activist.

YUH WEN LING
Policy Analyst, Department of Transportation
Washington, D.C.
Age: 28

Never underestimate the power of a tchotchke. It might lead to a job. Just ask Yuh Wen Ling.

Approaching graduation day from Princeton University with a master's degree in public affairs, Yuh Wen brainstormed her next move. She had flirted with a variety of gigs by that point—public radio intern, movie projectionist, investment banker—but this next step, she rationalized, should be one in a semi-permanent career direction. Getting paid in books, as she had been at the radio station, wasn't going to pay the bills, and the I-banking route wasn't for her.

The school's career center posted a job alert of a prestigious government-sponsored program, "Presidential Management Fellows," where graduate students vie for paid, two-year positions with a federal agency. This sounded interesting.

Yuh Wen, in her self-deprecating manner, downgrades the competitiveness of the program, saying she "somehow passed" the somewhat "arbitrary" test. "Actual question: 'Your peers think you are: (a) competent; (b) nice; (c) aggressive; (d) funny.' Me: 'Uh, I dunno . . . nice?' "

But despite that odd softball question, the barriers for acceptance are steep. Candidates must be sponsored by their school, submit a resumé, and take the three-hour written test designed to assess critical thinking, life experience, and writing fundamentals. The year Yuh Wen applied, so did more than five thousand other people. Of them, 784 were selected as finalists and invited to attend a PMF-exclusive job fair. If an agency hires you, then you become a "fellow."

Federal agencies crammed into a football field–size convention center in D.C. attempting to woo prospects with free swag. Yuh Wen showed up with one goal in mind: to land a job with either the Office of Management and Budget (in charge of preparing the president's annual budget and thus very influential on national policy) or the Department of Housing and Urban Development (oversees housing and community planning policy). After meeting the recruiters staffing those booths, she snaked down the aisles, pocketing the goods (free stapler from Health and Human Services! Foam toy buffalo from the Bureau of Land Management!) and stumbled upon the U.S. Department of Transportation in a corner.

"While the USDOT tchotchkes were sorely lacking in appeal—I think I got a pen," she jokes, "the recruiter was intriguing." The

DOT, he explained, has a hand in all nationwide-related transportation issues—from trolley cars to highways to freight trains—and they were beginning a tremendous shift to implement environmentally conscious policies. Plus, she'd be working three steps below the politically appointed secretary of transportation. One not-so-secret rule of thumb: if you're going to work in bureaucracy, be as close as possible to the politically appointed leaders. It's where the decisions are made, as opposed to the bottom rungs, which can be notoriously mundane.

For most people, the USDOT wasn't the sexiest sounding department, but it appealed to Yuh Wen's proclivity for big-picture thinking and the broad reach of infrastructure improvements into Americans' lives. "I don't think everyone has a clear opinion on the deficit or on national security, but everyone has something to say about their commute." Six months later, she started her job as a policy analyst.

Born in Singapore, Yuh Wen immigrated with her family to Toms River, New Jersey, when she was six years old. Academics came easy, and her tradition-minded parents encouraged her to follow a well-paved career route. "When you're an Asian immigrant, you're expected to become a doctor, lawyer, or concert pianist," she says. "I wasn't sure if I wanted to be any of those things."

Nevertheless, she hewed to a conventional track after graduating from the University of Chicago and accepted a job as an investment banker in the Windy City. By the second year, she knew it wasn't a long-term fit and applied to graduate school in hopes of finding clarity back in her academic comfort zone.

Princeton University accepted her, but she chose to defer. "I wasn't ready," she says. Work wasn't clicking; school wasn't, either. And rushing one or the other was bound to eventually backfire in regret.

Without a career plan and with an itch to travel, Yuh Wen looted her savings and indulged her peripatetic side. She took off, crisscrossing continents, often returning to New Jersey only to leave again days or weeks later: three months in Ghana working on a documentary and volunteering in a rural community, back to New Jersey; a month of French lessons in Bordeaux, back to New Jersey; Spanish immersion in Guatemala and scuba lessons in Honduras, back to New Jersey; and backpacking through China, Myanmar, Cambodia, Malaysia, and Singapore, back to New Jersey.

She tallied thirteen countries in one year. Feet once again planted on U.S. soil and the travel bug ostensibly at bay, she took her spot at school and began the core curriculum required during the first of the two-year master's program.

In theory, she loved the idea of working in international development, in part sparked by her globe-trotting experiences. In reality, her professional background paled in comparison to other students, and in order to get a full-time job, she needed to buff up her resumé.

Princeton offered a "middle year" to test the waters and so, you guessed it, she took off again. Through a combination of the school's career center and her own resourcefulness, she headed to Switzerland for a summer internship at a nongovernmental health organization, then to Seoul, Korea, for four months working to provide medical aid to North Korean patients, and finally rounded out the year with six months in Urumqi, China, as a fellow for the Clinton Foundation HIV/AIDS Initiative. It was an intense period of development work boot camp, learning both the administrative side (writing reports for international donors) and getting hands-on experience (field trips to program sites).

But she also learned that the aspects and nuances of development work weren't for her.

When she returned to the United States to complete her degree, she chalked up her expansive travels as a useful exercise to whittle down options. "I envy the people who know what they want to do from an early age. I didn't. For me, it's more like a process of elimination, like, 'Well, that was a good experience. Now I know better.' "

Fast-forward to grad school commencement and work orientation. Initially, the shift from campus life to everyday desk duty was difficult. "I must be truthful. I work in cube land," she jokes. A travel-inspired "transpo-themed" photo montage tacked to her cubby wall brightens her view: a smiling man waving from a passing train during a hike she took in Myanmar, a girl on a water buffalo, a postcard of a boy sprinting with a baguette.

Two weeks after she started, the department consolidated positions and asked her to work directly with the assistant secretary. The change doubled her workload and splintered her time, but she was a good sport. Lesson learned: sometimes, when you sign up for one job, you get another piled on top of it.

Pulling double-time for two bosses often created confusion. "I don't think people in my office (including myself, sometimes!) really know what I do because I've been doing too much of everything," she says. "I think I'd blame myself for this. I am pretty friendly and willing to help, plus, I apparently proved my competency too quickly in the office."

In the original gig, as a policy analyst, Yuh Wen joined an all-male, erudite group of economists assigned to assess transportation grant proposals from around the country. Her firecracker presence and tendency to dash down halls raised eyebrows at first. Her ability to get the job done lowered them.

The 2009 economic stimulus bill doubled the department's budget, and to spur job growth, it was allotted $1.5 billion in grant money to distribute for transportation projects. The team reviewed cost-benefit analyses of hundreds of selected finalists trimmed from more than 1,400 applicants. Projects included transportation priorities from across America—rural bridges needing reconstruction to urban start-up transit projects to street improvements that make way for improved bicycle and pedestrian access.

Choosing the awardees was more complicated than just number

crunching. Yuh Wen helped decipher the proposed projects' pros and cons not always quantifiable in Excel format. Take, for example, a city's request for funds to build a highway off-ramp to a low-income part of town choked off from commerce for decades. The benefits to that low-income community are huge. "If a city is trying to right that wrong, it's not necessarily in the numbers."

Is the job perfect? No. Office politics are inevitable, especially in the nation's political headquarters. Yuh Wen is still trying to determine how this experience fits into her larger career scheme. "I still haven't figured out what I'd like to do. I do think that I always wanted to do something that 'helped people.' That usually leads people to public service, and I think my current job could be considered as such, to some extent."

She does daydream about traveling again. "My goal was to visit thirty countries by the time I was thirty, but I don't think I'm going to make that." For the time being, she's staying put. "I've got most of it out of my system," she says. "I think."

There's a financial incentive to sticking around as well, at least for the short term. As a federal employee, Yuh Wen's salary is tied to a rigid pay scale. Most fellows, and those with newly minted master's degrees, earn about $50K per year. Their promotions rise steeply and quickly. After one year, the raise is $10K; after two, another $10K, and then the bumps plateau, possibly for many years, she says.

Whether she stays in bureaucracy or not, Yuh Wen finds comfort in a story her dad told her as a child: "At the top of rivers and streams, do you ever notice that there are so many rocks? They're ugly and rough, and they eventually fall in the water. They travel a long way in the river—the route is winding, cold, and those rocks get thrown around a lot. But at the bottom of the river, when all the rocks arrive, they are beautiful, smooth stones. You're just in the river going toward the end right now, and you'll get there."

His wise words often coach her to keep a greater perspective in focus. "It still helps me get through the bad days," she says.

> ## Postscript from Yuh Wen . . .
>
> **If I knew then what I know now, I would . . .** Probably have studied civil engineering / architecture / urban planning in college and grad school.
>
> **Three characteristics or personality traits you need to do this job:**
> 1. Patience!!
> 2. Ability to see policy within the picture (to justify your inane / silly daily tasks)
> 3. A certain level of cleverness and ingenuity in solving problems / getting the answers you need
>
> **Don't even try this if . . .** You can't think about how your job affects anyone other than yourself.

CARA SCHMIDT
Intelligence Analyst, Department of Defense
Washington, D.C.
Age: 23

Deployed in Afghanistan as an intelligence analyst, Cara Schmidt consistently logged sixteen-hour workdays, seven days a week.

What kept her adrenaline racing were the enormous responsibilities on her twenty-three-year-old shoulders. The prior year she was a senior in college completing a political science degree at the University of Illinois, Urbana-Champaign. Now, living in Kabul on a dusty American base camp at the crosshairs of the war in Afghanistan, she was a junior member of the Department of Defense team reporting to high-ranking military officials.

The gravity of how far Cara had come in such a short time span came into sharp focus at one particular meeting during the deployment, when she briefed the now former general Stanley McChrystal, the commander of U.S. and international forces in Afghanistan and a venerable, decorated war veteran.

The general, a notorious workhorse who infamously eats only one meal a day, was about to embark on a tour of the country's military bases, but first he required a thorough status report—regions under local police control, latest violence statistics, updates on district political elections.

For answers he called for a meeting with four members of the intelligence analysts team specializing in the region. Along with other agencies, like the CIA and the State Department, it's the DOD's job to understand how these South Asian countries operate. This is no minor undertaking: DOD must ingest and comprehend everything about Afghanistan, from tribal disputes in a village and the social network of insurgents to the platforms of national political candidates. The department employs nearly 150 analysts working out of the Pentagon in D.C. and about thirty in Kabul. The aggregated information is then relayed to the military higher-ups so they may shape the war strategy.

The night before, Cara and her bosses prepared two dozen slides for the meeting with McChrystal. They were taking him on a step-by-step update of the insurgency. Cara's boss would do the majority of the talking, but she was the point person for a portion of the briefing.

When it came time for her to present her slides, she couldn't help but feel a little out of her league: flanking the general were his top brass deputies, all men and all with decades of military experience.

Despite the boiler-room pressure, Cara rose to the occasion thanks to her preparations. From her first day on the job back in Washington, D.C, eighteen months before deployment, her routine had consisted of reading and researching the South Asia region. Intelligence analysts are trained to mine for information from a wide range of sources: human intelligence (i.e., embedded spies), signals intelligence (i.e., listening in on phone conversations and intercepting emails), imagery

("Google Earth on crack"). She poured over English translations of local Afghan-Pakistan newspapers, combing the text for hints of temperament changes or shifts in propaganda so that, for briefings like this one, she could accurately report to the "decision makers."

Clearing her throat, Cara, a fidgety person by nature, quit tapping her pencil on the desk and calmly began her presentation. Not five minutes into it an official interrupted her, challenging her analysis of the situation. For a second, Cara felt her cheeks start to burn.

"It's hard to stand up to a two-star general," she says, recalling the hour meeting and the fleeting moment she was put on the spot. In a breath, Cara regained her composure and explained her reasoning to the general's satisfaction.

Deployments to international base camps are anywhere from four-month- to twelve-month-long stints and are technically a volunteer opportunity. Cara chose to sign on because it's considered a significant career-building experience, and for the "hazardous" pay, which triples the base salary ranging from $35K to $80K, depending on level of experience and education.

In order to deploy, Cara was required to complete rigorous training and be medically cleared. She spent two weeks learning how to shoot a handgun and administer military-caliber first-aid tools like a special clotting dust that stops blood gushing from wounds on contact.

A "car getaway" simulation was a component of the "crash-bang" course. Cara was instructed to pretend an enemy was chasing her and the only escape route was to drive like hell—code for race upwards of 100 mph, drive backward and execute 180-degree spins.

The sober reality of the training impressed upon her the danger she would face. "The reason they're teaching you is because you might have to do it."

Finally, after completing the training, passing yet more chokepoints—a physical and a psychological exam—and getting vaccinated for "everything you can think of" (flu, anthrax, small pox), Cara boarded an Air Force cargo plane for Afghanistan.

South Asia was a part of the world not always on Cara's radar. Originally, the master plan was to go to law school. "It just seemed like what I was supposed to be doing," she says, echoing the sentiment of many recent college graduates without a plotted career chart.

In an abrupt about-face, she tabled law school and moved to D.C. to start an unpaid internship at the National Defense University, a graduate school offering degrees related to national security and policy. Most of the students are military veterans returning to school for an advanced degree, but the internship department attracts a younger crowd. A serendipitous placement in the Near East / South Asia division and a pairing with a faculty member-turned-mentor narrowed Cara's focus to international relations.

During the ten-week program, interns help organize university-hosted seminars for visiting foreign governmental officials. Between conferences, they work alongside faculty members who write and publish academic papers on topics ranging from counterterrorism to advanced war-fighting strategy. Under the supervision of a faculty member, Cara opted to carve her niche in South Asian relations.

For a young woman who had never traveled abroad or barely lived outside of her hometown of Watson, Illinois, exposure to this world was eye opening and mind bending. As she immersed herself in the dense aspects of fragile international relations, she began to picture building a career in the field.

Graduate school still seemed like a smart investment, only this time, she decided, it would be to pursue a two-year master's program in security studies at Georgetown University. She enrolled and girded herself for full-time academic life. A workhorse herself, however, she decided to take on a full-time job in addition to school and knew exactly what she was looking for.

First stop: USAjobs.gov—essentially the Monster.com for government gigs. She scoured the site's thousands of postings and found one opening for a DOD "intelligence analyst," to which she applied immediately.

Three months passed without hearing a response. She was ready to become a full-time student at Georgetown when the DOD called. A ten-minute interview a few days later covered—to Cara's surprise—relatively generic questions (Q: What are your negative attributes? A: "Taking on too big of a workload." Q: What are your public speaking skills? A: "Relaxed, but sometimes fidgety.")

"I thought I did okay, but not great," she says. "They told me they were interviewing five people for two positions, so I figured I just have to be better than three."

She was. A month later she had a job offer—pending results of a background check and a polygraph test.

The vetting process of government job applicants is exhaustive. Cara's personal life became fair game for scrutiny. Government agents visited her parents at their home in Watson, asking probing security questions: Did they have any reason to believe their daughter was not a good American? Has she ever been involved in any terrorist activity? Criminal activity? And they combed through her travel history and former addresses—a relatively simple task given Cara's previous domiciles were her parents' house, a campus dorm, and her apartment in D.C.

Once the background check and polygraph test cleared, Cara and her twenty fellow DOD analyst new hires (most of them male and with former military experience) took an oath to protect and uphold the Constitution of the United States and got to work.

These days, come 9:00 a.m., Cara swipes her security badge through the Pentagon turnstiles and heads down a labyrinth of corridors to a windowless basement. Maps wallpaper the perimeter of the room and computer monitors glow amid the sea of cubicles, while analysts crouch over "Classified" and "Top Secret" documents on their desks. Conversations drop to a whisper at the flashing of an overhead red light—an indication that a visitor or maintenance man is in the vicinity.

Toward the back of the room, Cara's five-person team shares a C-shaped desk—an office layout to encourage collaboration. At twenty-three, she's the youngest analyst on the team by several years.

Occasionally, Cara shuttles to Capitol Hill to meet with a senator or representative. The briefings range from general updates about the Afghan-Pakistan region to rundowns on the latest insurgent weapons and tactics.

Because the subject matter is sensitive, so, too, are the meetings. With many topics, especially complex ones like international relations, there are no black-and-white answers. Policy makers will ask vague, open-ended questions, like "Will our plan work?" This is impossible to answer, Cara says. Her job is to describe the situation on the ground and forecast what it will look like in the future, not to recommend a course of action.

"Sometimes it'd be easier if I was a doctor or lawyer, then people would know what I did," she says, often refraining from talking about work outside the office. During her graduate classes' debates on national security policy, she abstains from the discussion, receiving an all-knowing nod from the professor who understands her job prevents her from sharing her opinions.

One constant she can rely on is a sense of job security. "You have the peace of mind the government is not going out of business," she says. "It's pretty hard to get laid off. They've invested a lot in you with the clearances and training."

Not everyone who begins in the government sector stays there. Some analysts remain and rise to senior analyst positions; some choose to parlay their area of expertise—Middle East, Africa, or China—to a think tank or private sector job.

For the time being, Cara plans to continue to specialize on the

South Asia region, after which she'll reassess. One goal is to perhaps follow the career trajectory of Secretary of Defense Robert Gates, a man she admires. "He started as an intelligence analyst and went on to lead the CIA, Texas A&M, and now the Department of Defense," she says.

For a young woman just starting her career arc, she's learned very adult lessons. One, be ready for criticism and know how to take it, and two, whatever general or superior you're reporting to, know your stuff, because they're looking to you as an expert.

Postscript from Cara . . .

If I had to do it all over again, I would . . . Have spent less time thinking about going to law school because I thought it was what I should do and spend more time considering what I wanted to do.

If I knew then what I know now, I would . . . Not think I was underqualified for the job. A large portion of the analysts are in their twenties and early thirties, with limited experience.

Three characteristics or personality traits you need to do this job:

1. Understanding. The job is to put out the best product; you have to be able to take criticism and admit when you're wrong.
2. Confidence. You're the expert, or at least expected to be; senators and four-star generals are going to be asking questions that they want answers to.
3. Flexibility. You could find yourself on a plane to Afghanistan for four months or working in a different office with little notice because they think that's where they need you at the time.

Don't even try this if . . . You need to be in control at all times.

JERRY GREENSPAN
Chief of Staff for State Representative
Houston, Texas
Age: 25

Jerry Greenspan keeps a to-do list at all times, to a maniacal point, he admits. The yellow legal pad is a mess of almost illegible scribbles and notes to himself, but it's his Bible and without it, he'd be lost. Also tethered to his side is a beat-up BlackBerry, clipped to his belt for quick access.

Jerry is the chief of staff for a Texas state representative, an Hispanic woman who represents a predominantly low-income, Latino, inner-city district in southeast Houston known for its strong labor unions and growing gay, lesbian, bisexual, and transgender communities.

"Every two years, my boss has to ask 150,000-plus people for her job back," he says. "Therefore, I report to 150,001-plus people."

Jerry splits the year between Houston and Austin, the state's capital. June through December, the district office in downtown Houston is the bullpen. The small staff—an office manager, two interns, and Jerry—handles "constituent services," a catchall phrase for fielding community requests. "If district residents aren't getting the services they need from the state, we call the appropriate department and fix it, whether it be late food stamps, red tape surrounding a concealed handgun permit, or potholes on state highways."

The workday begins around 7:30 a.m., when Jerry opens the office and braces himself for a full plate of what he has learned to anticipate as organized chaos. "The chief of staff should really be called the chief of stuff," he says. First order(s) of business while he drains his coffee: check overnight voice mails, skim news headlines, and review the representative's day schedule crammed with meetings with colleagues and constituents.

When the crew trickles in about an hour later, Jerry switches into management mode, delegating who responds to mail, reviews legislation, schedules meetings. "It's rare that the staff doesn't have anything to do, but just in case, I make sure I have extra work available for everyone," he says, tapping his master list.

Ringing phones and drop-ins from the neighborhood jolt the office into high gear. "On any given day, so many people show up at our door who want to see our boss," he says, enumerating the (frequently unannounced) visitors: a lobbyist from a teacher's association rallying for extra pay; the Texas Farm Bureau rep lobbying for property rights; or a miffed resident ranting about a broken parking meter. As chief gatekeeper, Jerry decides who is granted a meeting with the rep, which requests can be handled by staff, and which queries can be put on hold. There are times when he has to head off protest groups masquerading under a different name whose only goal is to berate his boss.

Meanwhile, Jerry has received two or three calls and a text message from his boss checking in from the House floor or whichever meeting is slated for the morning. Because the job of a representative is classified as part-time (monthly salary of $600), most have full-time jobs in the private sector. Jerry's boss is a small-business consultant.

It's a rapid-fire pace that Jerry had to learn quickly. During college, he interned for the representative when she was serving on the City Council. When she was elected to the House, she asked him to come aboard as her chief of staff—a gamble both were willing to take. Jerry was young and inexperienced, but she was new to this tier of government, too. "There was a mutual trust there. I would never be so bold as to say I was the most qualified person for the job, but I was in the right place at the right time. And she knew I'd find a way to get things done," he says of those early days.

He didn't have much time to navel-gaze at his good luck. He was hired in late November, just over a month before the 150 House members congregate in Austin for a 140-day legislative session. Jerry scrambled and rented a second, sparsely furnished apartment in the state capital—a stretch for a COS salary capped at $50,400.

January begins the Austin-based stint of the job. Early mornings are spent prepping the representative on the docket of bills scheduled for a vote. Jerry collaborates with the rep's salaried legislative director, a twentysomething with five-plus years of policy experience. "We make sure the rep's floor packet is ready, with the backup information about the eighty to one hundred twenty bills being voted on that day." Jerry's on the lookout to flag sneaky last-minute amendments from adversarial reps whose edits can change the meaning of a bill, prompting a complete overhaul of the rep's position.

En route to the Assembly floor, Jerry shadows his boss as she pauses to chat with fellow politicos in the corridor. In between handshakes, she rattles off instructions. "Elected officials remember everything they give you to do," he says, astonished at his boss's capacity to follow up on her voluminous list. "'Did you call so-and-so back?' or 'What's the latest on the such-and-such legislation?' My job is to be ten steps ahead of the person in front of me. It's tough, especially when I'm trying to catch up on the last ten steps that I missed."

When the session begins and the rep is ensconced on the House floor, Jerry bolts back to the office to call the staff holding down the fort in Houston.

During the session from January through May, normal life shutters. It's all legislation, all the time. "The House and Senate meet whenever they feel like it, including Saturdays and Sundays," he says. "The job is stressful, period. It is hectic, at best out of control, and downright overbearing." A $1,500 "end of session" appreciation check helps lessen the sting.

In their first year working together, Jerry's boss filed nineteen bills—"impressive" for a freshman rep, he says. Of those nineteen, two became law, one related to reducing speed limits on residential streets, the other related to the licensing of court interpreters. By comparison, some seasoned legislators file more than one hundred bills.

"If all goes smooth during the day, and it usually doesn't, I roll with the representative to the many events that happen at night," he says, grateful because it's sometimes the first time he gets to eat all day. The evening outings are a welcome wind down to the harried days of politicking. People try to step off their soapbox and relax—a networking opportunity Jerry enjoys. "I love the connections. Between the diverse residents you represent, the other elected officials, lobbyists, and nonprofit organizations you work with, you have met more people than your BlackBerry lets you enter."

And to think he almost became a pharmacist. In high school, at his mom's prodding, Jerry took specialized health classes designated for students aspiring to work in medicine. As a senior, he spent one class period a day working at a local pharmacy, continuing on that track the next year at the University of Houston Pharmacy School. But once out from under his mother's parental push, he quickly switched majors to political science. "I don't think pharmacy school ever really stood a chance," he confides.

Besides, politics was part of his upbringing. Dinner talk at home in Brownsville, a small town near the Texas-Mexico border, centered around policy debate and elected officials. Mom was a former school board member and his dad worked for the sheriff's department, in the inmate transportation center.

During college, Jerry added a City Council internship to complement what he was learning in the classroom. "I am a firm believer that an internship should be a requirement of any college degree. It can, at least, tell you what you don't want to do with your life."

The chief of staff gig comes with its share of drawbacks, of course. "Friends think I am a glorified gopher," he says. In self-defense, he distills his job description into making "the jobs of those around me easier, whether it is to pick up lunch for the boss or the staff, drive the rep to an event, or anything that may or may not have anything to do with politics or policy."

And mistakes are part of the game. "I have had my share of big screw-ups. Most of them are 'classified,' but suffice it to say that when you're not supposed to leak certain information, doing so can cause some big headaches." The lesson: when your boss tells you something in confidence, especially about where she stands on a particular bill, don't let it leave the office.

After two years in the job, Jerry has hit the proverbial ceiling. "I am not planning a coup to become the elected official, so I've reached the peak of my office. Technically, becoming COS to a more senior member of the House or a senior staffer to a state senator could be considered an upward move," he says. "Since I am loyal to my boss, I wouldn't plan on taking a job with another House member."

Jerry is weighing his options and checking his own to-do list, but keeping an eye on the political sphere in one way or another.

Postscript from Jerry . . .

If I had to do it all over again, I would . . . Have trusted my staff from the beginning. The power of delegation shouldn't be a result of trusting your staff, it should be a tool used to build trust. I tried to take on everything on my own.

If I knew then what I know now, I would . . . Have not been so stressed out by everything. It will all work itself out eventually.

Three characteristics or personality traits you need to do this job:

   1. Loyalty to the boss
   2. Dedication to get the job done
   3. A thick skin

Don't even try this if . . . You are already skeptical of government. It can disappoint every now and again, but it's got its good days.

ANDREW SNOW
Photographer
Washington, D.C.
Age: 28

People are lucky to have a once-in-a-lifetime career-defining experience. Freelance photographer Andrew Snow has had two, both before his twenty-sixth birthday. The first was a six-month stint documenting the violent Palestinian rallies in the war-torn Gaza Strip. The second was traveling with John McCain's press corps during his presidential campaign run.

The Gaza Strip assignment had an unremarkable beginning. In the spring of Andrew's senior year of college in Washington, D.C., he applied to a news wire online job posting seeking a freelance photographer willing to travel to the Middle East and cover the escalating conflict. His resumé wasn't the strongest—a photo internship at a local paper during high school; photo editor of his college newspaper; odd pick-up jobs for friends—but he fit the other criteria. "Apparently, they wanted someone young who would work all the time, with little pay," he says.

"Are you fucking crazy?" his mom yelped when she heard the news. "Those were her exact words." After reassuring Mom ("I told her the situation wasn't as bad as it seemed, and that I was grown-up now"), Andrew boarded a commercial Gaza-bound flight, still hungover from college graduation festivities.

What awaited him twelve hours later was a sobering reality and scorching temperatures. A bald, no-nonsense man named Abu Ali introduced himself to Andrew at the airport—a "fixer" hired by the news service to drive, translate, and by and large, protect the young photographer. Abu Ali drove a beat-up car and stored a gun in there, just in case.

The two strangers settled into a routine. The fixer waited outside

Andrew's arranged accommodation ("a refugee B&B") in the pre-dawn
hours, chain-smoking inside the car, blasting air-conditioning. Andrew
would appear in the pitch black, already sweating from the extreme
heat, with camera gear in tow. Morning nods were exchanged; cigarettes, too. Then a clipped discussion about the day's destination—a
Hamas parade or a Spanish doctor treating patients—and silence again,
while Andrew tried to catch a few more winks en route.

It was early summer at this point, and the protests were peaceful.
Police occasionally arrested unruly demonstrators, but the 120-degree
heat waged the fiercest battle. Andrew was one of a handful of photographers, mostly working for foreign agencies. Once the conflict
heated up, Andrew was sparring with the hundreds of journalists sent
from all over the world, including "pushy" Americans. "It was hot,
hectic, and scary. And really exhilarating."

Through the lens of a Canon XLR, Andrew witnessed tem-
pers escalate. Peaceful rallies morphed into riots. Tear-gas bombs
were lobbed overhead, and gunshots pierced the air. The old days
of sit-and-wait became run-and-duck. Andrew crouched in corners
capturing authorities matching street violence with violence.

The day's work haunted him around the clock. The fixer delivered
him home and he'd crawl into his twin bed, cockroaches scurrying
underneath. Clutching his camera gear for fear of it being stolen, he'd
shut his eyelids and see the horrors play out all over again. Even today,
years later, the war's images have seared his brain, and friends and family urge him to seek therapy. He refuses.

Day after day for six months, Andrew did his job, blanketing the
Gaza Strip and into the West Bank, Sinai, and Israel. There were spells
when nothing was going on and he caught up on sleep, interspersed
with days of war unfolding before his eyes and camera. He shot thousands of frames, each capturing its own harsh reality: armed guards
pulling bodies from the rubble, medical staff overwhelmed by patients, maniacally smiling gun-toting rebels, and Israeli soldiers on

camel back. Children were part of the turbulent landscape, too. In the midst of grown men marching, Andrew's lens zeroed in on lost innocence: a young boy sitting atop a truck playing with a toy gun wrapped in a Palestinian flag.

Eventually, the violence and blood became just more violence and blood. One war zone blended into the next. "I was getting numb to the horrible things that were happening," he says. "It was time to go."

Returning to the United States was an abrupt adjustment. He spent a month at home in Oakland, California, before easing back into pre-deployment life in D.C. "Nothing had changed, but everything had," he recalls. Friends still lived in the same neighborhoods, hung out at the same bars, rooted for the same football team.

For work, he accepted a variety of assignments: beauty pageant photographer for girls four to seventeen, competing in nearly a dozen states; miscellaneous conferences and breakfast meetings shooting a speaker behind a podium. "I couldn't find meaning in what I was covering. I felt I had come back to cover stuff that didn't seem to matter," he says.

The tedium was beginning to feel endless, and moments of doubts surfaced. They still do. "There are times I think I should choose a more stable job—maybe property management like my dad. But then I recall a monotony of a summer in high school when I worked in a tiny cubicle of an ad agency looking for stock photos."

One of the gigs he picked up was shooting political fund-raisers and the cavalcade of donor hand-shaking and backslapping photo-ops. It also allowed him to tap into his entrepreneurial spirit. Prior to Senator John McCain's presidential campaign, Andrew covered the Arizona senator's home state fund-raising events. He lowered his rate in exchange for the right to sell additional copies of the 8 × 10 glossies donors receive as a memento. He also made the image available on other keepsakes, like mouse pads, T-shirts, key chains. Orders poured in. While Andrew outsourced the printing and shipping of the gizmo snapshots, the pictures fell to him to distribute. To keep up with demand, he hired an old boss's ten-year-old son to stuff, lick, and stamp envelopes for 10 cents a piece. "My old boss called me one day to tell me I had to fire his son," Andrew says. The kid was making $80 a day working for Andrew and neglecting his chores that paid a measly $1.

Meanwhile, Andrew had built up goodwill with the campaign insiders and was positioned to become full-time photographer. "At the beginning, there was no traveling press because McCain was fifth or seventh in polls," he explains. As the race narrowed and McCain's prospects improved, the campaign's media staff grew to nearly a dozen still photographers, plus ten videographers. Andrew snared one of the still photographer slots.

The campaign trail pace is grueling. Three or four scheduled photo-ops a day (sample itinerary: Cincinnati, Columbus, St. Louis), plus OTR (media-speak for "off the record") pit stops in iconic places: McCain snacking on custard in St. Louis or eating famous cheesesteaks in Philly. Andrew sometimes traveled in the press motorcade; other times he'd fly ahead to the next stop.

With equipment, he tried to keep it simple: four lenses, two flashes, and two camera bodies, all fitting in one carry-on exactly to TSA standards. Another backpack carry-on held essentials—extra shirt, pants, toiletries, and camera batteries—should his checked baggage get lost.

Campaigns work hard to present a seamless operation (whether they succeed is a different story). Behind the scenes that impression requires fine-tuned planning: every speech, wardrobe selection, and hand wave is choreographed. Camera angles are analyzed, lighting tweaked. Andrew understood his role in the production. "We're documenting the campaign. Of course, we're biased. If fifty people are expected to attend, they book a room for forty, so it looks crowded. We want things to look good," he says.

Down in the press pit—the buffer zone between the audience and the stage where the candidate is speaking—it can get a little heated, too. "There's an interesting dynamic between the traveling press and the local press," he says of the two camps' territorial attitudes. For the traveling press, covering the same stump speech feels like seeing the same movie over and over again. "By McCain's fourteenth speech, I could practically give it with him," Andrew says, adding he sometimes found himself mouthing the words along with the candidate.

Despite the big-league bragging rights earned from covering a war and a presidential campaign, Andrew's friends still insist on giving him grief. "The running joke is that I watch TV and goof off all day. But really taking pictures requires hours of paperwork, back-up, licensing, administrative chores." They have "normal people" jobs, like being an accountant. "I could never do that. I see a spreadsheet and my eyes glaze over."

But with a "normal" job comes a consistent paycheck. Working freelance doesn't. "If I worked for a wire service, the salary would be thirty-five thousand dollars a year for sixty hours per week. And they own you." Working for himself, "I've always managed to make more than that. If I wanted to take pictures of law firms and weddings, I could make more money, but I find it's a balancing act."

Part of that act is to keep dreaming big. "I still have the itch to do work on a bigger scale," he says. He's mulling how to work with a college buddy in the Peace Corps who has an idea how to educate people about AIDS through music. It harkens back to what an old boss once told him: "Whatever you do, don't major in photography or journalism. If you want to be a portrait photographer, study psychology; if you want to take shots of politicians, major in political science."

Does he see everything through a photographer's eye now? No. Behind the lens, he's also a twentysomething who likes to have a good time. "I do try to turn it off. I don't carry a camera with me everywhere like I used to. When I went to a friend's wedding in the Bahamas, I only took four pictures." All professional-caliber, picturesque moments? Nope. "All drunken blurry ones."

Postscript from Andrew . . .

If I had to do it all over again, I would . . . Have studied more business.

If I knew then what I know now, I would . . . Be more patient and stay in touch with more people.

Three characteristics or personality traits you need to do this job:

1. Free wheeling
2. Organized in a disorganized quick moving world
3. Ability to adapt and be what you need to be

Don't even try this if . . . You like a regular schedule and the ability to plan something more than five minutes out.

MENTOR'S INSIGHTS: *CONGRESSMAN JOHN LEWIS*

COURTESY OF THE U.S. HOUSE OF REPRESENTATIVES

Why You Should Listen Up—(a Selection of) Your Mentor's Resumé Stats:

- U.S. Congressman, Georgia, Representative for Georgia's Fifth District since 1987
- Senior Chief Deputy Whip of the Democratic Party, a member of the House Ways & Means Committee, a member of its Subcommittee on Income Security and Family Support, and Chairman of its Subcommittee on Oversight
- Atlanta City Council member for five years prior to being elected as a Congressman
- Dubbed one of the "Big Six" leaders of the Civil Rights Movement, along with Martin Luther King Jr.
- B.A. in religion and philosophy from Fisk University, and graduate of American Baptist Theological Seminary

The cover of John Lewis's biography, *Walking with the Wind, a Memoir of the Movement,* is a black-and-white close-up profile photograph of him as a young man. He wears a collared shirt and jacket. The half of his expression that is visible—chin down, eyes cast downward, brow furrowed—gives a sense of the intensity of his mind-set. Pan out wide and the context of the snapshot comes into greater focus: the early 1960s, in the height of the Civil Rights era.

As one of the Movement's most well-known leaders, Lewis spent his early twentysomething days waging a nonviolent struggle against segregation. He helped form the Student Nonviolent Coordinating Committee that organized sit-ins and peaceful protests engaging the twentysomethings of his day. Not even dark moments threatened to sideline Lewis. He was arrested and severely beaten on multiple occasions, always enduring in the name of the Movement's mission for justice.

One Photograph—Many Memories

At this particular moment (pointing to the book's cover image), I was standing in front of a restaurant in downtown Atlanta. It's a little place called Krystal's that denied service to people of color. I was determined to stand there and be a witness to what I saw, what I felt, and what I believed in. I wanted to change Atlanta, change the South, and change America and to make our society a better place—a decent place. To create what we called then a "Beloved Community"—an interracial democracy based on simple justice that values the dignity and the worth of every human being.

I saw this nonviolent protest only as one step, only as a means to move closer to creating this kind of community and a more perfect union. At that moment I didn't have any idea, didn't have a dream, that one day I would be a member of Congress, an elected official holding any position. I just wanted to change things.

At this moment in front of Krystal's, I am drawing from a sense of righteous indignation, asking "Why does this injustice exist?" And saying, "This is not right. This is not fair. This is not just. So I'm going to stand here, I'm going to protest with everything I have." It's like being anchored, and deciding I'm not going to be disturbed, be removed, or set off course. We used to sing a little song during a lot of our protests that went something like, "I'm like a tree planted by the water and I shall not be moved. Come hell or high waters. You can beat me, knock me down, arrest me, throw me in jail, but I'm going to stand."

Fast-Forward Forty-Plus Years, What Would You Tell Him?

I would say to this young man, "Keep the faith, don't give up, don't give in, don't give out, and hold on to your dreams." And I would say to this young man, "Don't forget what your mother said to you over and over again—be mindful. Don't get in a hurry. Whatever it is you believe in, wherever you want to make a difference in our society, take the long hard look." The struggle for justice is long, and it requires endurance. One must pace him- or herself for the long haul because this is a struggle that lasts not for one day or one week or one month or one year. It is the struggle of a lifetime.

Working in Government Is a Calling

To work and serve in government at the local, state, federal, international, or global level is a calling. It is a duty to create policies that look out and care for the people. It's wonderful work. I know if someone had told this young man when he was growing up very poor in rural Alabama that one day he would be serving on the City Council in Atlanta or serving as a member of Congress from Georgia, he would have reacted in disbelief. But today, this young man, other young men, and young women have an opportunity to just go for it. The sky is the limit. So just go out there and push and pull and don't be afraid.

It is my hope, it is my dream and prayer, that the young people who work with me on the staff, whether they are working in Washington or back in Georgia, learn something from what we do. I've always felt that in my younger life we didn't spend enough time learning from our elders, learning from individuals like a Martin Luther King Jr., Robert Kennedy, or John F. Kennedy and so many others. Sometimes you learn just by listening. Sometimes you learn just by being watchful.

Growing Up Quickly

There are hundreds and thousands of young people in Washington, D.C., and on Capitol Hill—especially during the summer when most of the interns come. During the past twenty-four years I've seen these young people literally grow up overnight. It's almost like living my life over again during the sit-ins and during the Freedom Summer. I saw young people grow up in a few months while they were sitting on those lunch counter stools.

Almost every single day I see a group of young people somewhere on this campus sitting or standing staring at the Capitol taking it all in. I want to say to them, "One day you may come back here as a member of the House, a member of the Senate. Maybe as president of the United States." Because they are learning—which is good. They have opportunities and chances that many Americans never had. In my own estimation, we are producing a better breed of citizen in this country than ever before.

If these young people can go out and share their own experiences in government, they could tell others that government service is not bad. It's a good thing. I think a lot of the young people coming into government today will be able to humanize government and make it more compassionate.

Govern with Caution

Yes, working in politics, a person can become drunk with power and very selfish. I run into legislators and leaders who love America and love the world, but they don't really like people. They don't want to get their hands dirty. You have to be mindful. You have to go back to your anchor, your center, and remember your purpose. It is important for any person to have core values you believe in and can stick to. And in your life and in your work you have to make sure not to let anything take you away from certain immutable principles.

Sometimes when I'm sitting on the floor or in a committee meeting, even back in my district, I have what I like to call "an executive session" with myself, and I remind myself of my commitment. I feel I have a moral obligation, a mission, to use this position to do my very best. I am obligated to give it all I've got. You only pass this way once, and it's your calling to do your best. I often think about what other people gave up, what other people sacrificed and died for in our democracy, people I got to know like President Kennedy, Robert Kennedy, Dr. King, and others. They served, but they didn't live to see the fulfillment of a lot of the things they tried to do. I feel like they are watching. I feel that if I fail to do my part, and if those of us in government fail to do our part, somehow, in some way the spirit of history will not be kind to us. I almost feel that if you don't do your part, if you don't do your best, then you will pay a price, a higher price than any human being can make you pay, but a price of the conscience.

Protests in This Day and Age

We've become too quiet. We've become almost immune to the problems and the conditions facing us. People should be a little more visible. Maybe it just goes around in cycles. Maybe it will take some leader or some symbol to emerge. Sometimes I think maybe people are afraid to have hope again. During the 2008 presidential election it seemed like there was a tremendous sense of hope and optimism. It reminded me of my own involvement in the political process as a young man. I think something is out there just waiting to take flight again.

There is something so beautiful about the unity of believing in something and taking a stand for an idea. There is a gratifying sense of bearing witness to the truth, and it creates a sense of coming together. A sense of solidarity. We shouldn't let that go, regardless of the outcome of a political campaign. That sense of unity is more powerful than any one candidate or election, and it can be used for good.

An Obligation to Do Something

You must be ashamed to leave here—this little piece of real estate that we call earth—until you have made some contribution to make things better for all humankind. I see people just go through life wandering, almost just wasting their time away aimlessly. You have to have a purpose. You should follow that star. Go down that path. Go down that road. Make the journey.

The storms will come. The wind will blow and the thunder roll and the lightning will flash. But you have to be anchored. Say to yourself, "Whatever comes, I will continue. I may get knocked down, I may get arrested and go to jail for a time. I may even become a public servant and still get arrested and go to jail, but it's going to be for a meaningful cause. A noble cause."

A Nonviolent State of Mind

Before you go on any mission, before you even take a job, or run a service project, you have to gather your mind. You have to have an executive session with yourself and say, "I'm not going to deviate from what I've been taught, from my core values, no matter what work I do. I believe it is better to love than to hate and to forgive." You have to decide that you're just not going to be pulled in, and go along with whatever happens. You have to decide you're not going to let your environment or let someone else distract you or set you on the wrong path.

7

Derailed Gigs

On Second Thought . . .

INTRODUCTION

In December 2007, the U.S. economy started a decline that wouldn't show significant signs of recovery for many years. Those years, some economists say, marked the worst recession since 1929 and the start of the Great Depression.

A storm of statistics exists to illustrate how bad the recession got, but one overarching number will suffice for our purposes: more than eight million people lost their jobs.

A portion of that eight million unemployment figure represents twentysomethings who had recently finished college or graduate school and were flooding the workplace with fresh blood, ready to make an impact. Weeks, months, or a couple of years later, the recession claimed their jobs, too. Loss of income wasn't the only casualty. Self-esteem took a beating, and confidence in career direction wobbled.

However this twentysomething generation may be perceived—ambitious or lazy, groundbreaking or entitled—they share the de-railed experience with other generations.

This chapter picks up at the "What now?" moment, with profiles of four twentysomethings who were laid off just as they were getting started. As so many people know firsthand, a derailment early in a career's trajectory—or anywhere along the timeline for that matter—can be a debilitating blow on many fronts. While some profiled here were more reflective than others, each demonstrated a commendable bounce-back attitude. They kept moving. To what, they weren't always sure, but the destination presented itself eventually. The trick was to keep looking.

One undeniable takeaway for everyone might be this: before a boss-employee dynamic becomes unsalvageable, look for opportunities elsewhere in the company. Some bosses are jerks; some employees are, too. But it's a shame to end a relationship with a company you admire on disappointing terms because the relationship with a boss didn't work out.

When Michael Pak was interviewing for law associate jobs, a point of pride for the real estate firm he was considering was that it had never laid off any employees due to economic downturns. The firm always found a way to save jobs by refocusing associates to other projects.

Those bragging rights would need a rewrite. Michael worked as corporate real estate attorney for twenty-seven months before the recession intervened. Perhaps it was just as well—with an honest, 20/20 self-appraisal, Michael wasn't entirely sure why he became a lawyer in the first place. A gregarious guy who excelled in school, and could talk sports, politics, and whatever else off the cuff, he had no specific job ambition except to make his parents proud and impress his fellow Ivy League peers. A misguided game plan if there ever was one.

Julia Riley, on the other hand, was anything but a conformist. When she graduated from college, she took note of where her peers were headed—banking, consulting—and intentionally went in the opposite direction.

That 180-degree strategy would be laden with dead ends. After getting fleeced by a bogus employer and a go-nowhere job in advertising, she ping-ponged around other advertising gigs, collecting a few bruises along the way. It's been a tough transformation for this young woman who entered the workforce expecting others to match her optimistic spirit. She's weathered a number of disappointments but has lessons to share from each of them.

Raised in a blue-collar family in Bristol, Florida, Carmen Williams's mainstays growing up were work and religion. The little-girl version of Carmen, however, had dreams that wouldn't fit in a small-town arena. She wanted to be a businesswoman, and the only place that would do was in the heart of the finance world: Wall Street, New York City. She followed all the "career ladder" rules—got her MBA degree and worked her way up to the venerable financial institution, Lehman Brothers.

The sequined finance industry would nose-dive barely two years later. Carmen's story is told through a twenty-four-hour period—the infamous Sunday that marked the beginning of the end of this famed house of finance.

Not getting along with a boss is a sure way to get derailed; just ask Amy Faulconer. The James Madison University graduate was stoked when she landed an international marketing job in the magazine publication division of a multimedia conglomerate in Washington, D.C. The company also produced award-winning films and documentaries, and was world renowned for creating innovative work.

Her enthusiasm waned when face-off squabbles with her boss intensified, ultimately leading to her lay-off three and a half years after she started. Now, she's living in Aspen, Colorado, and waiting tables for a winter season while figuring out her next move.

Acclaimed journalist Dan Rather knows how an unceremonious exit feels. After more than four decades working for CBS News, he found himself without a job.

Rather was the first person I thought of to mentor this chapter.

People rolled their eyes. "Good luck with that," they said, referring to the lingering contentious air between Rather and his former employer.

But a few years had passed. Maybe, I thought, he was ready to give some career advice on a tough and all too real downside of working.

Was he ever. My interview with Rather was scheduled to last thirty minutes. We spoke for one hour. He recalled details from his early career dates with rapid-fire quickness, including names of old bosses and street addresses.

Rather may no longer be filing stories for CBS, but he is still reporting. As anchor and managing editor of *Dan Rather Reports,* a weekly hourlong news program airing on cable's HDNet, his travel and reporting schedule is as packed as ever—proof that being derailed isn't necessarily a final verdict.

AMY FAULCONER
Former Marketing Executive
Aspen, Colorado
Age: 28

Everyone knows what a waitress does for a living. The gig at the vegetarian bistro during the busy ski season in Aspen, Colorado, where Amy Faulconer waits tables, follows the norm. She recites the specials (potato and leek soup), recommends her favorite dishes (the butter lettuce salad), and tries to up-sell wine selections ($80 bottle of Chateau Mont Redon of interest?).

But this behind-the-scenes snapshot isn't so much about what Amy does during each lunch shift, as the how and why she's here in the first place.

Amy retreated to this affluent ski town nestled in the Rocky Mountains to recoup after a blindsided layoff from a coveted marketing job in Washington, D.C. Landing that gig three and a half years earlier at a world-renowned travel and photography magazine seemed kismet. The position—international new business marketing manager—for a multimedia conglomerate blended her interests perfectly. Two years of managerial experience, an international marketing degree, and months traveling in Europe and Australia made her well suited for the role.

"I was really excited about it. I really wanted it," she recalls. "It was cool to be a part of an organization that nobody on the planet ever responded by saying 'What do they do?'" In addition to its magazine publication division, the company also produced award-winning films and documentaries.

Amy was psyched to be part of the family. The $50K salary came with generous medical benefits (full health and dental) and twenty-one vacation days (plus every other Friday off in the summer). The hours weren't crazy—forty per week on average. The "international" part of the title wasn't only for show: she traveled to European conferences that enabled her to network with sales reps and develop new marketing concepts.

"But, as with all jobs, it lost its luster after a while and became just that—a job," she says. Toward the middle of her run, the monotony set in. What once felt innovative turned mechanical. "If you lived outside the United States and you have a pulse, my mission was to get you to buy a year (or more!)" of a magazine subscription. To do that, the four-person department sent mass snail mailings of "all those pesky form letters that clog up people's mailboxes" and produced the postcard-size magazine inserts that invariably wind up "scattered over any gym floor." The bulk of the work was spent tethered to a computer where she coded HTML into subscription pages, edited marketing materials, set up spreadsheets for financial analysis, and managed all the sales reps stationed abroad. "Mondays were report days—how did we do for the last week? Fridays were, 'Let's file a few papers mindlessly 'cause I'm ready to get the heck out of this office for a few days.'"

Claustrophobia grew as she realized that room for growth was improbable, since both of her bosses had fifteen-year tenures. Amy's immediate boss was a pleasant guy, but territorial of his workload. Her relationship with the main supervisor, with whom she once got along brilliantly—they shared sarcastic senses of humor—was starting to erode.

From Amy's perspective, she was trying to take the reins of her managerial role and add input to the company's marketing strategy. But, she felt, her efforts to contribute were dismissed outright, and instead of being trusted to make the right decision, she was being micromanaged. Hadn't she been hired for a reason?

When a conflict with a client surfaced, the boss sided with the client without a nod to her expertise. Amy thought the boss was kowtowing to an unprofitable client; the boss thought she was not being a team player.

The simmering dispute boiled over into a showdown when he summoned Amy to his office to discuss the snag. When he asked her for the fourth time how she was going to reconcile the problem, she responded evenly, for the fourth time, that she would take care of it. Not satisfied, he stared her down and asked a fifth time, drawing the metaphorical line in the sand.

This time her smart-ass inner dialogue leaked onto her face and the sides of her mouth started to curl.

He was not amused. With the office door wide open for everyone to hear he ripped into her: "Stop smiling! This isn't a joke, it's business, and you can just wipe it off and leave it at the door!"

Amy knew her time was limited when he emailed that afternoon to reiterate how inappropriate her behavior had been. She knew her time was *severely* limited when the client company's president replied, too. Apparently, he had been blind copied on the email and accidentally revealed himself when he "replied all" with a "thanks," acknowledging receipt without comment on the issue.

But it would be nearly four months before the ax dropped. Amy was summoned to human resources on a Thursday morning, where her boss was waiting. "He told me that for business reasons they felt other people could do my job and they didn't need me anymore. That it would be my last day."

The dismissal stung. "I was definitely emotional. I went through all the mood swings," she says. "Shock at first, embarrassment of having to tell my coworkers we were no longer colleagues. Lots of crying. Anger."

Back at the lunch shift in Aspen, wearing the requisite black trousers, shirt, and apron, she doesn't hold grudges and refuses to harp on regrets. With some we've-all-been-there prodding, though, she warms to a self-analysis. Could she have chosen her battles more carefully? Could she have handled the toxic boss-employee relationship a little better?

A crack in the veneer: "I do have one regret," she says after a pause. About a year before the tension at work got bad, a position in another marketing department managing the international language editions popped up. Amy felt it was a little out of her grasp and let the job vacancy come and go without applying. "I should have gone for it," she says with a sigh.

Shaking it off, she's focusing on the positive. The Aspen hiatus presented itself serendipitously. While commiserating with a fellow newly unemployed friend, she decided to tag along on his road trip out West, where he was planning to spend a clear-your-head ski season. Fast-forward to a waitressing gig opening a few weeks later.

"It's a nice change of pace from waking up at seven a.m. every day and getting home at six thirty p.m. Monday to Friday. I can take off when I want to, although I don't get paid for those days."

Not everyone gets her laid-back attitude. The peanut gallery of friends and family slip in their opinions in not-so-thinly veiled comments. "You need to be finding a real job, even if it's as a secretary," scolded one friend, a patent lawyer in Virginia, where he felt Amy "should be."

To those naysayers, she shrugs. "I've just decided I don't care. It's something different. Do I want to be a waitress forever? Of course not," she says. But "nobody said you couldn't have fun while being unemployed."

As the season comes to a close, she has a decision to make. The restaurant management wants her to stay. They've eliminated the dinner service but are trying to shuffle lunch shifts to keep her busy. Meanwhile, most of the twentysomething temporary transplants are packing their bags and steeling themselves for the return to "real" lives. The road-trip friend, a congressional-aide-turned-taxi-driver, recently interviewed for a national nonprofit job.

Then again, she figures, you can only do this drop-everything, move-to-a-ski-town thing once. When Amy leaves, it will be for good. "I know I'll never move back," she says, "and I don't want to cut an opportunity short."

She's thought a lot about work in the big picture lately, and the value her peers place in a job title. Full disclosure: she did, too. From international new business marketing manager to waitress. What "title" will follow these, she's not sure.

But one perspective she does have clarity on as she weighs her options is a theory her dad always subscribed to: "Amy," he used to say, "summer's hot, winter's cold. They call it work because that's what it is."

Postscript from Amy

If I had to do it all over again, I would . . . Not change it. Life is what it is and I accept it for where it goes.

CARMEN WILLIAMS
Former Financier
New York, New York
Age: 28

Morning, Sunday, September 14, 2008. Carmen Williams's morning routine during the work week was timed precisely: 7:00 a.m. alarm goes off, two hits for five-minute snoozes, in-and-out shower, flat-iron hair, and out the door by 8:05 a.m.

But today was Sunday. No need to rush. A few extra hours of sleep were in order before church started at 10:45 a.m.

Church. Her solace. Her anchor. Each Sunday, Carmen walked the one block from her studio apartment on Manhattan's Upper West Side to the Baptist service where smiling familiar faces greeted each other warmly.

The Sunday tranquility came to a jarring halt when the phone rang.

"Come into the office," her boss ordered, sounding harried.

There would be no church today.

She was half expecting this call. The previous Friday, work was a circus. Carmen was an analytics associate at Lehman Brothers, one of the world's biggest and most influential investment banking and financial services companies. But that heyday was rapidly diminishing. The finance industry was hemorrhaging jobs across the board. Lehman Brothers had had four rounds of layoffs within the past year alone, and the future was getting bleaker. The bank's stock price plummeted 73 percent in the first half of 2008, and whereas other troubled Wall Street financial firms were being scooped up and folded into healthier banking institutions, no one seemed to want to rescue Lehman Brothers. Not even the government.

When Carmen left that Friday evening, her boss warned her to keep her cell phone close. "We knew that come Monday, the bank was either going to be there or not," she recalls.

Since church was off, she pulled on something casual—a pair of jeans and a shirt—and headed to catch the C train on 8th Avenue, just as she had for the previous twenty-one months. Transfer at 59th. Walk one block east. Go to 12th floor.

When she arrived by 11:00 a.m., a staff of thirty was already at work, but the place was oddly quiet. "It felt like a morgue," she recalls. "The energy was dead. People were somber and stoic."

She found her supervising boss. "What can I do to help?" she asked.

Getting to Wall Street, the financial nucleus of the world's economy, was a dream come true for this woman who grew up in the Florida panhandle town of Bristol. Her family still sells earthworms to bait and tackle shops. One young brother drives a truck for a living; the other two are in grade school.

But Carmen felt destined for bigger things. She idolized the businessmen she saw on television and the two-piece tailored suits that came with the job. Her eyes were transfixed on the epicenter of the industry: "I thought, Just get me to New York City and I'll figure it out."

Now that she was here, how could she help? The boss directed her to start pulling account details for the Securities and Exchange Commission, the government agency tasked with regulating the securities business. Vague instructions, but she understood.

Banks borrow and lend each other money on a regular basis. As with so many other businesses, banking and lending depend to a very large degree on relationships, trust, and confidence. Carmen was part of the treasury data analytics team. Translation? She spent all day, every day, making spreadsheets that tracked how much money Lehman and its eighty-eight relationship banks worldwide were borrowing and from whom.

With the benefit of hindsight, Carmen had seen this moment coming for months. The number of report summaries she was asked to complete had begun to drop precipitously—finally to a trickle. Where she once knocked out twenty transaction summary reports each week, barely five awaited her attention—her from-the-hip barometer of how the business was skidding. "We basically overextended ourselves, and when we got into sub-prime mortgages, that just killed us. We weren't brilliant enough to manage it," she says.

Sitting at her computer, Carmen clicked "print" over and over again. Hundreds of documents—exposure data and account details—queued up. She glanced around. Colleagues with red-rimmed eyes shuffled to the bathroom. Others traded questioning looks. "What have you heard?" they whispered to one another. One rumor in the mill was that the firm's CEO was in round-the-clock meetings with the Federal Reserve chairman and other heavy hitters trying to "figure out how to stop the sky from falling." Lehman Brothers going bankrupt was unfathomable. Someone would save them.

Afternoon. With Mexican food spread out across the conference room table, people filed in, spooned some beans and rice on their plates, and returned to their desks.

Carmen's colleagues had good reason to be upset, having invested ten, twenty years with the firm. Their entire identity, not to mention financial security, was wrapped up in the bank. Its demise was their demise.

Carmen, on the other hand, was more removed. New to the firm, she didn't have years of savings at risk. While the printer hummed, she peeked at a white booklet she kept tucked in a desk drawer, a daily devotional book entitled *The Daily Bread*. She kept her spiritual side private. "The workplace isn't a good place to broadcast stuff like that, I found."

What was broadcast freely was the wealth. The firm's cupidity was contagious, intoxicating those who thought they were immune to the so-called golden handcuffs. Even Carmen, the daughter of blue-collar parents, got caught up in the rush. The nearly six-figure salary afforded her a lifestyle not known to her neighbors in Bristol. When she received her first bonus, a few thousand dollars, she let herself splurge: $500 Louboutin shoes, a new computer, new clothes.

The shopping spree was, she felt, a well-deserved reward for meeting her goal. In college, she chose an accelerated five-year MBA program at Florida A&M in Tallahassee—a faster track to get into that two-piece business suit she always envisioned. To meet the program's internship requirements, Carmen spent a semester in Michigan interning in the human resources department of a major pharmaceutical firm's research and development facility, and another semester in Boston at a blue-chip accounting firm. When they offered her a full-time job after graduation, she accepted after she negotiated a transfer to the New York City office. Once there, friends regaled her with stories of Wall Street and the investment banking high life, prompting her to make the leap, too. After all, Wall Street was where the real suits come to play.

Now those suits were all over the news. Finance broadcaster Maria Bartiromo delivered the play-by-play on the flat-screen televisions in the conference room. CNBC streamed financial updates on computers. Media trucks and reporters were double parked on the street below.

In the late afternoon, a call from headquarters located in Times Square summoned a glimmer of hope. Another bank was considering buying them. Their jobs might be saved. "People believed it. We thought we were going to get bought. We just didn't know when or by whom." It was just a matter of time before this all went away.

Evening. That "Hail Mary" didn't play out. No rescue deal materialized. The evening news pundits speculated that Lehman would be forced to declare bankruptcy.

Around 9:00 p.m., Carmen walked out the front door and hailed a taxi.

A $12 fare later, and a block from her apartment, she passed the Baptist church. "That day was the worst day in a lot of people's lives and here I am, not my worst day." Next Sunday, she knew where she'd be.

Postscript. On Monday morning, a press release confirmed that the bank planned to file for bankruptcy protection. Some employees, including Carmen, were swept up as new hires for Barclay's Capital. But six months later, more rounds of pink slips were shuffled, and Carmen became another unemployed casualty of a historic banking debacle.

Postscript from Carmen . . .

If I had to do it all over again, I would . . . Have gotten more mentors from diverse backgrounds at the beginning of my career.

If I knew then what I know now, I would . . . Honor all parts of myself. I'm both right brained and left . . . analytical and creative . . . If I had figured this out years ago, I could've perhaps been in a more custom-fit career a long time ago.

Three characteristics or personality traits you need to do this job:

1. Self-starter. No one's going to hand-feed you, you're going to have to be a quick learner, and to ask a lot of questions when you get stuck.
2. Know how to play corporate politics. You can't escape it. If you

> want to climb the corporate ladder, you've got to have people
> on your side.
>   3. Self-awareness: You've got to have self-awareness to know if a
>   career/job/team environment is the best place for you to reach
>   your potential.
>
> ***Don't even try this if . . .*** You don't enjoy spreadsheets, databases,
> fast pace, and staying up with the news at all times.

JULIA RILEY
Former Advertising Associate
Orange County, California
Age: 24

Well that was easy. Julia Riley had just scored a job for doing what
came naturally—being popular. It was February of her senior year at
Duke University in North Carolina, and out of the blue, an Internet start-up company messaged her via Facebook. The company was
launching a travel website aimed at college kids and recruited Julia as
a college ambassador (err, "marketing manager") to help it go viral.
She had more than a thousand "friends"—a few plugs from her and
the site would have a built-in audience.

They promised to pay Julia $1,000 to distribute promotional
products—shot glasses, T-shirts, ping pong balls—on campus and then
flew her to Orange County, California, during her spring break for an
interview. An hour later they handed her a sweet job offer: marketing
director, salary $100K, plus stock options capped at $1 million.

She returned to campus on a cloud. The remainder of the semester
sailed by, concluding with graduation farewells and good lucks. Most
of her friends embarked on traditional paths—consulting or finance
or law school. So predictable, she thought. Not for her. She wanted
to be a risk taker.

This Internet start-up "risk" happened to come with a very handsome salary. Sure, it was a little unusual for a twenty-one-year-old with no experience, but who was she to question what her new employers saw in her? She whisked off to Southern California.

The red flags greeted her on landing. The company's two dozen employees, whom she had met months prior, had vanished. What were once three large offices was now one small room. Worse yet, the partners didn't seem fazed.

Julia began to realize what she thought was her three bosses' charisma was really well rehearsed spin-doctor hype. "Business meetings" consisted of the four of them. Little lies started to surface. Julia arrived early one day to discover the electricity had been cut off and they were about to be evicted. The bosses shrugged, deflecting the blame to the "rude management," and assigned Julia the task of begging the landlords for a few weeks' reprieve. She bit her lip and continued to perform her "marketing director" duties, like emailing venture capitalist firms soliciting investments.

This "Internet start-up" was supposed to be a travel website, a one-stop shop where young adults could book flights and swap travel itineraries with friends. But the little money they did raise went to pimping out the office with video games. The leftover chump change was spent on an inexpensive web designer. It showed. "The site looked awful," she recalls. Links were broken; it was disorganized. Error messages were rampant.

A chronic optimist and admittedly a touch naïve, Julia stuck it out for four months before jumping ship. "I should have been more skeptical. The CEO had no idea what he was doing, and they had no business plan" (except for the one she cut and pasted together). "I realized I was just spinning my wheels and this 'start-up' was never actually going to start up," she says.

And that $1,000 campus promo gig payday, $100K salary, and stock options? Julia was never paid a penny. Neither, it turns out, were dozens of original employees.

It was a wake-up call for this Palo Alto, California, native who was raised to believe any dream she had was attainable. She wasn't prepared for the potholes that lay ahead. "In two years, I went on sixteen interviews, had four full-time jobs, moved three times, and was laid off twice," she says. That's a lot to handle for a young woman who entered the "real world" brimming with hope and confidence.

That energy had been in abundance since she was a kid and wide eyed about media. "Ever since I was little, I'd scrutinize all the advertisements around me—billboard ads, TV commercials, even radio jingles—with the overwhelming feeling that 'I could do this,' or 'I could make this better.'"

Life was like that for this little girl. She couldn't help it.

Back to the grown-up drawing board. Lesson one: If it looks too good to be true, it is.

A family friend helped her land an interview at an advertising agency specializing in creating movie posters. The legitimacy of the place hooked her instantly, especially after being burned by the smoke-and-mirrors outcome of her last job. Look, over there—real employees! And there—meetings in glass-walled boardrooms. Catered food, mock-up posters propped up on easels, and finished glossy prints framed in the halls. "I was so excited to work somewhere that felt like a real job. I fell in love with the company right away."

A "coordinator" position was open (salary: $33K) and Julia grabbed it, hoping she'd learn the business and move up quickly.

Apparently, not quickly enough. The honeymoon period was brief—two months. "My job was easy, too easy." The entry-level coordinator title came with entry-level work, like answering the phone and dealing with deliveries—"basically a receptionist with a better title."

"They didn't need me and I didn't want the job," she says. "I got really bored and they could tell." She spent more time asking to help out in other departments than she did at the receptionist desk where she was stationed.

Not wanting to lose her, the company created an "assistant photo editor" position. New job description: find and purchase the props and wardrobe for in-house photo shoots used to illustrate the posters. Julia zipped around in her black BMW, a college graduation present from her parents, to the movie studios in LA and foraged through warehouses for masks, bathtubs, handcuffs, or fake weapons. "When I described my job to my friends, it sounded amazing. Who wouldn't want to spend their days shopping?"

She lasted four months. "The problem was, again, I felt dispensable. I wasn't using any of my knowledge or skills, and I certainly wasn't putting my Duke education to good use." When the company decided to eliminate her position due to "the economy," Julia didn't put up a fight.

Three positions in less than one year. Nothing was sticking. Perhaps she was partly to blame for having high expectations, but was it too much to ask to be stimulated at work? Lesson two: Find work that is intellectually challenging.

This time, she reversed the sequence of customary job-seeker steps. Instead of scrolling through pages of Internet job postings, she researched companies that impressed her and then checked to see if they were hiring.

One of her perennial bookmarks was Google. From a creative and advertising point of view, it was *the* place to work. Innovative. Legitimate. Practically every open position HR posted—media coordinator, account manager, production specialist—she had applied for, but she never got any traction. They wanted experience. Her spotty resumé never made its way to the top.

A couple of weeks into her hunt, she discovered a company that seemed to hit on all cylinders—a well-respected, technology-driven advertising firm upending traditional methods of ad design, packaging, and sales. It was well funded and had a position available immediately (salary: $33K).

The job was working on the five-month-old media consulting team for the TV advertising side. Because the company purchased air-time in bulk, it created affordable campaigns for mom and pop shops. For instance, a small family-owned golf shop could buy a fifteen- or thirty-second commercial to run on a major sport cable network for $500 per week. The consultant's objective was to decide when and where the target demographic was and how best to reach it.

"My first interview went so well, I was literally skipping out of the building," she recalls.

For her callback, she prepared an exhaustive PowerPoint presentation and, wanting to deliver beyond expectations, wrote and produced a mock commercial to showcase a sales pitch for a pseudo-company.

Julia's heart sank when she began to set up—her computer and the projector were not compatible. "Wing it," they told her. She fumbled through as best she could, leaving in near tears.

Despite the flub, she got the job. "They told me they truly admired my 'fortitude' and 'optimism,' " she recalls.

During the three weeks of training that followed, she absorbed real, tangible skills: using customer relationship management software, understanding important sales techniques, creating media proposals, as well as handling day-to-day customer questions, complaints, and requests.

She was getting the hang of it until the roller coaster plummeted again. On the Monday of her fourth week on the job, she was among one hundred employees sent packing when the departments were slashed, including the fifteen-person media consulting team. The future of ads, the executives decided, was in search-engine advertising.

"It was really tough," she says, utterly demoralized at the time. "I was starting to think, 'Can I keep a job for more than a few months?' It was disappointing because I felt it was something I could be good at."

She soldiered on, attacking the job search again like a woman possessed. She mined the contacts she had accumulated. Nearly everyone she knew received a phone call. Lesson three: Job security trumps risk.

As usual, she applied to Google. This time she got a phone interview. "They told me to apply again once I had a year of experience under my belt. This gave me the motivation to just find anything—salary was the least of my concerns."

She ended up scoring a job as an account manager (salary: $30K) at a company that owned and operated hundreds of websites, a division of which catered to niche communities like car enthusiasts.

Not the sexiest job, but she dug in, making up for lost time. In addition to managing the site's advertisers, she went above and beyond her title, studying ad "click" patterns and analyzing why some ads popped up more than others, then relaying her findings to the ad trafficking department.

Is it her dream job? No. Management guarded every nickel—overtime was frowned upon, and employees were told to bring their own food to holiday parties—and she was earning slightly more than she would babysitting. But, she thinks, when the next interview comes along, she'll be damned if she's not going to have something to show for it.

"Although the path I've taken to find my career hasn't been the smoothest or the fastest, it has definitely made for an interesting and valuable ride," she says, still retaining that optimistic glint in her eye. She can't help it.

Postscript from Julia . . .

If I had to do it all over again, I would . . . I'm a huge believer in the saying "everything happens for a reason," and I honestly don't think I would change anything if I had to do it all over again. I've learned more about myself—who I am and what I want—by experiencing the ups and the downs, the good and the bad. Had I gone the more traditional route and taken a less "risky" job from the get-go, I certainly wouldn't have grown to be as resilient and strong-minded as I feel I am now.

If I knew then what I know now, I would . . . Be more skeptical and less naïve . . . I'd understand "too good to be true" scenarios are most likely just that. Also, I would never underestimate the power of personal relationships and connections in helping to find and build a career.

Don't even try this if . . . You're scared of risk taking, rejection, instability, or uncertainty. If you're going to take that initial risk, I don't necessarily believe you should "prepare for the worst," but you most certainly need to hope for the best!

MICHAEL PAK
Former Attorney
Los Angeles, California
Age: 29

Only those who knew him well could tell he was faking. Even his parents didn't realize he was harboring a secret. On the surface, all signs pointed to his good fortune—fancy job title, new car, six-figure salary. But a closer inspection revealed a radically different story.

"I knew without a doubt that the job was killing my soul," Michael Pak says. Acknowledging that many people struggle with crummy jobs, and get paid a lot less than he does, he "felt the pressure to just suck it up and do it." Plus, the title made his parents, first-generation emigrants from South Korea, so proud. They positively beamed when introducing him to their friends: "Meet our son, a corporate real estate attorney."

Those introductions turned his stomach. "I felt guilty about not liking my job and complaining about it because it was a prestigious job. I know my parents and grandparents struggled to be able to afford me these opportunities." Michael's grandfather had chosen his eldest child, Michael's dad, to bring to the United States after the Korean War. They settled in Princeton, New Jersey, and each of the other three children arrived when they could afford to send one. Meanwhile, Michael's dad attended Columbia University in Manhattan and eventually married Michael's mother, who was "literally, fresh off the boat," he says. She put aside an aspiring career as a pianist to raise Michael and his sister, completely committing herself to housewife and mom duties, including emphasizing the role of education. "Growing up, the score card of how I was doing as a kid was my report card. As long as I was doing well in school, everything was okay."

Fast-forward to the 29th floor in a high-rise building in Los Angeles where for twenty-seven months, Michael reported to work. And each day he did what real estate lawyers do: reviewed leases, drafted contracts, and negotiated terms for clients whom he rarely met in person.

The year prior, business was booming and Michael was billing seventy hours a week at the seventy-five-associate firm. The schedule was torturous, but it was a lucrative torture: Michael's base salary was $140K.

The façade unraveled a few days after the New Year holiday. Come January, the economy was shattering and firms were shedding jobs. Associates did their best to look busy and keep their heads clear of the guillotine. Having dodged a few miscellaneous surprise layoffs in the past four months, they were painfully aware that a pile of pink slips was due—the first economically triggered layoffs in the firm's history.

"Around that time, every day I'd walk into my office with a beautiful view of the ocean and wonder how much longer I'd have it," Michael remembers.

A knock at the door by two senior partners put that question to rest.

Their spiel lasted about ten minutes. It started with a slight hint of empathy—something about paying for his state bar dues for the remainder of the year, and a three-month severance package paid in a lump sum. Then a stiff reminder of the reality of the situation—an impersonal order to vacate the premises "as soon and as quietly as possible," Michael recalls.

The partners left. Michael froze. "You hear the rumors and you're constantly looking over your shoulder, but until it happens to you, it's hard to fathom."

A wave of panic and disappointment overcame him and then, as if on an exhale, released its vice grip. After the initial shock, "I realized I was cracking this wry smile," he says. Might this be a *good* thing? He hadn't had the courage to leave the job on his own. Without this forced intervention, who knows how long he would have stayed?

The bigger concern was how had his feelings about work disintegrated so drastically? How had he let the situation get so bad? He knew the job was numbing his spirit. Every day was an exercise in coping.

Cross-examining the motives that got him here in the first place took some soul searching. Performing his career autopsy, Michael is brutally honest about where and when he went awry, and the misstep he took in falling in step with herd mentality.

At the University of Pennsylvania, he was influenced by a tight-knit circle of well-off friends, nearly 75 percent of whom were headed to Wall Street to start finance jobs after college, he estimates. "The first year in New York was like our fifth year of college. The focus for all of us seemed to be on getting rich with little regard for whether the job was satisfying, enriching, or even interesting. I followed the path blindly, partly because I didn't know any better and more so because I didn't know what else I wanted to do with my life, and figured that the 'conventional' path could not be wrong if everyone else was doing it."

Michael found a position as an analyst at an investment bank. "I was there for a year—the bare minimum to be able to leave with a straight face." Then he moved to the West Coast for a ho-hum office job in television production, scheduling station promos to fill leftover airtime slots.

Neither job mattered much to him. He was really just biding time before he could go back to school, an environment where he knew he excelled. Law school might give him time to think and, hopefully, expose career tracks he could get excited about. Plus, people told him, "there are so many things you can do with a law degree."

The first of which, he discovered, is to pay off debt incurred from earning that law degree. "Sadly, once in law school, the realities of student debt and the persuasive forces of career services steer nearly all students to Biglaw (i.e., law at a big firm)," he says. Many students starting school swear off the big firm life. But by the time they leave, the reality of carrying upward of $100,000 in debt for the next few decades coaxes them to accept a high-paying corporate gig. Michael was strapped with about $60,000 in loans to pay back. Without savings or any inclination to ask his parents for financial help, he, too, found himself signing up for big firm duty.

New game plan: Just make it through a few years of "Biglaw," pay down some school debt, and then figure out who he was and what he wanted to do.

But he was drop-kicked into big firm life at warp speed with scant time to think "big picture." Little on-the-job training was exacerbated by demanding bosses. The switch from the camaraderie in law school to having to report to rigid partners was jarring. It was not uncommon for Michael's boss to walk into his office on a Friday afternoon, drop a one-hundred-plus-page document related to an upcoming transaction, and slap a Monday due date on it. There goes the weekend.

That overtime contributed to a monstrous tally of "billable" hours—a law associate's abacus—which in turn produced a salary that helped soothe the drudgery. "I would be lying if I didn't admit that the high salary was my favorite part," he concedes. "It allowed me to live a life where spending too much was never a question." Overnight or weekend trips to Las Vegas or San Francisco were no big deal. A round of drinks for friends? Put it on his tab. Valet parking? Of course.

Life was good, right? Michael had a prestigious title that impressed his friends and made his parents proud. He was working with very wealthy people helping out on "big-time" deals, all of which helped stroke his ego and perceived status.

If they only knew. "Despite the fact you might hate the job, if your work raises eyebrows or respect among your peers, then it must be worth it, right? Yeah right." Pre-lawyer Michael was a frugal guy who drove a 1980 Volvo. A pair of $20 concert tickets was an extravagant purchase. Dinners out were special occasions. He kept copious notes of expenditures and cut coupons for groceries.

Reflecting on the irony of his meteoric climb up the corporate career ladder, he gave himself a gut check. "I've always been in positions that sound great to others but never felt good to me," he confides.

Until, that is, he listened to what that wry smile stuck on his face was telling him.

Less than thirty days after being laid off, Michael boarded a flight bound for Australia, where his sister was opening the Sydney branch of her finance firm. A subletter took over his apartment. He parked his new car in the garage and cashed his severance for travel money.

Some things are the same as when he started this twentysomething odyssey. He still doesn't know where he's going or really what he wants to do, but one thing is nonnegotiable: it's on his terms this time.

"When I was miserable at work, the world seemed so small and hopeless," he says. "I'm much more at peace at the prospect of breaking away from the conventions of my peers to find a life and gig that suits me best."

It just goes to show, sometimes it takes a derailment to get on track.

Postscript from Michael . . .

If I had to do it all over again, I would . . . Have traveled the world earlier in life.

If I knew then what I know now, I would . . . Not have followed the same path that all my peers did just because I was too scared, ignorant, or comfortable to look for what would really make me happy.

Three characteristics or personality traits you need to do this job:

1. Ability to thrive on or deal with stress effectively
2. Highly, highly detail-oriented and organized
3. Derive happiness from status, money, and ambition

Don't even try this if . . . You value your free time or don't like being told what to do.

MENTOR'S INSIGHTS: *DAN RATHER*

LYNTON GARDINER

Why You Should Listen Up—(a Selection of) Your Mentor's Resumé Stats:

- Anchor and managing editor of *Dan Rather Reports,* an HD-Net cable news broadcast
- Journalist for *CBS News* for forty-four years, including twenty-four years as anchor of the network's *Evening News*
- Has covered numerous historical events in the past sixty years, including the assassination of President John F. Kennedy, the Civil Rights movement, Washington's political scene, numerous wars (Vietnam, Afghanistan, Yugoslavia, and Iraq), and September 11, 2001
- Winner of several Emmy and Peabody awards
- Graduate of Sam Houston State Teachers College (now Sam Houston State University) in Houston, Texas

Dan Rather is arguably one of the most famous journalists of the twentieth century. His deep voice and faint southern accent are recognizable in an instant. The beginning of his extraordinary six-decade (and counting) career had humble beginnings in the small southern

town of Huntsville, Texas. Barely twentysomething, he started reporting for the Associated Press, climbing the ranks quickly to join a large
circulation daily newspaper, the *Houston Chronicle*. From there, he
branched into radio and television news, still using southern Texas as
a base camp. It didn't take long for the big-city CBS Network folks
to take notice, recruiting him to their news team, where he stayed for
more than four decades, culminating in the coveted anchor position.

Clearly, his resumé qualifies him as the "News Gigs" mentor. But
even the most successful people take some hits. Rather was abruptly
derailed from his anchor post at CBS News following a story he reported that cited sources who were ultimately discredited. Different
people called the exit different things—"pushed out," "fired," "encouraged to leave." The label doesn't matter. What does matter is that
Rather is reflective on a moment that stung—a moment that many
twentysomethings will inevitably encounter as they build their careers. The message he'd like you to take away isn't that setbacks will
arise—that's a given—but how to handle them and move on.

Work Ethic: First One In, Last One Out

My creed has been since early childhood (because I got it from my
father who got it from his father, and for that matter, my mother and her
mother and father): get up early, stay late, work hard and smart in between, and never give up.

When I was in my twenties, it was unusual for me not to be up by 5:30
a.m. Beginning at age 14, I worked on a pipeline in the oil field, which
was common for young people in my time and place. Given my father's
model (who also worked the pipeline and in the oil field, as did his father),
I wanted to be the first there and the last to leave.

During the day I would observe other people working and just say,
"I've got to be the hardest working person here." If someone was needed
to stay extra late, I always volunteered to do that. That's what I was taught
to do. These things sound so fundamental that there is a tendency to sort

of scoff and say, "Well, listen I know that yes, yes, yes." But what worked for me, particularly once I got into my twenties, was to remind myself of these fundamentals every day. I can remember getting up and as soon as my feet hit the floor sort of mentally going over a checklist, not unlike a pilot taking off in a plane. I never was the smartest person around, and I knew that. But I wanted to work as smart as I possibly could.

Keeping Moving to That North Star

I understand, particularly in one's twenties, that you ask yourself, "Well, gosh, I wish I had a guiding dream. I'm not sure what I want to do. I'm not clear what my destiny is." I did have the advantage, and it was an advantage, that I had a driving dream: to be a great reporter. I'm still working on that dream. I'm not suggesting that I've achieved that. Mentally, I hung that out there as a North Star. I certainly had my failures, sometimes abject failures, but when I would get down or when I would say, "I just don't know how I can do this," I just mentally envisioned a North Star and was always moving toward it.

Also, I kept in my pocket a card on which I had written, "Is what I'm doing now helping me to achieve my goal?" When I would reach in my pocket to get change or a pen or something it would always be there and it would be a reminder. Again, let the record show that I say this with a chuckle and a smile. It struck some people at the time who would notice as a little sophomoric if not childish. But my point here is that it helped me keep focus.

Close Career Calls

I had one of the shortest and least distinguished records in the whole history of the Marine Corps, but when I came out of the Marines there was a bit of a recession on and I had a very hard time finding a job. I was out of work for quite a little while. I interviewed for a job as a combination industrial relations–public relations person for a steel company. I remember that I was going over in my mind that this was not what I envisioned myself doing, but let's face it, I'm getting pretty desperate here. The job paid well and was with a very big company that had good benefits.

They called me back for what they said was a final interview, and a man appeared—I'm certain he was a psychologist of some sort. He was professorially dressed and smoking a huge pipe, drilling me with his eyes. He asked me some questions, such as "What's my life's goal?" Because my father at that time had never made as much as $10,000 a year (that sounds worse than it was in the sense that it was a different time and the money scale was somewhat different), I remember telling him that before I die I would like to make $10,000 a year and I would like to have a boat—I love to fish. He pulled this out of me. When he asked me, Did I have a dream job? I did tell him that I dreamed of being a good, maybe even a great journalist, but that I needed to make a living.

He told me at the end of that session that "I'm going to recommend you for this job, but I don't think it is the job for you." I found myself thinking at the time, well, you don't know how many checks I have out there floating around with no money in the bank to back them up. In fact, they never actually offered me the job because I was supposed to call back at a certain time and then I just didn't call back. I remember that very well.

The Low Points

There certainly were a lot of low points for me. One was when I volunteered for the Marines. Much of my childhood was taken up by World War II, and as strange as it sounds to say so, I was afraid the war was going to end and I wouldn't have served. I had rheumatic fever when I was a child, and it was called an "eliminating health problem." I'm not proud of it, but I lied about it. I wasn't going to be drafted, but I lied about it when I got in the Army Reserves and I lied about it to get in the Marines.

At any rate, they found out about the rheumatic fever. I was taken out of my training platoon, and they assigned me to clean non-commissioned officers' and officers' latrines.

I felt myself a complete failure. I had no prospects for a job, so I was saying to myself, "If I'm going to get out what am I going to do for a living?" It was a very low point. I thought North Star as I often have in the ups and downs of my professional life. Somebody had told me when I was in my middle teens that the magic words in life are: "If it is to be, it is up to me." Somehow that came back to me, and just at that low point I said, "Well, if it is to be, it is up to me." I was given a medical discharge despite my appeals.

That was a low point for me but it also was a terrific learning experience. The combination of eye on the North Star and "If it is to be, it is up to me" got me through that as it has any number of times since then.

Unceremonious CBS Exit

Look, it wasn't easy. I had been at CBS News for forty-four years. I believed in the mission of the institution, believed it was important. I was extremely disappointed how things had come together there at the end, but by that time—remember by that time I am at almost seventy-five years old—I never thought about hanging it up. I never thought about giving up. I said, "Well, I don't like this, don't think it is right, don't think it's fair, but I'm going to find something else. I am going to keep working."

Fortunately—how does one say this gently?—I had enough money to ensure that I would be okay. One option was, why not just retire? But, frankly, that lasted about a nanosecond. I couldn't imagine myself just going off fishing and doing what everyone does when you retire. But remember where I am in life at that point. I'm in my midseventies, and I didn't have anything to prove. Maybe if I had not been as lucky as I had been and never gotten at or near the top, I might have always wondered. But I had been there and was there.

At CBS, it is very hard for anybody to understand outside, but inside we considered ourselves in a magical, mystical kingdom where every correspondent was a knight and that we had important work to do. That was deep in my id, if you will. I had no idea what I was going to do, but I knew that I was going to continue working and continue working in my craft.

I have a lot of flaws—most of them are pretty well known. I think even someone who doesn't like me or my work—but who knows anything about me—knows I have a passion for journalism. That passion has burned with a hot blue flame since I was very, very young. By the time I left CBS it had increased in intensity and heat, not decreased.

For twentysomethings trying to figure what they are going to do with their lives or how to achieve what they may already dream, I think the most helpful advice is—I wish it were my quote originally, but it isn't, it's Winston Churchill's—"Never, never, never, never give up." Once you adopt it, it's not all that hard. It's really very, very important. When you are in your twenties and sometimes confused and sometimes discouraged, just always keep putting one foot in front of the other. Just keep on keeping on. It's what has worked for me.

Your Mentor's Mentors

I hear a lot of young people talk about cultivating "mentors." It may be possible to do that, but that is not the way it worked with me. I didn't go looking for mentors. I didn't "cultivate" mentors. They just came.

The John T. Jones family was an extremely wealthy family in Houston—they owned the *Houston Chronicle,* they owned the radio station where I worked, and owned just about everything in town. Mr. Jones, for reasons that remain totally mysterious to me, helped me, guided me. I was about the lowest employee that his empire had.

When I got to CBS, a couple of legends, rightful legends, in my craft helped me tremendously. A CBS news correspondent named Charles Collingwood, who was a Rhodes Scholar and one of the original Edward R. Murrow boys, really took mercy on me and in many ways saved me. The point here is that at each and every turn somebody that I either didn't know or barely knew helped me, to no advantage to themselves. Charles Collingwood is in everybody's journalism hall of fame.

Dress the Part

What is worth noting is if someone begins to try to mentor you, pay attention and try to make that bond as close as one can. I learned so much—small things and large things.

For example, this is a bit embarrassing, but when I was first working at the radio station, Mr. Jones said to me, "You probably ought to dress a little better." In that time and place one was expected to wear a shirt and tie—even though Houston has the climate of Calcutta—and I always was in shirt and tie, but I often wore short-sleeve shirts. Mr. Jones—very gently, kindly, and even fatherly—said, "Maybe you want to think about wearing a long-sleeve shirt," because, as a gentleman you wear a long-sleeve shirt.

He always wore a handmade suit, and he always had cuffs showing. I remember looking at him after that and noticing he had a long-sleeve shirt and some of the cuff showing. I adopted that. After he had that conversation with me, I literally borrowed money to buy a two-pants suit. Don't laugh. I went to some place called Bonds Clothiers and they were famous for the two-trousers suit. You could take your coat off during the day and sort of nurse it along, then you send one pair of trousers out to the cleaners.

After I bought this Bonds suit (part of my job was to cover the police beat, which is a very good apprenticeship but a pretty grubby line of work), I remember going into the pressroom at Sixty-one Riesner Street in Houston and the other police reporters were there. When I came in wearing my new suit and long-sleeve shirt, a guy named Jack Weeks, who was a typical stubble-bearded, cigarette chain–smoking, rough-and-tough police reporter, glanced up from what he was doing, looked at me, and said, "Well, Rather has gone Hollywood." I didn't take it as an insult. I really did walk a little taller and a little straighter and also had a sense that I was growing as a man and as a pro.

8

Outdoor Office Gigs

Nature's Cubicle

INTRODUCTION

You know the moment: You're ensconced in your gray, walled-in cubicle, toiling away on the computer or drowning in paperwork. You look up to glance out the window. Your eyes fix on a random image—a tree limb, or a parking meter maid, or the rain pounding the pavement—and you can't look away. "What would it be like if . . . ?" thoughts float to the surface.

And then the phone rings or the instant messenger notice dings, and that reverie ends abruptly. The "what-if . . . ?" daydreams disappear until next time.

But what if you decided that next time was this time?

Nine-to-five office life isn't for everyone, so what kind of outdoor jobs are there for twentysomethings?

The only data I could find on the topic was a bland chart on the U.S. Bureau of Labor Statistics website. Staggered bar graphs depicted hourly wages for what the BLS considers the nineteen outdoor occupations composing 1.1 percent of total national employment in 2007. That 1.1 percent included a random range of jobs—atmospheric and space scientists, landscape architects, utility meter readers, and groundskeepers.

Full disclosure: I didn't dig too deep for other stats because I looked up and caught a glimpse out the window. Inside the frame was a cloudless blue sky, tulips blooming in wild orange and lipstick pink, and students tossing a football on the lawn. The cruel irony of writing about outdoor gigs from a fluorescent-lit room was not lost on me.

In place of more stats, I thought this quote I read in a newspaper, by a hydrologist in Washington State, set the tone: "I used to say the worst day in the field still beat the best day in the office."

The four twentysomethings profiled in this chapter make a living working outdoors. As they'll share with you, outdoor jobs aren't without their own unique set of occupational hazards. It's typically physical work, and while working in the spring and fall can be in pleasant weather, summer and winter are on the clock, too. Regardless, they caught their glimpse, went outside and didn't come back in.

"I love my job," says Christine Vela, a zookeeper in New York State. "One day I'll be picking up a van full of hay and feed, then I'll be driving the porcupine to the vet, or helping tranq the bobcat for a nail trim."

Christine works rain or shine and on most holidays and weekends. The job requires taking care of and cleaning up after animals—and the occasional zoo visitor who forgets that the animals are in enclosures for a reason. "I'm always dirty, and probably smelly," she laughs, and she loves every minute of it.

I caught up with Danny Romes, a park ranger, by phone when he was en route to the closest grocery store—forty minutes away from his home. Another potential outdoor job "hazard" (depending on the way you look at it) is that cell phone and email service is spotty in nature. Luckily, this was part of the job's draw for Danny.

Danny started camping and hiking in high school, and when it came time to earn a living after college, he didn't want to demote it to a weekend hobby. He has rotated through parks in five states, and though each landscape is markedly different, the visitors' tendencies are the same. "Most people who work for the park service did not get a degree in everything e-ology. We don't know it all," Danny says. "People are disappointed when you can't tell them the scientific name for devil's foot (*Oplopanax horridus*) or how old a piece of granite is that they are holding in their hand that they just took from some place in the park they shouldn't have."

Adventure guide Travis McDaniel knows how good he has it. Even his conference calls sound fun. Maybe that's because he takes them while chilling in a kayak bobbing off Washington State's San Juan Islands. "I don't think they ever knew where I was during the phone call, but I saw an orca whale twice while hanging out on the water," he recalls with a wide smile.

Travis travels both locally and internationally guiding groups on hiking trips and kayaking expeditions, among other adventures. He can appreciate the lifestyle now because he used to have a normal office gig. Travis worked as a television production assistant, a job he enjoyed for a few years before he noticed how often he was staring out the window.

If Travis had hung around long enough in his kayak off the coast of Washington, he may have seen Eryn Longobardi motor by. Eryn is a stewardess on a $10 million yacht that boomerangs between the Caribbean islands during the winter months and the Pacific Northwest in the summer. After graduating from Pepperdine University in Malibu, California, she worked as a nanny while waiting for an "I want to be a ..." epiphany.

An offbeat answer arrived by accident when someone mentioned a "yachtie" gig, a job she had never heard of. She met with a crew agent in San Diego, who explained the business: very wealthy people employ year-round crew to staff their yachts and travel with them to exotic corners of the world. The job is a hospitality gig—the crew is there to work. Eryn could handle that aspect, so the agent "told me to pack my bags because she'd have me out of here in two weeks—and she did."

Whenever someone can go skiing, running, climbing, windsurfing, kiting, cycling, or hiking and it could technically be considered a work-related tax write-off, that's someone you want to get to know.

Meet Topher Gaylord, your outdoor gigs mentor. Given his outdoor sports experience (having achieved "expert" status in most of the activities mentioned above), and his professional history (president of The North Face and most recently, Mountain Hardwear, both well-respected outdoor apparel and gear manufacturing companies), Topher was a shoe-in. He shares career advice about how he got his start, and how to impress him, should you find yourself in his office for a job interview.

CHRISTINE VELA
Zookeeper
Bear Mountain, New York
Age: 24

Let's clear up some common misconceptions up front: no, the animals at the zoo where Christine Vela works are not her pets. "I don't give the bears hugs, take the coyotes out for walks, or pet the bobcat," she says. And those claws, you know, the ones on the birds? They're real, which was news to one guest who thought the eagles' talons were glued on by the staff.

Fielding these sometimes nutty questions comes with the territory as zookeeper. They induce an eye roll here or there, but generally Christine doesn't mind. What is irritating—and dangerous—are the times when people taunt the animals, throw garbage into the enclosures, or try to get behind the fences. None of the animals or people has been hurt, yet. "Even though they rely on us for food and shelter, they are still wild animals and deserve the same respect."

Christine is one of three zookeepers at a forty-acre zoo plopped in the middle of Bear Mountain State Park in southern New York. Trees filter the sunlight beaming through, while an animal symphony provides the soundtrack—coyotes howling, the bald eagle screeching, the otter chirping. The animals housed here are ones native to the state, or, in other words, ones you might come across if you took a hike in the state park. So don't ask where the giraffes, tigers, lions are (wrong continent), but do check out the red-tailed hawks and vulture enclosures.

The zoo opens to the public at 10:00 a.m. every day year-round, but Christine clocks in at 8:15 a.m., when she and her coworkers arrive to check on the animals and prep meals and medication. On the menu: fish and a mix of cat food and ferret food for the river otter; wood branches, rodent chow, and fruit for the beaver; red meat, chicken, and eggs for the coyote.

The animals' ailments may sound familiar. Raeba ("a bear" spelled backward), one of the zoo's three black bears, takes a chewable pill hidden in a fig newton for her arthritis; the twenty-three-year-old bobcat has meds sprinkled onto her food to help ease her aging joints.

And lastly, before the zoo gates open, come rain, sun, snow, or holidays, the enclosures get cleaned. It can be a dirty job. Besides general tidying—hosing, raking—Christine picks up "poop" and dinner scraps like rat guts, skins, bones. The chore used to make her squirm and she'd grab the closest shovel to keep her distance. That didn't last very long. Now? "I don't care," she says, laughing, having changed her method to latex gloves and a strong stomach. "I'm sure I smell horrible."

The three-member keeper staff, aided by three maintenance guys and two front office personnel, keep the zoo operating, both on- and off-site. Afternoons include more meal prep and making the rounds to answer questions and make sure visitors aren't misbehaving. Physical

work—enclosure maintenance and painting and shoveling snow—
eats up the afternoon.

Off-site, the staff mans the zoo van to respond to emergency calls
from the public reporting animals in distress—orphaned baby birds,
injured hawks, or rabbits—and follows up to ensure that they see a vet
and get to a rehab clinic.

Some days she'll work an eight-hour shift alone and mostly on her
feet. The solitude doesn't bother her. "The days I'm by myself and the
zoo's quiet are pretty nice. I can take the extra time to observe the
animals, watch the bears or coyotes play, and find some fun enrich-
ment item for the otter."

It's just as well—this is not a place where you come dressed to
impress. "I don't even bother with makeup because there's a good
chance I'll accidentally spray myself with the hose and have mascara
all over," she jokes. "My nails are always chipped, and my hair's a mess.
I have to stand around and talk with the public when my pants and
shirt are dirty from who knows what."

Christine grew up visiting this zoo. The eagle she takes care of
now is the same one she saw as a kid on a school field trip. Growing
up on the family's two-acre property, Christine didn't care for Barbie
dolls. Her toys of choice were stuffed animals that doubled as pretend
patients for her make-believe vet practice.

Eventually she graduated to real ones, like the stray dogs and cats
she fed while volunteering at the local humane society in middle
school. At a therapeutic riding center nearby, she prepared the horses
for lessons with kids with autism. In high school, she shadowed small
animal veterinarians making rounds with sick dogs and cats. In college at the University of Vermont, she pursued a zoology major—
predominately a biology degree, laced with animal-specific courses
that focused on the classifications of mammals and insects. She even
spent a summer interning at the zoo where she works now.

But before returning as a paid zookeeper years later, she'd be tested
with a post-college, six-month internship at an animal rehabilitation

clinic in central "middle of nowhere" Texas. "It was, by far, the hardest thing I have ever done in my life," she says. Along with six fellow interns, she lived in a doublewide trailer on the 180-acre sanctuary in the rolling hills backcountry, relying on food stamps to pay for groceries.

"It was 'baby season' at the clinic, which meant there were a lot of mouths to feed very carefully," she recalls. An entire day could be spent feeding a room full of thirty to forty squirrels, ranging from newborns in an incubator to hyper adults. The newborns required formula every hour, whereas the adults could be fed once or twice a day "as long as you were wearing welding gloves to protect your hands. By the time you made one round around the room it was time to start the second round of feeding." Same deal went for the songbirds, doves, raccoons, skunks, possums, and fawns.

Despite the challenges, Christine was gung-ho on zoo work at the end of the internship. But everywhere she applied required a minimum one year of experience. Christine moved to Long Island to attend vet tech school, but that lasted a semester. "I was tired of spending money to go to school and not having an actual job," she says.

Moving back in with her parents, Christine fired off fifty-plus resumés to zoos all over the country. "I was ready to move anywhere for that first entry-level position," she says, and after three or four months without success, she finally got a bite: the local zoo, the one she grew up visiting, was hiring.

Technically on the books as a seasonal employee earning just over minimum wage, Christine is restricted to working 1,750 hours a year—equivalent to ten months. That schedule may translate to two months "off," but it must be spread throughout the year in order to not leave either her bank account or coworkers in a lurch.

Snow days shut down the zoo to visitors on rare occasions, but the animals still need to be checked, a responsibility she takes seriously. "Since we are in control of everything—food, shelter, exercise—when something goes wrong, it ultimately comes back to you. Were they not getting proper nutrition? Were they too cold or too hot? Did I miss that first sign of illness?"

Thankfully, during the year that she's worked there, no major accidents have occurred and none of the animals has died. But that is a constant worry, as is leaving a cage door open. "The first couple of months at the zoo my entire drive home I would mentally go through the list—Otter? Locked. Eagle? Locked. Deer? Locked."

To those who can picture themselves cleaning up after animals all day, and enjoy it, apply everywhere, she advises. "It might take a year or two for you to get your first opportunity, but it is worth the wait." As for Christine, who still lives at home with her parents to save money and is ready to move out, her dream is to one day work for the Bronx Zoo or Central Park Zoo in Manhattan.

For now, though, she's happy where she is. The animals are a source of constant delight, as are the occasionally overheard wacky conversations from zoo visitors. Christine recalls one amusing example:

"Can birds fly backwards?" one young boy asked his father, reading aloud the trivia question posted near the animal enclosure.

"No," Dad replies.

Then the son reads the answer, "Yes. Hummingbirds can fly backwards."

Christine hears the dad retort, "That doesn't count, hummingbirds aren't *actual* birds."

"That poor kid," she says with a laugh.

Best to leave the zoo keeping to the zookeepers.

Postscript from Christine . . .

If I had to do it all over again, I would . . . Have started looking for a job/internship even before I graduated college.

If I knew then what I know now, I would . . . Not have spent so much money on work pants—they get beat up quickly.

**Three characteristics or personality traits you need
to do this job:**

1. Patience because you are working with animals. They do
   what they want, when they want; you are working around their
   schedule.
2. Reliability. The animals need to be taken care of every day . . .
   no matter what.
3. Motivation. There's always something that needs to be done;
   when you come to work, expect to be doing work . . . all day.

Don't even try this if . . . You're afraid to get dirty. You will be
outside shoveling and scraping poop, just to go inside to cut up rats
and mice (for animals' dinner).

DANNY ROMES
Park Ranger
Homestead, Florida
Age: 28

In two and a half years as a park ranger with the National Park Service, Danny Romes has managed to get by relatively unscathed—no
serious sunburns or run-ins with wildlife. Except for the time he
stood five feet downwind from a towering black bear in Alaska's back
country and accidentally pepper-sprayed himself in the eye (more on
that later).

Cubicle work this is not. No complaints of photocopy jams or
carpel tunnel here, more like poison ivy and omnipresent bug bites,
and that's just the way Danny prefers it. "When I come up to that sign
that says 'Welcome' to wherever National Park and I think to myself,
I work here, this is my office—that day is pretty sweet."

He has rotated through five national parks—one each in Ohio,
Alaska, South Dakota, Colorado, and Florida, and the only consistent
thing he does day to day is put on his uniform (think classic "Smokey

the Bear" get-up—starch-stiff green pants, gray shirt, name tag and wide-brimmed yellow hat). Each placement is for six months, and in lieu of a briefcase, basic survival gear is piled in a backpack—pocket-knife, compass, fire starter, mace, and a $3,000 handheld radio.

After graduating from Marquette University in Milwaukee, Wisconsin, with a B.A. in history and education, Danny knew he wanted to teach, but he couldn't come to terms with a future that would confine him to a traditional classroom. He spent the next two years traveling the country as an AmeriCorps volunteer, helping to rebuild houses in New Orleans after Hurricane Katrina and to landscape a garden at a monastery in South Carolina. All memorable experiences, yet it would be the assignment to camp in Lake Ouachita State Park in Arkansas that would stop him in his tracks, courtesy of an inspirational park ranger.

After a day constructing a wooden trestle bridge to span a trail, the ranger led an impromptu kayaking excursion for some of the group. As they paddled around the lake, he pointed out the variety of vegetation and explained the history of the area.

At dusk, the group beached on a sandbar for a constellation lesson. The stars in the sky weren't the only ones aligning. Something clicked. Here he was, Danny thought, learning about things that interested him and being surrounded by nature, a passion stemming from years of backpacking and hiking. "This totally makes sense," he mused. "I could be doing this."

And so he did. He completed his final year of AmeriCorps and hurled himself through a four-month application process that would result in the round robin of national park ranger work. Based on his recollections, here are postcard-style snapshots:

Cuyahoga Valley National Park, Ohio. Winter. 51 square miles. Terrain: rolling hills bordering dense hardwood forests, with the Cuyahoga River zigzagging through it.

Relieved to finally have my foot in the door as a park ranger, though I'm not entirely sure what I'm supposed to be doing. I work at the winter ski rental store and give cross-country tours. That is, when there's snow on the ground. Otherwise, I get to use my carpentry skills maintaining the gear (snow shoes, skis). Along with a few volunteers here, it's just me manning the place. It's not rocket science, but I enjoy it. Two cool job perks: one, when there's nothing to do, just go hiking, and two, I snow-shoed to work the other day.

Living accommodations are pretty nice—a two-story restored farmhouse in the middle of the park. My roommates are two interns who are my age and a park mechanic in his fifties.

Kenai Fjords National Park, Alaska. Spring and summer. 1,760 square miles. Terrain: 60 percent ice and 40 percent fjords.

Before I got here, I had never seen a glacier or a whale. Now I see glaciers for miles in every direction. And whales? I counted thirty in one day recently.

Today I had a close call with a black bear while giving a tour on the Harding Icefield. I'm leading forty or so people on a path bordering a glacier, and as we crest a hill, we see this huge bear in the bushes, ambling around on all fours. Of course the tourists go nuts, grabbing their cameras, pushing me closer to him to get a better picture. Ridiculous. I tried yelling to scare him away, but he's only getting closer. I'm thinking, "This thing's gonna mess me up." I reach for the mace, flip the lid to spray it, and the wind shifts, blowing it back into my eyes. Great. The bear eventually got bored and walked away while the group traded cameras to compare their shots. I should have just let them put their kids on him for a photo-op. They'd have loved that.

Normal days are calmer. I give glaciology presentations to school kids a few times a week. Otherwise, a partner and I patrol the hundreds of miles of coastline in motorboats or kayaks, rarely coming across another person, which I kind of like actually. I think there are probably about twenty people in the entire park. I do manage to get to town (Seward, population about three thousand) to have a few beers with the locals though.

Badlands National Park, South Dakota. Winter. 381 square miles. Terrain: cliffs and mounds of dirt and mud.

Winter in South Dakota. Really? What was I thinking? I am *always* freezing. The wind chill is insane—temperatures are consistently in the negatives. I heard it dropped to negative 50 the other day. Basically, I run whenever I have to be outside.

Honestly, this probably is my least favorite park so far. I chose this over the Florida Everglades because I was told I could help build the distance-learning program—education via web cam—and it'd be a "good resumé-building experience." But by the time I arrived, the program was up and running just fine. I am learning a lot though. Because the schools are so small here and the park is too far away for a field trip, I give lessons via web cam in real time. So the kids watch from their classroom as I give a lesson about, say, the Native American people who lived here hundreds of years ago (and some still do), and artifacts we have, like bison bones or a bison bladder.

Rocky Mountain National Park, Colorado. Spring and summer. 415 square miles. Terrain: snow-capped mountain peaks, plush grass at lower altitudes.

I'm based at Alpine Visitor Center, the highest in the park service at almost twelve thousand feet. We had six thousand people come in the other day (summer is peak season). Some are lonely and think since you're wearing the uniform, you have to talk to them.

The altitude makes some people go nuts. They get dehydrated, dizzy, fall down and twist ankles, even assault one another on the trail. All of us rangers are EMTs, so we have a good handle on how to take care of these patients—averaging 1.5 per day to be exact (I compiled the annual medical stats). That's a ton. For comparison's sake, in Alaska we had about three for the entire park in six months.

I've been able to do a lot of hiking, too. Went twelve miles the other day to take care of some garbage at a campsite. Sometimes I'll run into hikers who seem a little lost and are really happy to see me.

Everglades National Park, Florida. Winter. 2,343 square miles and third largest park in the United States. Terrain: wetlands, also known as the "river of grass."

Made it to the Everglades after all! Everyone, including the city kids who come up from Miami for school field trips, confuses the terrain with "swamps." I try to correct them, explaining that the Everglades is actually a slow-moving river. Very slow—at the rate of about a quarter mile per day.

The students are great. We walk to two spots that are guaranteed to get a rise out of them. They can be pooped on by birds and intimidated by alligators. They can touch sawgrass, feel periphyton (a slimy algae that is extremely important to the ecosystem), walk over snakes, wander through a jungle-like habitat (called a hardwood hammock). And, possibly most impressive, experience a profound silence far from the city's hustle and bustle.

Judging from their reactions—squealing to laughing to shrieking—I'm making an impression. The feeling is reciprocal. It never ceases to amaze me when they ask, "How many people a day get eaten by an alligator?" or "Is it real?" when referring to the snakes or turtles. They can't imagine an animal roaming free or not in a cage.

★   ★   ★

Danny's love affair with the outdoors started when he was sixteen, on a high school retreat to the Appalachian Trail. The first day was a fiasco. A whiteout snowstorm blindsided the group, forcing them to bail on hiking to a proper campsite and instead pitch their tents on the side of the trail.

But the second day was breathtaking. The sun was shining on a landscape coated with snow. Besides nature's noises, it was completely silent. So this is the Appalachian Trail, Danny thought, riveted by this new outdoor playground ripe for exploration.

After that, he couldn't get enough. Every break from school he roped friends in for backpacking trips. Some signed on a few times, but their enthusiasm tapered off as Danny's treks got more intense, prompting them to name the hikes "Death marches with Romes." No worries—when friends wouldn't commit, he'd go by himself.

Even his parents were good sports and tried to connect with their teenage son on his terms. To prep, they beelined for the sporting goods store, spending a small fortune on fancy gear. A grocery store run provided food provisions for a small feast. Car loaded, Mom, Dad, and Danny drove twelve hours to the AT area classified as "easy."

By hour two on the trail, it was hell. "At one point, our packs were so heavy we had to push and pull each other over the rocks, even a twelve-inch-high rock," Danny recalls. Carting around all this crap, Dad asked his son how to cut down on the weight. "I'm thinking his five-pound knife and ten-pound boots to start. We camped that first night on the side of the trail—we didn't even make it to shelter. The next morning we got to the nearest road and looked at each other and said, 'Let's get out of here.'" Suffice to say, camping isn't a Romes family activity.

But Danny's still at it. Some park rangers, like Danny, work seasonally; others have permanent positions. At the two-year mark, people tend to fish or cut bait with regard to making a career of it, Danny explains. Depending on overtime and locale, the annual beginner salary ranges from $28K to $31K, and moving expenses from park to park are not reimbursed. With about two moves per year, that adds up.

"This is the part they never tell you when you first join the park service," he says, taking a rare serious tone. "You get that first seasonal position and then you think it is all smooth sailing from there, but it really isn't." Take note: seasonal employees do not receive benefits, or retirement, or health insurance. And working a rotation at a park does not guarantee a permanent spot, if one opens up.

And that's a big "if." "It's not unheard of to have four hundred to seven hundred people applying for one job that may only pay thirty thousand dollars a year. It is tough to move up, and a lot of people quit."

Danny doesn't plan on being one of those people. He's in it for the long hike.

Postscript from Danny . . .

If I had to do it all over again, I would . . . Have worked for the park service in the summer so it would have been an easy transition into the workforce.

If I knew then what I know now, I would . . . Have taken more courses in science and gotten some certifications out of the way sooner, like my EMT certification and Wildland Firefighting certification. And if you are planning on making this a career, talk with someone who is experienced in the hiring process and can steer you through all the hoops and pitfalls.

Don't even try this if . . . You can't tell which way the wind is blowing when spraying bear mace, especially when the bear is approaching and you have about forty tourists behind you.

ERYN LONGOBARDI
Yacht Stewardess
Long Beach, California
Age: 26

How's this for an outdoor office? A $10 million, 130-foot, triple-deck mega yacht, outfitted with two hot tubs, two jet skis, three fully stocked fridges and bars, three flat-screen TVs, and a film library of more than six hundred DVDs.

Welcome aboard the playpen of its owner, a Southern California–based businessman, and the "office" and home to its six crewmembers. A few times a year, when the owner fancies a vacation with his wife and son, he alerts the crew—captain, engineer, deckhand, chef, chief stewardess, and stewardess—to meet him off the coast of, say, Juneau, Alaska, where the family will fly to board at their convenience.

In the eighteen months she's worked on the boat, chief stewardess Eryn Longobardi has logged sea ferrying jaunts to Canada, Alaska, Costa Rica, Mexico, and through the Panama Canal to the Bahamas in the Caribbean.

Depending on the boat's speed and the number of pit stops, the sea commute varies. Long Beach, California, to Juneau, Alaska, takes between five and ten days; Long Beach to the Bahamas about two weeks.

Once the crew is anchored at the exotic locale, they prep the boat for the owner's arrival. In the meantime, a broker typically books the yacht for a private charter of seven to ten days for a group of up to eight people. Price tag? $70,000 per week.

For "Yachties," the industry shorthand for employees on these particular boats, work is divided into two categories: "on charter" or "off charter," referring to when guests are on board and when they're not. This is ultimately a hospitality business, albeit one provided on magnificent boats, so if you can get over the fact that it's not your yacht and you *will* be serving very wealthy people, it's a great way to get paid to chase the sun and see the world.

Depending on the amount of "heads up" the crew gets before a charter, prepping the boat for guests can become a mad dash. The crew descends on the local town, dividing and conquering to cover all the to-do's. The chef tracks down the markets to purchase the freshest produce and ingredients for each day's three home-cooked meals—for the crew and guests—plus appetizers and snacks.

The captain or Eryn scout the tourist attractions—glacier helicopter tours, privately guided hikes, top-rated spas and masseuses. Eryn also drops off the flower vases to be filled with hundreds of dollars' worth of the most beautiful stems, and purchases specialty drinks requested by the guests.

Back on board, the second stewardess starts ticking off the cleaning chores: polish silver, vacuum floors, wipe down phones and all fingerprints, confirm towels and linens are in the correct cabins, clean AC units, straighten bathrobes on fabric hangers. The deckhand, engineer, and occasionally the captain wash down the entire boat, gas up the jet skis and tender boats, inflate the kayaks, and troubleshoot last-minute electrical glitches that arise.

Once the boat is sparkling, fridges are stocked, and rooms are triple-checked, the crew takes a deep breath and gets to have some of their own adventures. During the Alaska trip, the captain dispatched Eryn and the engineer in kayaks on a mission: explore the glacier shoreline and do a test run of a kayak tour, looking for cool inlets and wildlife to show the guests. "We found this massive glacier, but in order to actually walk on it, we had to wade through a river of ice water, with mini icebergs floating next to us," she recalls. They braved it, shoes in hand, before reaching the "turquoise ice, marbled with dirt and sediment."

The guests' arrival sends the crew into full-service mode. The guys are required to shave every day, uniforms are to be ironed, and appearances must be pristine. Guests are not to lift a finger, "unless, of course, they want to," Eryn adds.

"To provide the absolute best service to all eight guests means not just turning the hot tub on, setting someone up on a jet ski, and waiting for them to ask for something again," she cautions. "We are constantly trying to think two steps ahead of what the guests might need." At the ready are sunscreen, clean towels, snacks, drinks, and music to fit the mood of the moment.

In this high-maintenance job, Eryn's sharp multitasking skills serve her well. Not only is she monitoring drink levels for refills and fielding questions about the area, she's also keeping an eye on where the guests are at all times. When one leaves a room, she slips in to tidy disarray. A toilet flush sends her scurrying in to refold the toilet paper into a perfect diamond. When a guest wants an onshore spa appointment, Eryn accompanies him or her with the boat credit card to swipe for payment. The guests aren't hassled with a bill, which can add up to $100,000, until the trip ends.

She's constantly anticipating, watching, moving. "I ran a marathon in college and don't remember my feet hurting as badly as they do after seven 16-hour days of running up and down three decks serving drinks, offering towels and cleaning cabins!"

Eryn credits her indefatigable hostess spirit to having "a servant's heart," one of the tenets of her Christian faith. High school summers and college spring breaks doubled as mission trips to Mexico, Holland, and Albania. When Eryn was a youngster, her mother graciously welcomed guests into their home and spent days preparing the house for their arrival. Once they felt at home, "my dad would start telling jokes, instigating game nights, and making them feel special. When you grow up around amazing hospitality, it makes it easy to reciprocate when you're in the position to do so."

Entertaining families who are accustomed to only the best takes a certain amount of creativity. Add party planner to Eryn's list of talents.

While on a charter in the Bahamas, guests walked into their cabins to find grass skirts and leis spread out on the beds, with handmade notes inviting them to their own exclusive luau. Outside, on a private beach cove, tiki torches cast yellow light on chairs in the sand and a buffet table overflowing with food. "The guests and crew had a great time and no one wanted to leave, so we all joined in a hilarious improv game of charades as the sun set over the water," Eryn recalls.

Not all the customized events have to be on a grand scale. Some ideas come simply from paying attention. "If you just listen to people and observe, it's easy to figure out a common ground. Once you do, it's much easier to make their vacation personalized instead of doing the same thing each week."

Like the time a family brought a football on board. Turns out they were New York Jets fans. Eryn also noticed how stressed the dad was, inconspicuously checking his BlackBerry for work updates. Their favorite team was scheduled to play, inspiring Eryn to set up a "Jets Sports Lounge," so he and his eleven-year-old daughter could watch the game together. Eryn made green and white banners and put out a beer mug for him, apple juice for her.

"I went up at halftime to see if they needed more popcorn, and she was cuddled up next to her dad on the couch," Eryn says. "I could tell for that moment, even though he's a bigwig at a Fortune 500 company, he's never been happier than to have his baby girl enjoy his presence so much. Moments like that are priceless, regardless of whether you're guest or crew."

Occasionally, the distinction between guest and crew blurs, as was the case when a mom pulled Eryn aside and confided that she needed help. This was the first vacation that her family—four kids and busy executive husband—had taken without another family, and she was nervous that they'd have little to talk about once seated around the dinner table. They were used to being so busy and apart for meals. Would Eryn help make some conversation at dinner?

Eryn, as usual, overdelivered. She brainstormed a Jeopardy game designed around the family's chartered trip—where they'd visited, fish they'd caught—and turned what could have been awkward dinner silence into a meal of sharing laughs and recounting adventures. She clearly made an impression: "This family ended up visiting us again in Costa Rica, and took me zip-lining through the rain forest with them on Christmas Day."

Eryn is always happy to help, but keeps a sense of humor of where she falls in the food chain. "People hear I work on a ten-million-dollar yacht and assume I live the lifestyle of the rich and famous. Not quite, I serve beverages to the rich and famous."

Lest she forget, the crew's quarters down below are a quick reminder. "Think tiny, one-bedroom European apartment. Then make it rock," she jokes. She sleeps in a bunk bed that has the dimensions of a coffin in a room about five feet by six feet. Not everyone can handle the accommodations, or the work, which explains why Eryn has had ten roommates since she started. Don't even ask about the closets. "At the end of the day though, I do call a mega yacht home."

For those who do stick it out for a few years, the salary provides a comfortable lifestyle. The crew's pay rate varies based on the size of the boat, number of crew aboard, and job title. "Typical starting salary for a stewardess or deckhand with minimal experience is twenty-five hundred dollars per month, generally with regular pay increases at the end of each season. Chief stews make around double that," Eryn explains. Each charter ends with a customary cash tip—$2K to $3K per crew member. Multiply that times several charters per year, deduct most expenses (no rent or food costs), and "Yachties" can earn a solid living.

"I absolutely love running around all day serving people and making their vacation as relaxed and memorable as possible," Eryn says cheerfully. She has the tan to prove it.

Postscript from Eryn . . .

If I knew then what I know now, I would . . . Be more picky about what boat I got on. I absolutely love my owners and the boat I work on, but a buddy of mine got on a boat that is going around the entire world in two years. He practically wakes up with a new view out his cabin window every single day.

Three characteristics or personality traits you need to do this job (successfully . . . I know plenty of crew members who don't have any of these qualities and still do the job)**:**

1. Hardworking
2. A servant's heart
3. Assertive

Don't even try this if . . . You're claustrophobic or a shopaholic. The bunk beds are small and the closets are smaller. On the other hand, if you're looking to simplify your need for things, this is one way to do it.

TRAVIS MCDANIEL
Adventure Guide
Glendora, California
Age: 28

Sign you've got a cool job: when you don't have to duck a call from the office because you're kayaking around the San Juan Islands or caught in mid-ascent rock climbing in the Sierra Mountains.

Better sign you've got a cool job: when you get paid to be kayaking around the San Juan Islands or go rock climbing in the Sierras.

Yep, business as usual for Travis McDaniel, a guide and co-owner of an adventure company in Southern California.

Travis is "outdoorsman" personified. Tall and lanky with a stubble beard and a bottomless well of patience, he doesn't so much walk as bound. And he is all too comfortable on the side of a cliff dangling on a rope clipped to a tiny bolt hanger.

When he joined the company five years ago, it consisted of five die-hard outdoor enthusiasts offering local canyoneering courses. Now, the "family" is seventeen-strong with forty adventures on offer, ranging from $135 single-day hikes to ten-day programs climbing in Ireland for $3,500. A nationwide sporting goods store is a corporate partner and advertises the adventure company on its website. Other clients come from word of mouth.

In the span of a given month, Travis can be found leading groups on white-water rafting trips on the Kern River in central California, canyoneering (i.e., rappelling down waterfalls) in the San Gabriel mountains, or leading backpacking trips in Joshua Tree National Park, a nearly 1,250-square-mile desert outside Palm Springs, a popular remote destination.

When people have discretionary money, 80 percent of sales are attributed to those guided tours. In tougher economic climates, that share drops to 15 percent which leads the company to focus on other revenue sources like producing stunts for television and film.

For instance, when the reality TV series *The Amazing Race,* whose contestants compete on an around-the-world scavenger hunt, needed players to rappel down a forty-three-story hotel in Las Vegas, Travis and his team stepped in to design the logistics. They were also on site (and on camera) to help clip the contestants into the ropes, give safety instructions, and be at the ready for a possible rescue.

It's a jaw-dropping job. "I can start adventure programs literally just about anywhere on earth and get paid to guide people there," he says, still incredulous of his good fortune. The Black Canyon of the Colorado River, a Class I section of the river below the Hoover Dam, had been on his adventure wish list for years. He pitched a three-day tour to his partners for which he outlined travel details, camping sites, provision lists, and a suggested package price. Now it has a permanent spot on the company's menu of destinations. Next locales for the taking: Antarctica and Africa.

"I like that I'm getting paid to provide people with happiness. I get to hear at least once a week that one of our adventures has been the best day of a person's life so far." The inspiration is reciprocal. "I have learned that you are never too old to start something new," Travis says, referring to the clients in their seventies and eighties whom he has taught to rock climb and canyoneer.

Flashbacks of his life pre–outdoor adventure come rushing into focus each time his car comes to a crawl in city traffic. "Every now and then I get on Los Angeles freeways and sit in wretched traffic, and I can't believe people do it every day. They say that there's no other way to make a living—there is! But you have to make scary decisions and challenge yourself."

He's speaking from experience. Before getting paid to tackle the outdoors, Travis logged hundreds of miles a week on those LA freeways commuting an hour one way to his job as a television production assistant. Once he clocked in, it was a matter of minutes before he was back behind the wheel, dispatched on various errands for the production office.

He chalked it up to paying his dues for what was, at the time, his ultimate goal: to work as an assistant director, the person on television and movie sets who organizes the shooting schedule and is the director's right hand. Travis enthusiastically applied for the Directors Guild of America assistant training program, the industry's standard entry point for the gig.

When the fourth rejection came in, he said forget it. He didn't want it badly enough to keep fighting for a spot, especially when he had a second passion that he daydreamed could be just as fulfilling. But that pipe dream always felt out of reach, that is, until he had the audacity to try.

Travis was spending all his free time and money planning outdoor trips anyway. "Literally, the second filming ended on Fridays, I'd be out the door driving somewhere awesome and wouldn't be back until first thing Monday morning. I cherished those weekend and holiday adventures, and started to realize they were more important to me than my job."

Travis couldn't help but wonder: Could going on these adventures *be* a job?

It sure looked that way, judging from the smiles beaming on the instructors' faces. After the fourth AD blow, he treated himself to a series of weekend canyoneering lessons, and when the TV show he was working on wrapped for the season, he decided he wasn't going back.

Instead, he approached the company where he had been a student with a bold proposal: "I'd work for them every day for six months for free. If at the end of those six months, there's a position available, then you'll hire me; if not, I'll move on." By week four, Travis had made himself an indispensable part of the team. He believed in the group so much that he cleared out his savings to invest in the company, thereby becoming one of two co-owners.

It's not as if he wasn't qualified. This kid had been kicking up dust and hungry for a fresh-air fix ever since his parents took him on a hike as a five-year-old. By his teenage years, Travis was surfing and kayaking off the coast of Southern California and familiar with poison oak rashes from backpacking trips throughout the local mountains.

College? He bolted for the outdoor mecca of Oregon, where he majored in biology at Willamette University. Summer jobs were spent shepherding tourists down rapids in Montana and Wyoming, where he also got a taste of the office operations of running an outdoor company.

"After college, there was the requisite soul searching from the driver's seat of my VW bus. I had enough near-death experiences on frozen rivers and deserted islands to know that sometimes it's not so bad to settle down in one spot for a while." Hence the production assistant gig. But you can't stick an outdoor guy indoors for long.

Spoiler alert: even outdoor gigs come with indoor responsibilities. As co-owner, Travis wears many hats: updating the website, purchasing equipment, performing gear checks, sending pre-trip info to customers, overseeing finances, maintaining a blog, and updating social media.

By far the most time-consuming chore is dealing with the reams of permit paperwork each month. In the name of park preservation, the U.S. Department of the Interior regulates access to parks by organized tour companies. Permit allowances are different for each park, and the logistics to apply for them are extensive.

Maui, Hawaii, on the other hand, isn't a paperwork headache because currently the island prohibits tour companies from running trips in the canyons. Its canyoneering and hiking are too good to pass up, though, so if Travis and his cohorts can't get paid to lead groups there, they go on their own self-guided adventures. They're not messing around—the company bought a three-bedroom house where employees can stay for free, and Travis set up an automated travel alert to notify him when airfare drops.

And the best sign of all you've got a cool job: when you love what you do, especially since adventure jobs aren't the most lucrative. "I think the argument is that people are willing to work for less just for the experience of being outdoors. I can tell you firsthand that 'experiences' don't pay bills." Guides generally earn $100 to $180 a day, depending on the program. As an owner of the company, Travis receives an "operations salary" between $60K and $70K a year, depending on the income of the company that year. It helps that nearly all his expenses are paid for: cell phone, satellite phone, car insurance, travel, health insurance, food, gas, even his gear. "We get one client on average per week applying for a job with us, so we must be doing something right."

Being outdoors was something Travis loved throughout his youth. Why must it stop once "adulthood" sets in? For Travis, it didn't. Learning to rock climb or rappel down waterfalls was easy. Taking the leap to follow his dream took guts.

Postscript from Travis . . .

If I had to do it all over again, I would . . . Have never offered to learn HTML to help the company save expenses on website design. Learning web design work has expanded my personal skills, but has sucked up endless hours of my time for projects that never saw the light of day. The dark side of technology.

Three characteristics or personality traits you need to do this job:

1. Inventive. Between little things going wrong in the field (running out of propane) and marketing a company in an eighty-year-old industry, you have to stay inventive and fresh to make it work.
2. Passionate. If you don't like teaching people, being patient, and being outdoors, then this job definitely isn't for you.
3. Dependable. When you're working, being stuck in traffic isn't a valid excuse. You have to be fully rested and hydrated day in and day out. A group of people is dependent on you for guidance and safety every time you're in the field. If you're not at 100 percent, then their safety and well-being isn't at 100 percent.

Don't even try this if . . . You like to party. A celebratory drink at the end of a long trip is always appreciated. But when the clients are enjoying a beer around the campfire, you have to be prepping gear, cleaning the kitchen, being sociable, and getting rested for the next day. If you think adventure and partying mix together, you're going to be bummed out after the first day.

MENTOR'S INSIGHTS: *TOPHER GAYLORD*

Why You Should Listen Up—(a Selection of) Your Mentor's Resumé Stats:

- President, Mountain Hardwear, a premiere outdoor apparel and equipment company, based in the San Francisco Bay Area
- Fifteen-year career at The North Face, a respected outdoor apparel manufacturer and retailer, climbing the ranks from sales agent to president
- All-star athlete: Expert rock climber (Yosemite National Park, Austrian Alps); hardcore Alpine skier (expert only runs throughout the United States and Europe); ultra-running star (numerous top 10 placements in fifty-mile and one hundred-mile-plus races)
- Experienced sailor, windsurfer, cyclist, hiker, camper, and backpacker
- Bachelor of Science, California Polytechnic State University, San Luïs Obispo

Let the record show: Topher Gaylord has three resumés—one for his adventure sports accomplishments, one for his ultra-running finishes, and one for his professional work experience. The stats above barely give this mega-outdoorsman justice. The outdoor Curriculum Vitae runs more than a page, referencing as far back as age twelve when he started windsurfing. Fifteen or so years later, in his mid-twenties, he took a break and decided to add ultra-running to his hobbies. (To give you a sense of this "break," one of his victories was as the first American finisher in a race around Mount Blanc, the highest mountain in the Alps. The racecourse loop cuts through parts of Switzerland, France, and Italy. Gaylord ran the 167-km race in 24 hours, 51 minutes.) And finally, his "regular" resumé reads like a business-acumen pro, tripling revenue here, expanding global brand there.

Who *is* this guy? To find out requires ratcheting back the clock to his childhood, when he was growing up the youngest of ten siblings in the Adirondack Mountains in New York and the Wasatch Mountains of Utah. Along with Mom and Dad, that makes for eleven adventure-ready coaches, competitors, and teammates. It also means a lot of secondhand gear. Gaylord hasn't forgotten. "It's kind of the ultimate payback now being in the outdoor industry," he jokes from his office in Richmond, California, located northeast of the San Francisco Bay Area. "I get all the new stuff and they're getting the hand-me-downs. That was a big motivator in getting into the outdoor industry."

All jokes aside, Gaylord, energized from his morning ten-mile run, shares with you how he blended an extreme passion for extreme sports into an extremely successful "outdoor" gig. Here's a hint: start moving.

The Early, Early Years

Our house was the ultimate playground. We had a whole house just for our gear—not a complete house, it was like a barn. It had everything: ski gear, row boats, small sailboats, fishing gear, camping gear, windsurfing

gear, lacrosse, tennis, and anything to do with the outdoors. Imagine before they had plastic ski boots, my parents were out lacing up ten kids
in their lace-up ski boots, which would be crazy these days. We used to
drive around as a family in a bus—a full-blown green school bus! We did
a camping trip across the country one year when I was probably eight
or nine years old. We loaded everyone up in the bus and just drove west
and camped out. I think we spent all summer on the road discovering the
natural world around us.

From a young age I pursued sports with focus and passion. I was skiing before I was walking. I was windsurfing at the age of eleven, before I
could even carry my board to the beach. I'll never forget when I was just
twelve years old, my summer vacation consisted of visiting a brother who
was running a river guiding operation down the Colorado River, another
brother who was living in Maui at the time and had a sailboat—sailing
around the Hawaiian Islands with him, and then visiting another brother
who was a cyclist—cycling around Lake Ontario in New York and Canada.
I had an incredible family that really helped support and foster the concept of getting out and discovering and exploring and seeking adventure
in the natural world, which I just loved. It also taught me that in a family of
ten, you've got to be assertive to get food at the dinner table. It's not an
environment to be sitting by the side waiting for something to happen in
life. I learned quite quickly that if you want to eat or be heard, get yourself
to the front of the line and speak up.

Our family was very involved as investors in the Snowbird, Utah, ski
area. They built the Cliff Lodge, which is one of the primary hotels there.
The family has lifetime passes and we go skiing there every year together.
It is such a great way to connect as a family—out on the mountain. Now
we have extended family of nephews and nieces—we've got twenty-five
of them, so it is a big crew.

College and Internships—A Time for Exploring and
Test-Running Careers

One of the most exciting things about college or university is every
semester, every quarter you are taking anywhere between four and six
classes that are all different. For me, it was really an opportunity to whet

my palate and feel what got my blood flowing. I remember sitting in a landscape architecture class. At the time, I thought perhaps I wanted to go that route—I loved the outdoor world and I was exploring design. But I realized, this is not what I wanted to do. I wasn't feeling the energy and I couldn't focus in class the same way I could when I was sitting in a marketing class. I loved the energy of bringing ideas to life in a team environment.

I don't think there is any secret ingredient (to finding a passion) other than really being honest with yourself to understand what gets you excited. More than anything: do not follow the direction of what your friends think you should do, or what your parents think you should do, or what your counselors think you should do. College is the time you really need to reflect on what's important to you as a human being and pursue that with everything you've got. It is easy to say and hard to do, because so many young adults are incredibly influenced by their parents and peers and by mentors and coaches in their lives. I think it is important to have all those sounding boards, but there is an old saying that I like to live by: "Listen to everyone and follow no one."

I used summer internships and summer work experiences as ways to test what I really wanted to do. When I took a job selling real estate I was cold-calling high-net-worth individuals in an office in San Francisco and prospecting for real estate investment. After about three months of doing that, I knew exactly what I didn't want to do—work in a standard corporate environment, not providing meaning to peoples' lives beyond whether their fund was going up or down. Real estate didn't get my blood pumping. That was as important as understanding what I wanted to do.

You need to understand who you are and who you are not. The earlier you learn that in life, the earlier you can start a career that is meaningful to you. I have a lot of nephews and nieces right now who are challenged with this same phase in their lives and trying to understand where they want to go. Do I want a job in marketing? Do I want a job in sales? A lot of times they are thinking, "I'll take any job, or maybe I need to get a corporate job." My response to them is before you can decide what kind of job you want, you need to look at who you are, but equally you need to look at who you are not.

In Your Wildest Dreams, Did You Ever Think You'd Pull This Off?

When I first looked at the outdoor and action sports industries in college, I really thought I had pursued every kind of sport and activity that I've been involved with as far as I can take it. At the time sports-related marketing and branding was just emerging. Nike had been the leader for many years, in the 1980s, but that form of marketing was still emerging. That is really where I honed in and thought, "What is it that I can contribute to a company that is also unique and distinctive from any other applicant that might be interested in a job in the outdoors?"

I thought, "Well, I spent years in my youth as a sponsored athlete both in the ski industry and in the windsurfing industry," so I knew at a very young age the marketing power of athletes in terms of helping drive both product research design and development, advertising, and sales for companies. I had the formal business skill education combined with an innate understanding and psyche of how an athlete thinks and how to take athletes' talents and add value to companies. That helped me in college drive toward that as an initial entry into the outdoor industry.

A Tribal Way of Life

The ski, surf, windsurfing, and kiting industries, and the climbing and ultra-running communities—they are all part of the greater outdoor tribe. They have their subcultures or subtribes within the greater outdoor community, and I think they are all connected through a kindred spirit—a similar connection to their natural world. With technology coming faster than it has ever come before and people being surrounded with information in digital form, there's almost an insatiable need now to get back to feeling what life really feels like. I think those outdoors sports that are not 100 percent winning based and are about discovering your own human potential can bring you back to a grounded way of living.

If you are in a mainstream sport, many of those athletes are in it simply because it's a form of recognition and it's a form of money. I look at these more non-mainstream, adventure sports, which back in the day were called extreme sports, that are pursued more in a purity of the love of the sport and the ability to expand one's mind and potential. I also think that the mentality is not always, "I want to win. I want to be recognized, and I want to make a lot of money." It's a different mentality because if you aspire to go to the top of your game in windsurfing, kiting, climbing, and ultra-running—there is very little money at the top. The recognition is within a very small peer group or tribe and part of a broader lifestyle of creating community beyond competition.

People ask me, "Aren't you exhausted after running one hundred miles?" I say, "Yes, physically, but my mind is more pure than ever." The beauty of it is that it doesn't take a hundred miles to clear your mind and achieve that sense of accomplishment. You might find a five-kilometer run provides the same sense of rejuvenation.

How to Impress This Boss

It's not only about finding people who have a passion for the outdoors. I've had plenty of people who have come through my office and said, "Hey, I love the outdoors." But they don't have a desire necessarily to grow and learn and develop and do some of the more mundane work that is part of any job. When I look at applicants, it's people who have the desire, but also a level of both aptitude and commitment and ambition to grow in their job, not simply take an outdoor job for the sake of being outdoors more often.

It's about being real in an interview. I've had plenty of applicants who have come in and they're just not genuine in the way that they interview. What I see a lot of times is people who are not themselves. They are trying to be someone they are not. People talk about first impressions being so important, and it's true for any job or any other kind of profession you're interviewing for. It's a strong handshake, it's a direct look in the eye, and it's being confident in how you present yourself. It's also having a certain humble appreciation for the person who you are speaking with. It's a really important process. Unfortunately, there aren't a lot of classes in school that help you learn this.

One piece of advice I would share with a job applicant is: When you walk into an interview, assume there are three to five other applicants who are more qualified than you. Whether that's the case or not, you need to go in with that kind of mind-set. I think too often people are going into job interviews somewhat wavering—don't know if I want the job, I'm not sure if it's the right location, I don't know if I like the people, I'm not sure if it's the right company. You can decide all those things after you get the offer letter. Always better to get the job and be in a position to decide whether you want it later than to hesitate in the job interview.

I think too often people come in kind of with the attitude, "Well, what can you do for me? What will your company do for me?" You need to go into an interview with the exact opposite mind-set and what you are going to do for the company and how you can add value to the company regardless of the functional area. Job applicants, regardless of their experience base, should walk in there as if there were no other person on the planet who could do that job better.

There's a fine line between projecting your passion for the industry and sounding like you just want to join because you want more holidays or to be outside more. You have to be able to show what value you will add because all businesses are—for the most part, at least—designed to make money and to grow. It's important whether you're in the outdoor industry or any other industry that you share with the people who you are working for how you can help accomplish one of those two components of the business—either helping it grow or helping it be more profitable. That's something you can just never forget—the game is played exactly the same in all businesses.

Acknowledgments

The saying goes "It takes a village to raise a child." Well, I've learned it takes the same to publish a book.

Thank you, above all, to my generation—a group of inspiring, hardworking, optimistic young adults who will leave their mark on this world in a memorable way. I'm proud to grow old with you and see all that you accomplish.

To the twentysomethings whose stories appear in these pages, and to those who went through various stages of the process with me but will be saved for the sequel, thank you for letting us peek into your lives. You shared your jobs and your souls. It has been a privilege to tell your stories.

I'm grateful to a multitude of people who helped push this book from concept to reality.

William Wooten, one of the first people I confided this idea to, thank you for not skipping a beat when you replied that you believed it was a good one. Molly Moran, had you not perked up to mention your connection to a literary agent, it's very possible none of this would have happened. Meredith Dawson, that esteemed agent at Movable Type Literary Group, your guidance has been invaluable since day one. To Amy Pyle, my superb editor, and the whole team at Kensington Publishing, thank you for believing in this project and for trusting me to execute it.

Connie Hameedi, I'll always wonder if your cover design and layout for the original book proposal was what really cinched a deal.

Diane Livengood, your speedy transcriptions of mentor interviews were crucial to hit deadlines. A heartfelt thank-you to other family on all coasts, too.

To a cluster of very supportive professors at Columbia University Graduate School of Journalism, thank you. You read drafts, made mentor referrals, and fueled momentum.

David Funkhouser, your writing, coaching, and critiques made this a better book.

To a tight circle of friends, thank you for the encouragement that sustained me more than I'm able to eloquently express.

I'm indebted to the industry mentors who agreed to speak to me. Each of you went above and beyond expectations, and because of your candid advice, I anticipate many will follow your lead.

Benjamin Spray, you were an unwavering source of enthusiasm and support. Thank you for your tacit understanding.

And to a friend, coach, and mom, who helped me weather the lows and celebrate the highs of this book-writing odyssey, thank you. I could not have done it without you. Now it's your turn.

Sources

1. Healthcare Gigs

   www.bls.gov/oco/cg/cgs035.htm

   www.bls.gov/oco/cg/cgs035.htm#reated

   www.portfolio.com/industry-news/health-care/2009/10/19/
   quest-diagnostics-general-mills-police-bad-health-behavior-
   among-employees/

3. Do-Good Gigs

   74.52.60.18/~npt/index.php?page=1600-s

   pewresearch.org/pubs/1031/voung-voters-in-the-2008-election

   wwww.nytimes.com/2010/07/12/education/12winerip.html

4. Green Gigs

   www.nrdc.org/media/2009/090213.asp

   www.nrdc.org/globalwarming/f101.asp

   Pew Center on Global Climate Change and EfficiencyFirst,
   America's Home Performance Workforce.

www.efiiciencyfirst.org/static/files/HOME_STAR_Talking_
Points.pdf

5. News Gigs

www.businessweek.com/magazine/content/10_30/
b4188027495608.htm

mediadecoder.blogs.nytimes.com/2009/10/20/playboy-cuts-its-
circulation/

www.stateofthemedia.org/2010/online_summary_essay.php

www.tvb.org/rcentral/markettrack/us_hh_by_dma.asp

6. Government Gigs

www.bls.gov/oco/cg/cgs042.htm#emply

www.bls.gov/oco/cg/cgs041.htm

www.wired.com/epicenter/2009/08/what-the-obama-
administration-is-learning-from-facebook-google-and-
ideo/#ixzz0fdq8OFr5

7. Derailed Gigs

thehill.com/homenews/house/70657-dems-push-jobs-bill-
despite-best-jobs-report-of-recession

www.nytimes.com/2008/08/29/business/29wall.html?_r=1&em

8. Outdoor Office Gigs

www.nytimes.com/2009/03/08/jobs/08start.html

www.bls.gov/oes/2007/may/figure2.pdf